Smokeless Tobacco in the Western World

SMOKELESS TOBACCO IN THE WESTERN WORLD

1550–1950

Jan Rogoziński

 PRAEGER

New York
Westport, Connecticut
London

Library of Congress Cataloging-in-Publication Data

Rogoziński, Jan.
   Smokeless tobacco in the western world, 1550–1950 / Jan
Rogoziński.
      p.   cm.
   Includes bibliographical references.
   ISBN 0-275-93600-7 (alk. paper)
   1. Smokeless tobacco—History.   I. Title.
TS2230.R64   1990
394.1′4—dc20   90-6899

Library of Congress Catalog Card Number: 90-6899
ISBN: 0-275-93600-7

First published in 1990

Praeger Publishers, One Madison Avenue, New York, NY 10010
An imprint of Greenwood Publishing Group, Inc.

Printed in the United States of America

The paper used in this book complies with the
Permanent Paper Standard issued by the National
Information Standards Organization (Z39.48-1984).

10 9 8 7 6 5 4 3 2 1

For Paul Francis Hauch

Contents

Tables

Preface

I have enjoyed writing this book. And I hope that I have been able to communicate some of the subject's inherent appeal to the reader. The ways in which men and women have consumed tobacco over the past five centuries is in itself an interesting topic. Moreover, since it has been used in virtually every region of the globe since about 1600 A.D., tobacco—especially smokeless tobacco—has been present in widely differing societies. Thus, the many different ways this product has been grown, manufactured, consumed, and regulated provides a kind of heuristic key (or touchstone) that is useful in understanding life in various societies.

Cane sugar is perhaps the only other substance of comparable importance in so many places over so long a span of time. And it would be interesting to compare the use of these two products during various eras. However, these two substances do differ in one crucial respect. During the nineteenth century, cane sugar began to decline in importance with the introduction first of beet sugar and then of substitutes such as saccharin. In contrast, there still is no substitute for tobacco, which thus remains unique in its market.

As the notes indicate, writing a history of smokeless tobacco consumption throughout the world and during more than four centuries is in large part a cooperative venture with earlier scholars in several fields. For assistance in gaining access to these sources, I owe thanks to the staffs of the Library of Congress and the Arents Collection at the New York Public Library. For their encouragement and assistance with technical matters, I am grateful to William Douwes, president of Dowes Communications, and Harry W. Peter III, senior vice president of UST Incorporated.

Chapter 1

Introduction

1.1 SUMMARY

This study is concerned with the consumption of tobacco in smokeless forms—those that do not require the tobacco to be burned through the introduction of fire—from about 1550 to 1950. The primary focus is the consumer of tobacco in the European states, in their colonies, and in the independent states that succeeded the European colonies in the Americas and the Pacific Basin. Indigenous to North and South America, tobacco was introduced to Europe during the sixteenth century. When European explorers reached the Americas, they found their inhabitants using tobacco in many ways—chewing it and taking it as nasal snuff, as well as smoking it in pipes, cigars, and a kind of cigarette rolled in vegetable matter.[1] Both smokeless and smoking tobacco were adopted during the sixteenth century, and both forms subsequently have been used throughout Europe and the European colonies.

During these four centuries, consumer preferences have evolved following habits and rhythms of taste that often are complicated. In some societies—France and Italy until the 1840s, the United States before 1900—smokeless tobacco has been preferred. In others, the majority of individuals smoked pipes, yet smokeless products still formed a large portion of total sales. Since the end of the nineteenth century, the use of smokeless products has tended to fall, and cigarettes have become universal in many areas. Nevertheless, snuff and chewing tobacco continue to be taken by consumers in almost every country, although they now represent a relatively large part of tobacco consumption only in the Scandinavian countries.

To the extent records permit, my emphasis is thus on the individual consumer enjoying tobacco in its various forms. In order to describe accurately how consumers have used smokeless tobacco, it is helpful to define the terms that will be used throughout the study. While smokeless products have not changed dramatically during the past centuries, the processes by which they are made have a history, as does tobacco itself. Chapter 2 thus presents a brief, nontechnical description of the tobacco plant. All the tobacco grown in the United States today—and perhaps 90 percent of that now grown throughout the world—is some form of the one biological species *Nicotiana tabacum*. As human energies have spread it throughout the world during the past five centuries, tobacco has diverged into a bewildering number of types. But all of these, including the Oriental strains, are varieties of *N. tabacum*.

These many varieties exist because tobacco is highly adaptable yet sensitive to many different environments. Although it is a tropical plant that loves heat and humidity, tobacco tolerates a wide variety of temperatures, rainfall, and soil conditions. Thus, it can grow and has been grown in radically different habitats throughout most of the world—in Africa, China, Japan, Korea, India, and the Middle East, as well as in most parts of Europe and North and South America.

Although tobacco can be raised almost anywhere, various areas produce different types of leaf, with the soil and climate influencing what characteristics will be produced. Broadly speaking, all tobaccos are either *light* or *dark,* with dark tobacco being characterized as having "stronger" qualities and light a more "mild" taste. The ways in which tobacco is cured also affect the qualities of taste, flavor, and aroma. After it is harvested, tobacco is dried and cured to remove much of the moisture and then is allowed to ferment and age before it is subjected to the manufacturing process. Human ingenuity has played a major role in the evolution of modern tobacco types. Over the past centuries, planters both have guided the evolution of the species, and they also have developed new methods of curing that enhance the appearance or flavor of the leaf. During the nineteenth century, for example, planters in the United States developed flue-cured Bright and air-cured Burley, both of which were favored by manufacturers of pressed chewing tobacco for their attractive appearance and their ability to absorb flavoring or sweetening agents.

The cured and fermented tobacco may then be put through one or more of several processes, which vary according to the likely use of the product. Users of tobacco absorb its flavors into the body in several ways. They chew tobacco, they place moist oral snuff behind the upper or lower lip, they inhale small particles of powdered snuff into the nose, or they set fire to tobacco and inhale the smoke into the mouth. Chapter 3 both describes the manufacturing processes that have been associated with these end uses, and it also traces the early history of these practices through an examination of the literary evidence.

Of all the ways of using tobacco, the oldest perhaps is chewing. During the nineteenth century, pressed chewing tobacco or plug represented more than half of all tobacco manufactured in the United States. To meet the needs of U.S. consumers, American manufacturers developed a number of distinctive products, whose history is described in Section 3.2. In Europe (Section 3.3), although chewing tobacco always has been used, it is more difficult to assess the precise incidence of the practice. Prior to the 1850s, European manufacturers produced large amounts of a kind of multipurpose plug (generally unflavored) which the end users might grind for snuff, slice for chewing, or cut up for smoking. Since their development, generally by the 1870s, products specifically intended for chewers have appealed to a minority of European consumers. Except in the Scandinavian countries, chewing tobacco thus has represented no more than 10 percent of the total market in Europe.

The development and early history of nasal snuff is discussed in Section 3.3. As is the case with chewing tobacco, there again are significant differences between practices in the United States and in Europe. In the United States, nasal snuff probably was less common than chewing or pipe smoking throughout the eighteenth century; although significant amounts of snuff are still sold in this country, most is used as an oral rather than a nasal product. In Europe, in contrast, literary evidence shows that nasal snuff is one of the original forms in which tobacco was borrowed from the American Indians. Snuff has been taken for as long as Europeans have used tobacco in any form, entering each nation with the introduction of the leaf itself. Thus, powdered tobacco was used during the second half of the seventeenth century in Portugal and in Spain, whence it spread to France and also to the Spanish dominions in Italy. By 1600 it also was present in England, Holland, and Germany. During the eighteenth century, snuff taking developed into an art form at the royal courts in Paris, London, Berlin, and Vienna. Although smoking did not entirely disappear, it was considered coarse by the aristocracy and those who copied their habits. The frequency of snuff taking among the less fashionable classes is more difficult to estimate. At the end of the eighteenth century, however, nasal snuff accounted for about 80 percent of all tobacco sales in France, about half those in England, and a third of sales in the Habsburg empire.

Section 3.4 discusses the use of moist oral snuff. Nasal snuff, which is inhaled or sniffed up into the nostrils, is one of the original forms in which tobacco always has been taken. Since at least the first third of the nineteenth century, snuff also has been consumed orally, with this practice being most frequently found in the United States and the Scandinavian countries. Rather than inhaling it into the nose, consumers place moist snuff between the lip and the gums—with Americans traditionally placing it behind the lower lip, and Swedes behind the upper lip. Oral snuff represents a development of snuff intended for nasal use, some of which was sold in a coarse-cut and moistened form during the eighteenth century. Thus, we cannot establish precisely when snuff first came to be used as an oral product in the United States. Literary evidence shows that it has been used in this way at least from the first third of the nineteenth century and perhaps already during the eighteenth century, and several of the products currently sold have been made in the same form since the 1830s.

Although no evidence of a direct connection has been found, oral snuff also became widespread in Sweden during precisely the same decades of the 1820s and 1830s. At first oral snuff seems to have been substituted for pressed chewing tobacco. By the 1840s, however, snuff had established itself as the most popular tobacco product in Sweden, where it consistently outsold both smoking tobacco and pressed plug for almost a century. In Norway and Denmark, sales of pressed chewing tobacco were larger than those of oral snuff at the beginning of this century. But the latter has represented a significant and—in the case of Denmark, growing—portion of the national market.

Sections 3.5 through 3.7 describe the alternatives to smokeless tobacco. Until the nineteenth century, nasal snuff predominated in Spain, England, France, and Italy. In contrast, cut smoking tobacco was mainly found in the Netherlands, in the Germanies, and in Central Europe. Perhaps because of the popularity of smokeless products, Europeans were slow to adopt the cigar or the cigarette. Outside Spain, cigars were introduced about 1800, but their sales remained very small until the 1840s. And cigarettes, although they were first offered for sale in the 1840s and 1850s, did not represent a significant portion of the market until the end of the century.

Chapter 4 summarizes governmental policies toward tobacco cultivation and marketing. From the very beginning of tobacco's introduction into Europe, governments have tried to control or influence its production, manufacture, and pricing as well as its consumption. These governmental policies never have been totally effective; for example, as much as one-third of the tobacco that left America during the eighteenth century was smuggled into Europe. Nevertheless, by affecting the supply or the cost of various products, governmental controls also must have affected usage, whether directly or indirectly. To take one example relevant to a study of smokeless tobacco—none of the state tobacco monopolies in Europe advertised or promoted either tobacco consumption in general or specific products. Thus, changes in product preferences in countries under monopoly regimes can be attributed to the unguided evolution of individual tastes.

As described in Chapter 4, since the seventeenth century, the tobacco trade has been treated as a governmental monopoly in France, Italy, the Iberian Peninsula, and throughout Central Europe. In all these regions, the domestic cultivation of tobacco was totally prohibited; and manufacturing, distribution, and retail sales were strictly controlled. At first, most of these governments could not administer this monopoly as a department of the state. Thus, they "farmed" their monopoly rights to one or more corporations; that is, in return for cash up front, they auctioned off the sole right for a set period of years to manufacture and sell tobacco products. The concessionaire groups enforced these rights both by employing their own police powers and by calling on those of the state. Starting at the end of the eighteenth century, these farmed concessions were brought under direct state control in the Habsburg empire (1784), France (1810), and Italy (1882); all the successor states to the Habsburg empire have retained a state monopoly. There are two European countries that have followed less typical policies. Although the United Kingdom left manufacturing and retail sales to private firms, it strictly prohibited the domestic cultivation of tobacco until 1910 in order to collect high duties on imported leaf, and the Swedish government, after permitting a free market during the nineteenth century, erected a farmed monopoly from 1915 through 1966.

Chapter 5 analyzes the evolution of consumer preferences in regions where accurate governmental data is available from the end of the eighteenth or the beginning of the nineteenth century—the Habsburg empire (which included northern Italy), France, and Sweden. When our records begin, nasal snuff was the preferred product in France and northern Italy, and it represented at least a third of sales in the Habsburg empire. The continuing popularity of snuff into the second half of the nineteenth century is striking. Virtually every history of tobacco assumes that snuff consumption fell off rapidly during the early nineteenth century. In fact, 1881 saw the highest annual snuff sales in the Habsburg empire (about 5 million pounds). In France also, snuff sales in absolute terms continued to increase until 1861. After the final third of the nineteenth century, sales of prepared snuff did decline in proportion to total sales—but at a comparatively slow rate of about 2 percent per year. Given the relative tenacity of snuff users, the state monopolies throughout the nineteenth century willingly budgeted funds to maintain or even improve their snuff manufactories. If the use of snuff became less common, it did not quickly disappear from either France or Austria, and it continues to be enjoyed today. Similarly, although never as widespread as snuff in these countries, chewing tobacco also continues to be purchased in small but steady amounts.

In Sweden (Section 5.5), the history of smokeless tobacco followed a course almost exactly opposite to that in France and Central Europe. As in other countries, the first half of the nineteenth century was marked by a shift from multipurpose plug to products intended for specific purposes. In many countries, however, the nineteenth century witnessed the growing acceptance of pipe smoking and a slow fall in the consumption of smokeless tobacco. In Sweden, precisely the opposite happened, as the Swedes adopted oral snuff as their primary way of using tobacco. The use of moist snuff as an oral product has been comprehensively documented starting from the end of the nineteenth century; these official production and sales records suggest that the Swedes adopted this product as early as the 1820s and 1830s. At the same time, pipe tobacco, which represented some 40 percent of sales in 1810, fell to only 10 percent or less by the 1870s. While a minority of individuals did continue to smoke, oral snuff represented a majority of tobacco sales for almost a century after 1840. In Sweden, as in other countries, a small group also remained loyal to pressed plug tobacco, which took about 5 to 10 percent of the market between 1885 and 1925.

By the beginning of the twentieth century, other countries in the industrialized world also began to keep records of tobacco consumption, and nearly every state did so by 1925. Overall, four main patterns may be distinguished in the use of smokeless tobacco from 1880 to 1950.

1. In France, Italy, and the Habsburg empire, cut smoking tobacco became the most common product, but the state monopolies continued to sell significant amounts of nasal snuff and chewing tobacco.

2. The inhabitants of the Scandinavian states have been especially likely to use oral snuff and chewing tobacco, as described in Section 6.2. Like the Swedes, the Icelanders primarily have taken snuff. In contrast, the Norwegians and the Danes initially joined with the North Americans in choosing plug chewing tobacco (Table 6.2). After 1925, however, sales of plug fell in Norway while those of snuff remained more stable; by 1950 Norway was second only to Sweden in the use of oral snuff.

3. At the end of the nineteenth century, North Americans favored chewing tobacco over all types of smoking products (Section 6.3); in 1880, plug thus represented more than half of all tobacco sales in the United States, with cigars and cut tobacco more or less tied for second place. But per capita consumption of chewing tobacco had already reached its peak in 1880. During the next seventy years, U.S. tobacco users gradually adopted cigarettes, and consumption of cigars, pipe tobacco, and chewing tobacco all have fallen. Sales of snuff—mainly taken as moist oral snuff—have been more stable over time than those of pressed plug tobacco. As a consequence, although its sales were only a small fraction of plug sales in 1880, snuff had by 1950 almost overtaken plug chewing tobacco to become the best-selling smokeless product in the United States (Table 6.4).

4. In the United Kingdom, in Germany, in the Netherlands, and in the successor states to the Habsburg empire, cut pipe tobacco was the best selling product before World War I, with cigarettes generally replacing the pipe by 1950. But both chewing tobacco and snuff also have been used in every European country. Although per capita consumption was lower than in North America, chewing tobacco was particularly prevalent in the United Kingdom, in Germany, and in the British dominion of Australia. In Central Europe, most of the state tobacco monopolies erected in 1918 also have sold snuff and chewing tobacco, but use of these products traditionally has been lower than in Western Europe. Almost everywhere, chewing tobacco consumption has declined more precipitously than that of snuff, and snuff thus has replaced plug as the best-selling smokeless product in several of these countries.

1.2 NOTE ON SOURCES

This study focuses on tobacco products and their use for pleasure by the consumer. At the same time, the history of tobacco cannot be separated from the overall development of European and American culture, of which it forms an integral part. Because these affect the availability and prices of the products offered to consumers, Chapter 4 briefly describes marketing practices and governmental regulations that have a direct bearing on an analysis of consumer preferences. Indeed, changes in attitudes toward government and concomitant

U.K.
c. 1790?

changes in governmental policies even influence whether we can measure these consumer preferences at all. Prior to the last decades of the nineteenth century, governments were not expected to manage a nation's economy, and they did not collect information about the economic activities of private individuals. For this reason, we have numerical or statistical evidence describing (more or less accurately) the consumption of tobacco products only from those countries that were under state monopolies administered as a department of the government— the Habsburg empire (from 1784), France (1818), and Italy (1868). Before about 1880—and thus during the entire first three centuries of tobacco's use— no records exist describing what types of products were purchased by consumers either in countries with free markets or in countries where the state farmed its tobacco monopoly to a private concessionaire.

Some records relating to tobacco consumption may have been lost. In most cases, this information probably never was collected, and it certainly was not retained for future reference. In countries without state monopolies, the manufacture and retail marketing of tobacco was in the hands of hundreds or even thousands of small firms, which did not have the resources or the need to maintain records of product formulas or sales.[2] The very distinction between manufacturer and retailer is anachronistic prior to the second half of the nineteenth century. The first products with a manufacturer's "brand" were introduced in the United States and England only about 1850,[3] and retailers long continued to create their own snuffs or smoking mixtures by blending tobaccos they purchased in large quantities from firms processing the leaf.[4]

As also occurred in several other industries, tobacco manufacturing in the United States, the United Kingdom, and the German empire was reorganized and rationalized into large *trusts* toward the end of the nineteenth century. Although governments subsequently broke up these putative private monopolies or trusts, the industry in countries not under state monopolies has remained concentrated in a few multinational corporations.[5] In order to manage their worldwide operations, today's larger companies must maintain internal accounting systems. However, they are as loath as their smaller predecessors to allow competitors or—in an increasingly litigious age—potential claimants access to this information.[6]

During the eighteenth century, private groups farmed the tobacco monopolies in France, the Habsburg empire, and some of the German and Italian states; a farmed monopoly was retained in Italy until 1883, and this system also survived on the Iberian peninsula.[7] Only the farmed monopoly in France has been subjected to intensive analysis, and an exhaustive study of its surviving records has unearthed little information about product composition and no evidence about the sales of specific products prior to 1789.[8] Unlike private companies in a market system, these monopolists did not need to protect trade secrets from competitors. But the process by which the state conceded a monopoly to a private company gave the latter a strong incentive to make as little financial information as possible available to outsiders. As described in Chapter 4, governments effectively auctioned off their monopoly powers during a period of years in return for cash up front from the highest bidder. Assuming that the process was not rigged, it was in the interest of the current concessionaire to discourage another group from offering to pay the government a higher fee. For this reason, private monopolies tended either to avoid the release of accurate sales data or to report that their sales were lower than was in fact the case. The company that farmed the French monopoly during the 1770s, for example, deliberately falsified the sales records it provided to the government in order to conceal the extent of its profits.[9]

During the past eighty years, national and even provincial governments have begun to collect, preserve, and release information about production, sales, employment, and savings as part of their efforts to manage the growth of the overall economy. While some officials did accumulate records during earlier centuries, they generally preserved only information about tax collections that was perceived as directly relevant to the government's own fiscal needs. Throughout the nineteenth century, the largest centers for the manufacture and marketing of tobacco products in non-monopoly countries were found in the United States, England, the Netherlands, and Alsace. National governments in the United States and the Netherlands, which collected no taxes on domestic tobacco and only small duties on imports, had no reason to measure production and consumption.[10] The national government in the United Kingdom and the government of Strasbourg in Alsace did tax tobacco imports, with the English duties being levied at an extremely high rate. However, they imposed these taxes as a uniform charge on each pound of tobacco leaf imported by manufacturer without regard to the purpose for which the latter used the leaf.[11]

Governments in these major non-monopoly states thus made no attempt to follow what happened to tobacco leaf as it traveled from the grower or importer, through the manufacturing and distribution process, to the retailer and purchaser. In these countries, the retailing of tobacco products was largely unregulated, and they were sold in thousands of coffee houses in the cities as well as by virtually every general store, grocer, and baker in the smaller towns and villages.[12] And no government saw any reason to ask this multitude of retailers what kinds of tobacco were requested by their customers.

Indeed, since their concern was to collect the duty on the current year's imports of raw leaf, officials in the United Kingdom were slow even to keep records of the taxes paid on imports in prior years.

Before the beginning of the eighteenth century there does not seem to have been any thought of collecting the statistics of tobacco imports and consumption either for publication or reference. They were sometimes given in answer to a question in the House of Commons, but were not printed, being bound up with the miscellaneous papers of the session in the Commons' library, and were destroyed in the fire of 1834.[13]

Not until 1786 did the British government retain the official Custom House figures.[14] In the same way, the archives of Strasbourg in Alsace, which also levied a duty on imported leaf, contain an accounting of the amount collected only since 1726.[15]

For the United States, the largest consumer of tobacco products in the Western world, virtually no sources exist that can provide quantitative data about tobacco consumption before about 1880. The records of the decennial census from 1840 to the present permit estimates of the total production of leaf in some years, and other sources suggest what amount of the crop may have been exported.[16] However, we do not know how manufacturers used the leaf that was retained for home consumption. The first U.S. census that provides reasonably accurate data about the total output of manufactured products is that conducted in 1880; while chance has preserved the production records of a few companies from isolated years, we do not know what share of the market they enjoyed. Records of imports also provide little guidance. Only in the case of cigars were substantial amounts imported, and domestic production seems to have satisfied the demand for other manufactured products.[17]

The federal government has taxed manufactured tobacco products continuously since 1862. As described in Chapter 4, the tax is imposed on the manufacturer only when products are "withdrawn" from the factory or warehouse for distribution. Because there is thus a relatively brief time lag between collection of the tax and retail sales, the amount of tax collected for each type of product may be considered a generally accurate measurement of sales and consumption. In many years, when the same rate of tax was levied on chewing and smoking tobacco, these tax records discriminate only between cigars, cigarettes, and "other manufactured tobacco." By analyzing tax receipts against other records, however, the research staff at the U.S. Department of Agriculture has developed and published a statistical series reporting on the production of the major categories of tobacco products beginning in 1880.[18] While a substantial amount of tobacco was still cured at home by small growers in the 1880s and 1890s, the series published by the Agriculture Department provides a credible measurement of consumption over time for the entire United States—but unfortunately only during the twentieth century.[19]

As did that of the United States, many governments in Europe toward the end of the nineteenth century began to take an interest in the overall level of private manufacturing. To measure economic activity, they collected data on domestic production either—as in the new German Empire—on a continuing basis or intermittently, through a "census of production" similar to the already-existing censuses of human population. After the United States and Germany, Scandinavian countries such as Denmark (1897) and Norway (1909) were among the first non-monopoly countries to gather these *produktionsstatistik*. The English Dominions, whose governments then tended to espouse Liberal or Laissez-faire philosophies not congenial to governmental intervention in the economy, were somewhat slower to carry out production censuses. The government of the United Kingdom performed the first such exercise in 1907, followed by Australia in 1908 and Canada in the 1920s, but the government of

New Zealand apparently did not do so until after World War II. Some of the smaller states, such as Switzerland and the Netherlands, did not publish information specific to the tobacco industry until the 1950s.

Some of these censuses of production can supply statistics measuring overall domestic production—but only during the past century. Moreover, the published governmental reports are sometimes insufficient for the present purposes in one or more ways. Some goverments, such as the United States, measured production only in terms of the aggregated dollar value of a factory's output rather than in physical units of output; although this practice is certainly defensible in many cases (the radios made in one factory are not fungible with those produced by another factory), it is not immediately helpful for our purpose to know that a group of factories turned out 30 million dollars worth of cigarettes and "other manufactured tobacco." In other countries, such as the German Empire, the government did gather numerical measurements of physical things; perhaps in response to the complaints of manufacturers, however, it did not release this information in some years and instead published reaggregated trend data that obfuscate changes in the type of product manufactured.

Before World War II, only a limited number of production censuses provide precisely what is needed—the output, in pounds or numbers of items, of specific types of manufactured tobacco products. In these cases, the census, which measures only domestic output and does not take account of imports and exports, might be open to criticism as a measure of total consumption. However, at least in the case of tobacco products prior to 1950, domestic production in most countries does seem to be more or less equivalent to consumption. That is, in every case that has import and export data in a form that permits comparison to the published production data, domestic output—which may, of course, use imported leaf—does seem to account for the overwhelming majority of tobacco products available for sale.

In 1913, for example, the Danish Statistical Bureau helpfully published an accounting in comparable units (kilograms) that includes domestic production, imports, and exports. As Table 1.1 shows, domestic production supplied all

Table 1.1
Consumption of Tobacco Products in Denmark during 1913 (in thousands of U.S. pounds)

	Snuff	Chewing	Cut	Cigars[1]	Cigar-ettes
domestic	295	2,820	4,103	3,300	496
plus imported	103	--	400	299	207
less exported	71	2	152	117	13
net consumption	327	2,818	4,351	3,482	690

[1] Includes cigarillos.

Source: Denmark, Statistiske Department, *Statistiske Meddelelser,* 4th Series, 50.2:65.

the chewing tobacco used in Denmark as well as almost all the snuff (90 percent), pipe mixtures (94 percent), and cigars (95 percent) consumed by Danes; only in the case of cigarettes, which were new to the Danish market, did imports take a significant share of sales. Moreover, and perhaps most telling, imports and exports of imported products tend to be proportional both to domestic production and to total consumption of the same products. (In this case, for example, cigars represent 30 percent of domestic production, 38 percent of net imports, and 30 percent of all consumption.) Except in unusual circumstances, which are taken into account, import data would not change my conclusions; hence, when there are no sources measuring consumption, governmental production data can serve as a legitimate surrogate.[20]

In countries with a free market and in countries where the state monopoly was farmed by a private group, there are almost no records from individual manufacturers or retailers, and governments did not collect information about the production and distribution of tobacco products. Before the 1880s, to obtain the objective overview of total consumption that is provided by quantitative measurements, it is necessary to rely on the records of those governments— the Habsburg empire (from 1784), France (1818), and Italy (1868)—that treated the tobacco monopoly as an administrative department. To these records we may add those collected by the Swedish government since 1780. Prior to the erection of a concessionaire monopoly between 1915 and 1967, tobacco products were manufactured in Sweden by a mix of both private and public companies, but the rulers of this small state sought from an unusually early date to obtain measurements of production in order to guide industrial development.[21]

In contrast to the executives of private companies or contract monopolists, the administrators of these state monopolies found it in their self-interest to respond to public criticism by releasing more or less detailed information about their operations. The French and Habsburg *régies* (administrations) in particular generally have followed what is perhaps the most effective method of maximizing profits in a case of total monopoly; that is, they have attempted to sell tobacco to each consumer at the highest price she or he is willing to pay for it. Both tobacco administrations always have carried a variety of goods, ranging from low-priced products made of domestic *tabac inférieur* (as it is described in the accounts of the French régie) to expensive imported snuff and cigars. The better the quality, the higher is the price extorted. And, in the absence of alternative suppliers of decent tobacco, the prices charged at the high end notoriously have exceeded the retail price of the same or similar products in neighboring countries without a monopoly. Given that the wealthy individuals who purchased the better goods tended to be literate, they were aware of and resented this discrepancy. Throughout the history of these state monopolies, charges were made that their exorbitant prices would garner much higher profits for the state except for the inefficiency and dishonesty of the régie's administrators. It was thus politic for those administrators to release relatively detailed statistics purporting to show that the costs associated with leaf purchases, manufacturing, administrative overhead, and executive perquisites were not out of line with those in private industries.

In many cases, the published reports of these state tobacco administrations also give information about the sales of specific products, much as the post office today might issue a press release detailing the number of items it had carried the previous year at express, first-class, third-class, and parcel rates. However, a description of sales quantities was always secondary to a report on expenses and revenues measured in monetary units.[22] Since the amount of added sales data supplied each year always varied with the initiative or even the whim of the particular individuals in charge, it is thus not provided in a consistent manner over time. In some years, because the information about sales is aggregated into patently meaningless categories, it therefore is necessary to substitute production data when the latter is more precise.

Between 1784 and the 1840s, for example, the Austrian state tobacco monopoly reported sales broken down into only the two categories of snuff and all other products, with the latter—more than 70 percent of total sales—simply lumped together under the catchall rubric *Rauchtabak*. Furthermore, although they begin to give abundant details (including the sales of individual brands) from the 1840s, the reports of the Austrian régie continued for another sixty years to aggregate pressed chewing tobacco and fine-cut smoking products. The French have prided themselves on the logical clarity of their thought processes, and the reports of the French monopoly do provide usable evidence about tobacco consumption during the nineteenth century. Again, however, the logic of these reports was intended to meet the needs of financial accounting rather than those of marketing. In some years, for example, large amounts of the cheapest cigars, cigarettes, smoking mixtures, and chewing tobacco thus may have been reported together as one item—because the retail price was the same for one kilogram of chewing tobacco as for ten cigars (weighing half as much).

To the extent possible, Chapters 5 and 6 present an objective analysis of changes over time in the consumption of tobacco products. Whenever feasible, the text and the accompanying tables present the same type of data at regular intervals.[23] In the case of individual countries, for example, the tables report sales of the same products at ten-year intervals. When, for the reasons described above, sales data are not available for a given year, comparable production data has been substituted. If the sources supply no meaningful information for a particular year, the tables report on the next year for which we have data.[24] Consideration has also been given to the political circumstances. For example, the text and tables report sales during 1925 as well as during 1920 and 1930; especially in the new states that were created following World War I, markets remained disorganized in 1920, and certain products were not bought simply because they were unavailable for purchase.

NOTES

1. Brooks, *Tobacco in the Library of George Arents*, I:19.

2. For the United States, see Note 4 to Chapter 3. Based on the manuscript census records, there were about 300 tobacco factories in the states of Virginia and North Carolina in 1850; about one-third of these had a capital investment in plant and machinery of less than one thousand dollars according to Robert, *Tobacco Kingdom*, 171. In the United Kingdom, also about 1850, there were still 732 licensed manufacturers, with the 52 largest firms accounting for about one-third to one-half of retail output; these supplied about 185,000 retailers and dealers: Alford, *W. D. & H. O. Wills*, 95, 111. A century earlier, tobacco manufacturing had been carried out in literally thousands of small shops, employing tobacco and snuff workers under a skilled foreman: George, *London Life*, 456.

3. The firm of W. D. and H. O. Wills introduced its first branded products, two cut tobaccos and one shag, on January 1, 1847 (Alford, *W. D. & H. O. Wills*, 97). In the 1850s, manufacturers in the United States also began to give their products names that they hoped would be distinctive and seductive to the purchaser; however, paid advertising by manufacturers became common only after the Civil War, perhaps because trade names could not be patented until the 1880s: Robert, *Tobacco Kingdom*, 218–21; Heimann, *Tobacco and Americans*, 131–38.

4. The elite tobacconists catering to the gentry created their own expensive products, but small shops in rural villages also blended products aimed at the local market: McCausland, *Snuff*, 51–53, 76–78; Arlott, *Snuff Shop*, 57–59. See Price (*France and the Chesapeake*, 468–71) for the French monopoly's continuing and unsuccessful attempts to prevent retailers from grinding their own snuff.

5. Tucker (*Tobacco: An International Perspective*, 69) estimates that in 1980 the five largest multinational corporations together supplied about 35 percent of the cigarette market worldwide; counting in the Communist dictatorships, sales by state monopolies account for another 55 percent of the total world market. Tucker's estimates refer to the retail market and do not take into account homemade cigarettes consumed in Africa and Asia.

6. According to Tilley (*R. J. Reynolds*, xviii–xix, 445), in 1953 the president of one U.S. tobacco company ordered its employees to destroy virtually all internal records relating to past operations, partly to prevent lawyers and accountants from searching for references that might be made to support a law suit.

7. A farmed monopoly also existed in Sweden from 1915 to 1967; see Section 4.8.

8. Price, *France and the Chesapeake*, 427.

9. Ibid., 391.

10. For taxation in the Netherlands, see Gray and Wyckoff, "International Tobacco Trade," 3–4; Barbour, *Capitalism in Amsterdam*, 92–93.

11. Rive, "Consumption of Tobacco," 63; Chapter 4, Note 48.

12. See Note 3 for the retail tobacco trade during the nineteenth century. For the Netherlands, see Brongers, *Nicotiana tabacum*, 239. In eighteenth-century England, not only did coffeehouses and taverns supply tobacco, but tobacconists also sold gin: McCausland, *Snuff*, 23–27; George, *London Life*, 33. In countries under a state monopoly, only licensed retailers were in principle allowed to sell tobacco; but this prohibition could never be enforced in France, where "keepers of public houses of every description . . . sold the consumer his tobacco by the quarter pound, the ounce, or even the

pipeful'' (Price, *France and the Chesapeake*, 140). These under-the-counter sales were at least as frequent in Central Europe and Italy; see Chapter 5.

13. Rive, ''Consumption of Tobacco,'' 56.

14. Ibid., 63.

15. Hanauer, *Études économiques*, II:597.

16. Robert, *Tobacco Kingdom*, 128–31; Gray, *History of Agriculture in the Southern States*, 214–15.

17. Gottsegen, *Tobacco, a Study*, 7–8.

18. Gage, *American Tobacco Types*, 106–15, for a detailed discussion of the statistical series published by the U.S. Department of Agriculture.

19. See Chapter 3, Note 3.

20. It might be argued that neither domestic consumption nor domestic production statistics take into account sales to visitors from other countries; thus, it is hypothetically conceivable (though extremely unlikely) that most of the snuff produced in Denmark was not used by Danes but rather was sold to German, Swedish, or Norwegian tourists while they were visiting Denmark. However, mass travel for pleasure is a very recent phenomenon; except in very rare cases (such as during a world's fair in London or Paris), consumption by tourists is so minute prior to the 1950s that it safely can be ignored. Moreover, my purpose does not require a totally accurate measurement of consumption in individual nation states, whose borders have changed frequently over the past three centuries. If some of the chewing tobacco made in Denmark was consumed by Swedes, this has no bearing on (and is irrelevant to) my conclusion that Scandinavians use oral snuff more frequently than Mediterranean peoples such as the Italians or the Greeks.

21. See Chapter 4, Notes 40–43.

22. The Habsburg yearbooks, for example, indicate that an accounting of revenues and expenses is their primary goal by the very title *(Tabak-Gefall)* that they give to the tobacco statistics.

23. For ease of comparison and visual consistency, sales or production of tobacco products consistently are expressed in units of one thousand U.S. pounds; the sales or production data in the original sources has been converted to pounds from kilograms, English stone, or Viennese Zentner. In some cases, when governmental sources report the number of pieces of chewing tobacco or the number of cigars produced or sold each year in thousands of pieces rather than in terms of weight, the weight of these products has been calculated using the standard conversion factors reported by industry sources in those countries. Large and small cigars and cigarillos have been treated as one item, since the distinction between large and small both is subjective and also varies from time to time. All references refer to standard-size cigarettes; king-size and 100s did not become common until after 1950.

Converting all consumption or surrogate production data to one consistent standard—weight in thousands of U.S. pounds—allows a comparison of the use of tobacco products in different regions or in different eras. It is possible that one pound of, say, chewing tobacco is not always equivalent to one pound of snuff or cigars; that is, consumers of chewing tobacco in some eras may have used, on average, more or less of this product each day than consumers of snuff or cigars. But there is simply no evidence one way or the other. During the first half of the nineteenth century, the Habsburg state monopoly assumed that on average its customers purchased about eleven pounds each year or about half an ounce a day; this daily amount is equivalent to less than a pack of standard (but not king-size) cigarettes. Other individuals may have used more or less snuff each day. We cannot know what the typical consumption pattern was, or even if there was one.

24. Throughout, the tables signal by a broken line—which is inserted between the years affected—these lacunae in the sources or unavoidable changes in the base described by the statistics. For example, a broken line between the data for 1910 and 1920 signals that during the intervening years the Austrian tobacco monopoly had lost the vast majority of its customers, who now had to purchase their tobacco from the state monopolies in Czechoslovakia, Poland, and Yugoslavia.

Chapter 2

The Tobacco Plant

2.1 GENERAL CHARACTERISTICS

Biology assigns tobacco to the genus *Nicotiana,* one member of the very large family of plants, chiefly tropical, called *Solanaceae.* Altogether, this large family contains about eighty-five genera, within which are eighteen hundred species that include other useful plants—the potato, green pepper, eggplant, and tomato—as well as ornamentals and the deadly nightshade. Botanists further divide the tobacco genus into three subtypes, *rustica, tabacum,* and *petunioides,* which when taken together contain about sixty different species. All the tobacco grown in the United States today—and perhaps 90 percent of tobacco now grown throughout the world—is some form of only one of these sixty species, *Nicotiana (N.) tabacum.* Although the latter is in turn classified into many varieties, whose differences are important to producers and can be noticed by the consumer, all these varieties are biologically identical.[1]

A second type of tobacco, *N. rustica,* has been grown for local consumption in parts of Europe and is still produced for this purpose in the Middle East and in some Asian countries. Under the name *makhorka, rustica* was consumed in large quantities into the twentieth century in Russia and eastern Poland. Although highly appreciated in these areas, it has seldom formed part of the international or even a national market, and virtually all the tobacco products mentioned in the sources have been derived from one form or another of *N. tabacum.* Thus, unless otherwise specified throughout this work, the term *tobacco* always refers to this latter species.

Tobacco is perhaps unique in that the valuable part of the plant is its leaf, which is usually more or less pointed and generally twice as long as it is broad. Overall, the plant often is shaped something like a pyramid, with the largest leaves growing nearest to the ground. The size of the leaf varies with the variety and with soil conditions, and it has also been deliberately modified over the centuries. However it has always been very large in comparison both to the plant's root structure and to its small flowers and minute seeds. A mature leaf is often one to one-and-a-half square feet in area (or even larger for some recent varieties), and a single plant with eighteen leaves can thus produce twenty-five square feet of leaf. With six thousand to ten thousand plants per acre, the yield in leaf per acre can be truly prodigious.[2]

These leaves contain a complex of chemical compounds, which are affected by climate and by soil type as well as by the process of curing and manufacture. Taken all together, these compounds contribute to the subjective qualities we call taste, flavor, and aroma. These qualities cannot fully be explained by chemical analysis even today. Over the centuries, moreover, tobacco types have changed and evolved, largely reflecting the evolution of consumer taste. Thus, the dark leaf available today is not necessarily the same as the dark tobacco produced in 1750. In listing these tobacco types or in reporting consumer opinions regarding taste either today or hundreds of years ago, I cannot be more precise than my sources.

Among the chemical compounds in tobacco are a number of alkaloids, of which the best known is nicotine. Analysis of these compounds became possible only during the nineteenth century, and nicotine was isolated only in 1829.[3] At the present time, *rustica* can furnish products with up to 16 percent nicotine; the more common *tabacum* yields products that contain less than 8 percent and usually vary from 1 to 4 percent nicotine. The nicotine content of each variety may be hereditary; however, since it is affected by climate, the manufacturing process, and the presence of additives, there is no way of knowing precisely how much nicotine was present in, for example, the pipe tobacco or the nasal snuff used during the eighteenth century.[4] Again, I can only report that some tobaccos were considered stronger than others, with no way of knowing precisely what was meant by that description.

Both *N. tabacum* and *N. rustica* originally are native to the Americas, where *rustica* was grown in the northeastern half of what is now the United States, while *tabacum* was cultivated in Central and South America and in the West Indies. (Curiously, biologists have never found *tabacum* growing in the wild state; it apparently is a natural mutation that was cultivated by the Native Americans and was reliant on human assistance.) Although some writers have attempted to show that tobacco was known in Asia or Africa prior to its discovery in the Americas, it seems certain that all the tobacco now grown derives from plants brought from the New World.

In spreading throughout the world during the past five centuries, tobacco has diverged into a bewildering number of types. However, all of these, including the Oriental strains, are varieties of *tabacum*.[5] These varieties exist because tobacco is highly adaptable and yet sensitive to many different environments. Although it is a tropical plant that loves heat and humidity, tobacco tolerates a wide variety of temperatures, rainfall, and soil conditions. Thus, it can grow and has been grown in radically different habitats throughout most of the world.

Tobacco enjoys a relatively short growing season, needing under optimum conditions only about 80 to 90 days to come to harvest. While it matures more slowly in cooler climates, it can be grown in any locale with 120 to 150 days between killing frosts. During these (3) months of growth, the plant prefers an average temperature of about 80° Fahrenheit, but it will survive a range of temperatures from about 60° to 100°. And although rapid growth and large leaves require liberal, well-distributed rainfall, tobacco will also provide a crop in times of drought and in relatively wet seasons—as long as the soil is well-drained so that the plants do not drown.[6]

Given this adaptability, tobacco has been grown in fair quantities at latitudes from 60° north (Sweden) to 50° south (New Zealand). At the present time, the bulk of production is north of the equator and south of 40° north; and the most commercially desirable crops seem to grow between 10° north and 35° north (in China and Japan as well as in the band between Cuba and Tennessee). However, over the past five centuries, tobacco has been successfully grown virtually everywhere in the world—in Africa, China, Japan, Korea, India, and the Middle East, as well as in most parts of Europe and in North and South America.[7]

Tobacco thus can be raised almost anywhere. But various areas produce different types of leaves, with the soil apparently the main factor determining what type of leaf will be produced. Again, a type of tobacco will grow in many kinds of soil, but the same type grows differently in each soil. Moisture content and adequate drainage is particularly essential, especially in areas of heavy, sporadic rainfall. The plant may be said to prefer light, aerated soil that provides a mixture of sand, humus, and limestone in which water circulates freely. Thus, it grows quickly and well—producing large leaves that are low in nicotine and not too thick—in sandy soil provided with humus and limestone. It can also flourish in clay soils if humus again is present to hold in moisture between rains. While sizeable crops have been produced in soils that are mostly clay or that contain larger portions of limestone, the leaves will be smaller and thicker with fatter stems.

With the exception of Burley tobacco, which was introduced in 1864, a general rule of thumb has been that light open soils tend to produce a thin leaf that is light in weight and color and that has a less heavy aroma. In contrast, heavier soils produce a thick, heavy, strong leaf of darker color with a stronger flavor and higher nicotine content. Neither dark nor light tobacco is inherently superior; instead, the two types have been preferred for different purposes at various times.

Light sandy loams or loamy sands can thus produce abundant crops. But tobacco must be generously fertilized—particularly during the last two months when the plant accomplishes 90 percent of its growth. Substantial amounts of

nitrogen and potassium are required as well as lesser portions of lime and phos-
phoric acid. Today chemical fertilizers are used. In earlier centuries, these nu-
trients were largely provided through the application before planting of dung
and manure, in which they abound.[8]

2.2 AMERICAN TOBACCO TYPES

In several aspects, tobacco is not unlike the grapes from which wine is made.
As do wines, various types of tobacco differ significantly in flavor, taste, and
aroma. These differences are perhaps least noticeable in modern branded cigarettes, which are blended from several tobacco types and manufactured in carefully controlled ways to achieve a uniformity of taste that does not vary from
package to package. They are more readily discerned in the case of some traditional pipe tobaccos or in some smokeless tobaccos. And they were clearly
more noticeable before the end of the nineteenth century, when the mechanization of tobacco manufacturing made it possible to obtain consistency over
time.

Although these differences in taste, flavor, and aroma are obvious to the
consumer, they have not been precisely measured. In 1928, the United States
Department of Agriculture established a comprehensive system of classes and
types, and classification has been mandatory since 1935.[9] However, these standards are based on physical type and not on flavor, which remains largely a
matter of subjective judgment. Moreover, while the major tobacco types do
tend to exhibit certain general characteristics, these are affected both by the
soil in which they are grown and by the processes of curing and manufacture.
(It should be noted that some of the terms—such as Virginia or Oriental—that
originally referred to tobacco grown in specific areas now refer to general types
that are present throughout the world.)

In the ways discussed above, the climate and soil type affect the nature of
the chemical compounds that give each tobacco its particular taste, flavor, and
aroma. Broadly speaking, all tobaccos are either light or dark, with dark tobacco being characterized as having stronger and light more mild qualities.
These qualities are affected also by the processes involved in curing, fermentation, and manufacture. After harvesting, tobacco first is dried and cured to
remove much of the moisture, and then is allowed to ferment for at least a
year. During the curing process, the leaf is exposed to warm air that has been
heated either by the sun or artificially in enclosed barns.

Although some of these methods have been used only since the nineteenth
century, there currently are four main ways in which tobacco is cured; these
are summarized by Table 2.1. At the present time, flue-cured light leaf, which
primarily is used for blended cigarettes, probably represents the majority of
world tobacco production. Dark tobaccos usually are air- or fire-cured; while
the French, Spanish, and Central European monopolies have used dark tobaccos to manufacture cigarettes, they are primarily consumed in pipe tobacco,

Table 2.1
Major Forms of Cured Tobacco Leaf

Curing Method	Color	Type
flue-cured	light	Virginia
		Bright
air-cured	light	Burley
		Maryland
	dark	Black
		cigar wrapper
sun-cured	light	Oriental
	dark	
fire-cured	dark	Virginia

cigars, chewing tobacco, and oral and nasal snuff. However, these practices are not invariable, and there have been significant changes over the past four centuries in the types of tobacco used as well as the ways in which they have been consumed.

Throughout the eighteenth century and into the nineteenth, virtually all the tobacco consumed in this country and much of that used in Europe came from what is now the southern United States. It was the wealth from this export trade that gave rise to the fabled Tobacco Kingdom, which has received detailed study from American historians. What is less well known is the reason for the dominance of this industry in the Old South. No environmental or economic factors made Virginia's export trade inevitable. As Chapter 4 shows, the quasi-monopoly in the United States was, at least in part, the artificial creation of European monarchs who sought to enrich their treasuries through a state monopoly of the tobacco supply. Since they could not adequately control the crops of their peasantry, these rulers simply prohibited any cultivation of tobacco within their own realms.

Prior to the American Revolution, European importers recognized only two major classes of tobacco—Spanish and Virginia. Virginia tobacco was in turn sometimes further subdivided into Oronoko and *sweet scented*—although these rubrics were imprecisely used, and tobacco inspectors, finding it difficult to distinguish various types, sometimes tended to classify all American tobacco as Oronoko. Oronoko apparently resembled what is now know as fire-cured — dark leaf, and it generally was characterized as strong and heavy. It grew best in the rich, heavy soils of the bottom lands of the James, York, and Rappahannock rivers in the tidewater region of Virginia. Sweet scented, which differed from Oronoko in having a shorter and less pointed leaf, was somewhat milder in flavor and required more sandy loam. Throughout the seventeenth century, most tobacco was air-cured, but fire curing also came to be used in the 1700s in damp weather or to give a bright yellow color to the best grade of Oronoko, known as Kite's-foot.[10] Most of the tobacco grown in colonial Maryland also seems to have been of the Oronoko type; it is only during the last century, when many growers began to dry their tobacco in barns without heat, that Maryland became a distinct type.[11]

Strong dark tobacco of the Oronoko type continued to be produced in Virginia until the Civil War, and dark air- and fire-cured tobacco is still grown in comparatively limited quantities today. However, two additional types of tobacco were developed during the last third of the nineteenth century that have come to comprise the majority of the leaf grown in the United States—flue-cured Bright and air-cured White Burley, both of which are milder and lighter in color than the original colonial leaf. Bright tobacco is not a hybrid; it is produced when tobacco leaf grown on light sandy ridges is subjected to the hot air from charcoal fires. Burley apparently is a true hybrid and the result of a spontaneous mutation. Both varieties, however, were carefully developed over a period of years to provide a milder, smoother leaf of light color.

Dark, fire-cured tobacco is highly suitable for use both in pipes and in smokeless tobacco. Since these were the main ways in which tobacco was consumed in Europe throughout the nineteenth century, European manufacturers imported only limited quantities of light or yellow tobacco.[12] Consequently, as long as American farmers produced tobacco mainly for export, they primarily cultivated the darker leaf. However, as the growing American population increasingly came to chew or to *dip* oral snuff, the market price of light tobacco increased, providing an incentive for the development of these new forms.

During the nineteenth century, chewing tobacco came to be sold in square *plugs,* for which a light-colored, smooth leaf is desirable as a wrapper. Since they also contain much less sugar than the older, dark tobaccos, Bright and Burley also can absorb more of the flavorings—licorice, rum, sugar, and honey— favored by some chewers.[13] Both types were thus in demand by manufacturers of plug. At the end of the century, both also were found to be suitable in the manufacture of mild, blended cigarettes, and the area devoted to their cultivation thus increased even further along with the rising popularity of cigarette smoking during the twentieth century.[14] Today, both Bright and Burley are cultivated throughout the world and represent at least three-fourths of the leaf grown for the market.[15]

At the beginning of the nineteenth century the American pioneers brought the tobacco industry west to Tennessee and Ohio and also south to North Carolina, where they attempted to cultivate leaf on the coarse, light sandy soil of the ridges along the border with Virginia.[16] A well-publicized story attributes the discovery of curing with charcoal fires to Stephen, an eighteen-year-old slave belonging to Abisha Slade of Caswell Country, North Carolina, just south of the Virginia border. According to this story, having allowed the open wood fires in Slade's barn to go very low, Stephen stoked them with charcoal and found that the leaf "kep' on yallowin' and kep' on yallowin' and kep' on yallowin.' ''[17] In fact, experiments with charcoal fires for curing had begun twenty years earlier; and a system of flues to distribute the heat came into use only in the 1850s and was not generally adopted in North Carolina until 1872. Indeed, charcoal and flues had been in use in Maryland and Ohio in the 1820s. Moreover, charcoal curing in itself is not enough to provide Bright, which requires the combination both of light sandy soils and also of relatively rapid curing with smokeless heat.[18]

Bright represents a combination of soil and curing method. Burley (or White Burley) is a true mutation of a dark air-cured type (Red Burley), which was first noticed in 1864 in Brown County, Ohio.[19] Although farm management and soil types can produce Burley that is darker or lighter, it is characteristically a relatively light and mild tobacco that can be grown on deep, fairly rich loamy soils. Because it can absorb even greater amounts of sugar and other sweeteners than Bright, Burley was rapidly developed as an alternative and ultimately came to dominate the chewing tobacco market.[20] It is today grown throughout the world for use in cigarettes and as pipe tobacco.

2.3 EUROPEAN TOBACCO TYPES

Throughout its history, tobacco has been spread from the Americas to Europe, Asia, and Africa. With the exception of the Oriental tobaccos, all the tobacco types that are cultivated at the present time for the international market originated in the Americas. As outlined in Chapter 4, domestic cultivation was prohibited until after World War I in regions that today are comprised in the United Kingdom, France, Spain, Italy, Austria, and Czechoslovakia. A substantial amount of tobacco—apparently of the original dark air-cured varieties—was raised in the Low Countries, in Alsace, and in Pomerania and Brandenburg in eastern Germany; and both dark leaf and makhorka (N. rustica) were grown in the Ukraine and the other eastern provinces of Poland.[21]

From the seventeenth through the nineteenth centuries, Amsterdam served as the international clearing house for the tobacco trade.[22] Based both on the history of market prices in Amsterdam and on literary sources, the best of this leaf was that grown along the Dutch coast—in Amersfort in the province of Utrecht and in the neighboring provinces of Gelderland and Overyssel. While Amersfort tobacco could command prices only somewhat lower than Virginia, all the other types of European leaf sold at a substantial discount from either Virginia or Varinas Canaster from Venezuela, which was the luxury tobacco of the eighteenth century.[23] Overall, European tobaccos prior to the twentieth century are characterized by our sources as harsh and strong. Some kinds, such as Dutch inland tobacco, also are said to have had an unpleasant aroma; although the Dutch variety could be manufactured into inexpensive chewing tobacco and snuff, it was not suitable for smoking.[24]

These characteristics of European dark leaf presumably result from the influence of different soils on the original American types. The Oriental tobaccos represent more fundamental changes in the American types that have evolved over the centuries in response to the infertile soils and hot, dry summers associated with the Mediterranean climate in what are today Turkey, Greece, and the southern provinces of the USSR. True Oriental leaf is characterized by its small size and mild but characteristic aroma. The so-called Semi-Oriental types resemble low-quality Oriental leaf; they are produced when Oriental seed is cultivated in environments or climates that are not wholly suitable, such as are found in Macedonia, the coast of what is today Yugoslavia, or southern Italy.[25] The Oriental types primarily are used in smoking tobacco and especially in cigarettes. Thus, they were not widely imported into Western Europe until the last third of the nineteenth century.

Since the 1920s, governments in Latin America, Asia, Africa, Australia, and New Zealand have made concentrated efforts, with varying degrees of success, to foster cultivation of the milder air- and flue-cured leaf for the international market as well as for internal consumption. In Europe, however, at least until World War II, most leaf continued to be of the dark air-cured types, which were increasingly grown for use in cigarettes, pipe tobacco, and smokeless products in France, Spain, Italy, Belgium (but no longer in the Netherlands), Switzerland, and Sweden, as well as throughout Central Europe in Yugoslavia, Rumania, Hungary, Czechoslovakia, and southern Poland. In addition, Oriental and Semi-Oriental production increased throughout the Balkans, and makhorka continued to be widely cultivated for home use in Russia and Poland. Italy, whose state tobacco monopoly both protected and closely regulated production, developed the most diversified industry outside the United States; in addition to the traditional dark types, Italian growers in various regions successfully cultivated Burley, Bright Italia, and Semi-Oriental types.[26]

NOTES

1. Hitier and Sabourin, *Le Tabac*, 9–13; Garner, *Production*, 3–4.

2. Akehurst, *Tobacco*, 3–4.

3. Compare Rival, *Tabac, miroir du temps*, 205. In England the government established the first laboratory to examine tobacco for foreign and "adulterating" substances in 1842, following the passage of the Tobacco Act of that year: Mackenzie, *Sublime Tobacco*, 222–23.

4. Hitier and Sabourin, *Le Tabac*, 17–20.

5. Akehurst, *Tobacco*, 10–13, 42–44, 249–50. For the diffusion of tobacco from the Americas to Asia, Africa, and Australia, see Chapter 7; Brooks, *Tobacco in Arents*, I:146–54; Laufer, *Tobacco in Asia*, 1–5; Laufer, Hambly, and Linton, *Tobacco in Africa*, 4.

6. Garner, *Production*, 375–77; Hitier and Sabourin, *Le Tabac*, 28–31.

7. Akehurst, *Tobacco*, 7–10.

8. Garner, *Production*, 350–54; Hitier and Sabourin, *Le Tabac*, 32–37.

9. See Chapter 4, Note 8.

10. Gray, *History of Agriculture*, 216–18; Robert, *Story of Tobacco*, 17–19; Garner, *Production*, 23–25; Garner et al. "History and Status," 407.

11. Garner, *Production*, 34.

12. For the eighteenth century, see Price, *France and the Chesapeake*, 600, 774.

13. Heimann, *Tobacco and Americans*, 133–35.

14. Robert, *Story of Tobacco*, 183–86.

15. Akehurst, *Tobacco*, 29; Tucker, *Tobacco: International Perspective*, 2.

16. Heimann (*Tobacco and Americans*, 150) provides a useful map of this area. See the maps charting tobacco production based on the decennial censuses in, for example, Gray, *History of Agriculture*, 759, and Robert, *Tobacco Kingdom*, 142, 147, 156.

17. Heimann, *Tobacco and Americans*.

18. Gray, *History of Agriculture*, 777; Akehurst, *Tobacco*, 36–37; Tilley, *Bright Tobacco*.

19. Gage (*American Tobacco Types*, 19–20) reprints a firsthand account of the discovery of White Burley.

20. Akehurst, *Tobacco*, 32; Tilley, *Bright Tobacco*, 512–15, 588–89.

21. Price, *Tobacco Adventure*, 86–88; Price, *France and The Chesapeake*, 485.

22. Price, *Tobacco Adventure*, 6, 98; Price, *France and the Chesapeake*, 720; Barbour, *Capitalism in Amsterdam*, 13, 92–95; Roessingh, *Inlandse tabak*, 500.

23. Price, *Tobacco Adventure*, 7, 103; Roessingh, *Inlandse tabak*, 456.

24. Price, *Tobacco Adventure*, 87; Brongers, *Nicotiana Tabacum*, 76.

25. Akehurst, *Tobacco*, 243–48.

26. Ibid., 233, 209; Hutson, *Consumption in Europe*, 92–93.

Chapter 3

Manufactured Tobacco Products

3.1 SUMMARY

After tobacco leaves are cut from the plant, dried, and cured, they go through a process, which is sometimes prolonged, of fermentation and aging. The cured and fermented tobacco may then be subjected to one or more processes, which vary according to the likely use of the product. Users of tobacco absorb its flavors into the body in three main ways. They chew tobacco, they inhale small particles of it into the nose, or they set fire to it and inhale the smoke into the mouth. Until about 1850, medical doctors also recommended absorbing the smoke through an anal enema for medicinal purposes, but this method was probably not generally employed for pleasure.[1] Like other herbs, tobacco can also be diluted in water and drunk as a kind of tea or infusion, but this method also does not seem to have been widely appreciated.

Of these practices, the oldest is perhaps *chewing*, in which the consumer places the leaf or prepared tobacco in the corner of the mouth in order to absorb its flavors.[2] For this method of consumption no real preparation is needed, but users for three centuries have been offered both pressed twist and plug and also coarse-cut moistened tobacco. Before it can be consumed as nasal snuff or smoking tobacco, the leaf first must be cut, shredded, or pulverized. Strictly speaking, snuff requires no additional preparation before use, but it often has been submitted to additional processes. Until the 1800s, for smoking purposes, the end user placed cut, flaked, or shredded tobacco into a container called a pipe. Alternatively, either the manufacturer or the end user can fix or arrange cut tobacco into some sort of column bearing a covering or wrapper, which is itself made either of tobacco (cigars and cigarillos) or of some other flammable substance such as paper (cigarettes). The latter forms are the most recent, with cigars having been adopted only since the 1840s, and cigarettes becoming popular only during this century.

From the sixteenth century on, Europeans have consumed tobacco in these three ways, which were those known to the American Indians. And chewing, sniffing, and smoking remain the most frequent ways of using tobacco to this day. The products offered to consumers have grown more diverse and have shown significant evolution over the centuries, and the methods and machinery used to prepare these products have also grown more complex. Nevertheless, for analysis these varying products may be grouped into five groups—spun, twisted, or pressed tobacco (called plug in the United States); powdered or shredded tobacco, called snuff; cut smoking tobacco; cigars; and cigarettes. There are obvious similarities between the products in these family groups. Indeed, today's sophisticated machines may make them better and more consistently, but they are not required to make any of the five types. A substantial amount of tobacco has always been prepared at home by small growers, in the United States, Europe, and Latin America; and most of the tobacco used today in Africa is still homegrown.[3]

3.2 PRESSED CHEWING TOBACCO

When tobacco is not consumed by its immediate grower, some method is needed to facilitate transportation and storage by the manufacturer, the retailer, and the consumer. Perhaps the earliest form of manufacture was to spin the leaves into a twist of whatever size was desired. This method would have been obvious to men and women accustomed to spinning wool and rope, and a simple tobacco wheel was soon in use during the seventeenth century. In the United States, where most factories were small and located close to the grower, manufacturing remained at this fairly simple level almost until the time of the Civil War. In Europe, and particularly in France and Spain, where manufacturing was concentrated in fewer and larger factories by the state monopolies, more elaborate machinery was introduced by the eighteenth century.

3.2.1 Pressed Chewing Tobacco: United States

Before the American Revolution, only a limited amount of manufacturing was carried out in North America, which exported the raw leaf and imported prepared products. The few factories sometimes folded the twist into rolls, commonly weighing as much as twenty pounds, from which the retailer or consumer could cut portions for smoking, chewing, or grating into snuff. In imitation of the French practice, prepared tobacco was also put up in the form of *carottes*, rolls about twenty inches long that were wrapped with cord.[4] Early in the nineteenth century, presses, which initially were of wood and later of iron, were introduced to form the twist into more convenient plugs. Initially, pressure was applied through a screw and lever operated either by hand or by a mule or horse attached to a long pole. Although the first hydraulic press was not patented until 1858, its value was quickly appreciated, with fourteen factories in Virginia reporting its use in the following year.[5]

At first the tobacco continued to be twisted before it was pressed into plugs, but a description from 1873 describes a more advanced but still highly labor-intensive procedure that omitted this stage. In either case, the first step was to remove substantially all the stem and mid-ribs from the leaf. The *lump* or inside filler of the plug was normally made from strips of leaf from the upper part of the plant, which were of poorer quality than the outside or wrapper leaf. From the 1840s or 1850s on, this filler was immersed in some kind of sauce, often composed of licorice and sugar. It was then dried and sprinkled with additional flavorings before being trimmed and wrapped in a leaf of smooth texture; as indicated in Chapter 2, the need to produce a wrapper leaf of agreeable color and texture contributed to the development of Bright tobacco starting in the 1820s. After being wrapped (and sometimes before as well), the lump was pressed to form a plug of uniform weight.[6]

By 1880, most of the plug or twist tobacco sold in the United States was flavored (often very heavily) with additives that produce a sweet taste. Sweetening agents became common by 1860, although existing records do not indicate either the stages by which manufacturers adopted this practice or the exact formulae they used. Prior to the Civil War, tobacco manufacturing was carried on by thousands of small companies whose records are now lost; given the weak copyright laws at the time, these companies jealously guarded the secrets of their successful products. Honey was perhaps the first additive used to sweeten tobacco. Early farmers apparently used wild honey to sweeten their homemade twists, and a factory in Mecklenburg County, Virginia, is said to have pressed twists in aged bee gum during the eighteenth century. Sugar was also added at an early stage—in Jamaica as early as 1779 through the application of molasses. Licorice, however, which later was as common as sugar, seems not to have been added before 1830.[7]

Presumably because products containing these sweetening agents enjoyed higher sales, more and more manufacturers added sweeteners in increasing quantities during the 1850s. Descriptions of the manufacturing process in 1820 and 1839 do not mention the addition of flavorings.[8] However, they were common by the 1860s, when Burley's ability to absorb sweetening agents contributed to the rapid spread of this type. By the tenth census in 1880, manufacturers of tobacco in Virginia and North Carolina used enormous amounts of licorice and sugar as well as "rum, sweet oil, tonqua beans, essence of oil of almonds, oil of bergamot, lemon, cardamon seed, cloves, mace, styrax, nutmeg, cinnamon, caraway, and fennel seed." The sugar content of some plug reached as high as 25 percent.[9]

3.2.2 Pressed Chewing Tobacco: Europe

The history of spun and rolled tobacco in Europe differs from that in America in three ways. Until at least the time of the Civil War, European tobacco products were manufactured in larger factories, especially in those countries under a state monopoly. Thus, European consumers enjoyed a variety of products of more uniform and perhaps higher quality. Second, European products took the form of softer twisted rolls and harder pressed carottes, and the oblong plug of the U.S. type was less frequently produced. Finally, these spun products apparently were flavored with sweetening agents at least a century earlier than in the United States.

Until the last third of the nineteenth century, tobacco manufacturing was more centralized in Europe than in the United States; partly to control smuggling, the industry was particularly concentrated in countries with a state monopoly. Thus, Seville dominated the industry in Spain, as did the Paris region in France. During the 1770s, for example, the French monopoly maintained only eight manufactories, and the three factories located in the Seine area consumed 41 percent of all leaf imports.[10]

After Seville and Paris, the largest centers of production probably were found in Holland and in Strasbourg. Import and export data from the eighteenth century are notoriously inaccurate. (At least one-third of the tobacco consumed in the United Kingdom was smuggled and thus avoided customs records, and the companies that farmed the French monopoly deliberately falsified the tobacco data they supplied to the government.)[11] Nevertheless, the data do provide some measure of comparative importance if not exact consumption. About 1740, English and Scotch companies annually imported about 46 to 47 million pounds of U.S. leaf, and they in turn reexported about 16 million pounds to the French monopoly and 11 to 12 million pounds to Holland.[12] Based on tax data—which are at least as suspect as trade data—manufacturers in Strasbourg consumed on average between 11 and 12 million pounds of leaf annually.[13]

Although they tended to be larger than eighteenth-century American plants, tobacco factories in Amsterdam and Strasbourg, which were operated by private companies rather than by a national monopoly, were smaller than those in France and Spain. Tobacco manufacturing in Amsterdam was largely free of the guild restrictions on older industries, and most tobacco merchants preferred to establish their own plants where the leaf could be cleaned and processed before sale.[14] In Strasbourg, a 1787 report by a French official listed fifty-three factories employing 1,600 workers; taken together, these factories processed about 10 million pounds of leaf annually during the 1780s.[15]

Prior to the introduction of cigars and cigarettes toward the middle of the nineteenth century, European factories outside France produced four separate products. Specifically, they made powder for nasal snuff, cut tobacco for smoking, and two kinds of pressed products—soft rôles that each consumer might cut up for chewing or for smoking, and harder pressed carottes that the consumer could grate for snuff. At least in the Netherlands, manufacturers seem to have sold ready-cut tobacco starting in the middle of the seventeenth century, and some even supplied it in packages with distinctive identifying marks.[16] In contrast, as late as 1789 the French monopoly sold only minute amounts of cut tobacco in addition to the usual snuff, rôles, and carottes; those wishing to smoke were forced to cut slices off rolled tobacco.[17] Indeed, to prevent the use of smuggled or homegrown tobacco, the French company at first sold only high-priced ground snuff and the twisted or spun rôles marked with its seal. However, since these rolls were too soft to grate for snuff, retailers began to press together several strands into the carotte, a smaller and harder oblong roll, shaped something like a carrot and wrapped with strip. Because this offered retailers an obvious opportunity to mix the official and expensive products with other tobaccos, the monopoly was forced to introduce its own carottes about 1700; a law of 1721 prohibited retailers from possessing presses or grinders.[18]

In making rôles and carottes, the workers sorted, graded, and cleaned the tobacco, and cut out the midribs. The leaves were then dampened and twisted or spun into large rolls weighing from ten to as much as one hundred pounds. Some rolls (often those containing the less expensive leaf) might be sold at this stage or might then be passed under rollers and wound onto smaller rolls. Those made from more expensive leaf formed the basis for pressed carottes. These are sometimes described as spun à l'andouille (like stuffed sausage), probably because—as later in the United States,—the big outer wrapper leaves covered scrappier materials inside.

When ready, the entire roll might be dumped into a vat containing an appropriate sauce and allowed to ferment, usually for less than a week. Some of the sauces described in eighteenth-century accounts are quite complicated:

made for instance of extracts of the stalks and stems of the tobacco, leaves and seed of Campeachywood, cinnamon-bark, with the addition of white gum, molasses, etc. And, says an old recipe book: "leave everything to boil until it has turned into a thin syrupy mixture; this gives the tobacco a nice colour and great strength."[19]

The damp leaves were then shaped into carottes in iron molds that were placed under presses for from twenty-four to forty-eight hours depending on thickness; the large French factories used enormous presses that were operated by eight to fifteen men. From the 1720s on in France, the carotte was wound with string along its full length and is thus often also referred to as tabac ficelé (tied tobacco).[20]

Since these pressed and twisted products could be and were purchased by smokers and snuffers, it is difficult to estimate the popularity of chewing. Like pipe smoking and nasal snuff, chewing was one of the original forms present in Europe since the introduction of tobacco itself; initially prescribed for medicinal purposes, snuff also has been taken for pleasure since at least 1600.[21] In the 1660s, chewing briefly became a fad among officers and courtiers in England and perhaps also in France.[22] Since about 1750, however, it has always been the preference of a minority—taking more than 7 or 8 percent of total sales only in North America and Scandinavia.[23] Almost everywhere chewing seems to be found primarily among workers and especially among individuals, such as sailors, soldiers, and farmers, that spend much of their time out of doors.[24]

3.3 NASAL SNUFF

From the adoption of tobacco in Europe about 1550, all manufacturers produced tobacco in a powdered form, which was used as nasal and perhaps also as oral snuff. Powder or snuff today is usually made from blends of air- and fire-cured dark tobaccos, and this seems always to have been the case. Dark tobaccos were the only types available in Europe, and they also comprised the majority of the leaf grown in the United States until the introduction of Bright and Burley after 1850. Local leaf seems to have supplied the majority of snuff. Price lists from the eighteenth century include snuff said to be made from virtually every type of tobacco grown throughout the world. Merchants thus offered to provide snuffs primarily comprised of Virginia, Dutch Amersfort, French Saint Omer, and German leaf; and they asked higher prices for those supposedly produced of Varinas from Colombia and Canaster from Venezuela, as well as Cuban, Turkish, and even Indian and Japanese leaf.[25] Judging, however, by the sales of the French state monopoly, these exotic tobaccos probably appealed to a limited market. During the first half of the nineteenth century, as Table 3.1 indicates, fully nine out of ten French consumers purchased ''ordinary'' snuff,[26] which seems to have been made primarily of the very strong French dark mixed with Virginia dark.[27] It is true that foreign snuffs cost twice as much, but consumer tastes must also have played a role in so marked a preference.

The process by which tobacco leaves are made into a powder is relatively straightforward and seems to have changed little over the centuries. Drying them and reducing them to powder is as obvious a way of preparing the leaves for transportation and storage as is twisting them into a braid. When it was first introduced, moreover, tobacco was considered to have many medicinal values, and apothecaries no doubt crushed the leaves in a mortar and pestle in the same way that they crushed other herbs.[28] Over the subsequent centuries, rasps and graters have also been used, as have mills turned at first by hand, then by waterwheels or windmills, and finally by steam and electricity.[29] In most cases, the stems and midribs have been removed and only the soft parts of the leaf

Table 3.1

Sales of *Poudre* (Snuff) in France (in thousands of U.S. pounds and French francs per pound)

	1819		1845	
	amount	price	amount	price
foreign	127	6.35	27	5.03
ordinary	11,634	3.27	13,584	3.18
reduced price	1,768	1.27/1.59	1,194	.98/2.52

Source: France, Direction générale des manufactures de l'État, *Rapport concernant la fabrication et la vente exclusives du tabac* (1819, 1845).

have been used, at least for the more expensive kinds of snuff.[30] However, the Scotch and the Irish apparently used the entire leaf—particularly for a special type of Irish snuff made of the toasted or charred stems (then called Lundyfoot or Irish Blackguard and now called Lundy's High Toast).[31] And American manufacturers also sometimes have used the whole leaf or even added additional stems.[32]

During the twentieth century, manufacturers have usually allowed tobacco to ferment or *sweat* for several months before grinding it into powder. This is said both to remove unpleasant odors and to bring out desired aromas.[33] After grinding, the tobacco then may be salted or flavored, and sold more or less moistened. In general usage in the United States—but not in Europe—the terms Scotch and Strong Scotch have referred to strong-flavored snuffs that are sold finely ground, very dry, and usually unflavored. Rappee or French snuffs are less finely ground and are often perfumed. Both are usually inhaled. Swedish, Copenhagen, or Polish snuffs are coarse-ground or even flaked and frequently are flavored; consumers today often prefer to absorb these flavors by dipping or placing them into the mouth. Finally, Maccoboy—which is moist and flavored like Copenhagen but more finely ground—can be taken orally or inhaled.[34]

Today a minority of consumers use tobacco in its powered form. Until the middle of the nineteenth century, however, this form was preferred by many individuals of both genders and at every income level. In England, where there was no retail monopoly, it thus was prepared and mixed to order by retailers in hundreds of varieties—flavored and unflavored, perfumed and unperfumed—which were available in coarse, medium, or fine grinds according to taste.[35] Since preferences varied widely between and even within regions, generalizations must be qualified. Judging by eighteenth-century manuals, these products were then fermented for a briefer period than is the case today, which may have given them a somewhat stronger and more biting character.[36] Many consumers in Scotland do seem to have preferred a finely ground and very dry powder.[37] In London and on the Continent, however, before the introduction of modern packaging, some retailers devoted a great deal of effort to keeping their products moist.[38]

Given the available evidence, one should not be too dogmatic about the extent to which powdered tobacco products were perfumed. In England at least, snuffs were offered for sale under many names and in a variety of scents. Products incorporating lilac, roses, oranges, and tonqua beans were frequent; and more exotic varieties scented with musk oil and ginger or even with mustard and pepper were offered.[39] Many snuffs were offered in a perfumed form, but certainly not all, and perhaps not those most esteemed by connoisseurs. In England, according to the records of Fribourg and Treyer, a retailer catering to the crown and the aristocracy, about 1800 the most expensive snuffs were not scented with foreign substances but rather gained their distinguishing characters from a careful blending of various tobaccos of the highest quality. Martinique, the most expensive of these unscented blends, was light in color and subtle in character; it sold for one guinea a pound, twice as much as other snuffs. In Spain also, the most famed snuffs, made from Havana, Varinas, or Canaster leaf, similarly seem to have been appreciated for their own intrinsic aromas and flavors.[40] By the middle of the nineteenth century, most of the tobacco sold by the French monopoly—including some of the "superior" and more expensive types—also seems not to have been perfumed, or at least not heavily.[41]

In tracing the history of snuff, one faces in an especially acute way the problem of sources. For the reasons summarized in Chapter 1, there are statistical data prior to this century only from those countries that were under a monopoly system. In regions where it remained in private hands, until the late nineteenth century the tobacco industry was carried out by thousands of small companies that have not left records and that carefully guarded their trade secrets. (Neither do manufacturers today release an exact analysis of their products or their sales.) While some state monopolies do make public sales by product line, they began to publish this information only during the nineteenth century.

From about 1700 to 1815—during the century before the statistical series begins—snuff taking was a stylish practice among the high aristocracy in France and thus also among the groups that imitated the French aristocracy throughout Europe and its colonies, including what is now the United States. The stylish habits of wealthy aristocrats have always been the subject of gossip and emulation, and literary sources thus preserve many anecdotes describing the more interesting and often the more extreme examples of snuff taking among the great and the fashionable.

In estimating total snuff consumption, the difficulty lies in measuring how frequently the middling and lower classes copied these aristocratic habits. Until the introduction of mass production, advertising, and newspapers at the end of the nineteenth century, most of the populace did not emulate the habits of the aristocracy in the capital simply because they had no way of knowing what these habits were. Even today, when the whole people is subjected to national print and broadcast media, sales data show that not every fad in Manhattan or San Francisco reaches West Virginia. For this reason, the popularity of snuff among the aristocracy and the snuff habits of ordinary folk are two separate phenomena. And the popularity of snuff among the masses rises and falls independently of aristocratic fads. Today, when we are brought up to believe that all persons are equivalent, we sometimes are surprised by the antiegalitarian bias of earlier ages. Thus, the older sources attribute the adoption of snuff in every country to aristocratic patronage. Even when they are accurate, these attributions do not in themselves show that snuff was frequent among ordinary folk away from the court, and they must be supplemented by more general evidence.

While we cannot derive a quantitative measurement of snuff consumption until the nineteenth century, literary evidence shows that oral snuff is one of the original forms in which Europeans borrowed tobacco from the American Indians. Snuff has been taken for precisely as long as Europeans have used tobacco in any form, and it entered each nation with the introduction of the leaf itself. Thus, powdered tobacco was used during the second half of the seventeenth century in Portugal and in Spain, whence it spread to France and also to the Spanish dominions in Italy. By 1600 it also was present in England, Holland, and Germany. Initially its uses were medicinal. As the development of decorated boxes shows, however, it soon was being taken mainly for pleasure.[42]

Clerical records provide most of the earliest references to snuff—or to tobacco in any form. But this bias in the records does not prove that snuffing is primarily a priestly habit: Clerical corporations, which never die, simply do a better job of preserving records than do private individuals. After the conquest of Mexico and South America by the Portuguese and Spanish crowns, the native peoples continued to smoke, take snuff, and chew tobacco. Their European masters borrowed from the Indians all these ways of taking tobacco, but they initially seem to have preferred snuff, and took it in significant quantities even on ceremonial and sacred occasions. As early as 1570, the Council of Mexico is said to have prohibited the use of tobacco in the churches of Spanish America. The reference does not specify to whom the council addressed this decree, but rules adopted in 1583 for the province of Lima in Peru are specifically aimed at the Spanish clergy. As approved by the Roman college of cardinals, one of these rules, under penalty of eternal damnation, forbids priests "about to administer the sacraments, either to take the smoke of *sayri* or tobacco into the mouth, or the powder of tobacco into the nose, even under the guise of medicine, before the service of the mass."[43]

This prohibition, repeated in 1585 by a provincial synod in Mexico, does not seem to have been immediately effective, and snuff soon was prevalent among the clergy in Spain itself. By 1642, the presence of tobacco in the churches of Seville so scandalized Pope Urban VIII that he issued the first papal bull dealing with tobacco and addressed to the clergy of that city. Urban first stated that "in those parts the use of the herb commonly called tobacco has gained so strong a hold on persons of both sexes, even priests and clerics, that—We blush to state—during the actual celebration of Holy Mass, they do not shrink from taking tobacco through the mouth or nostrils." For this reason, the Pontiff forbade any person to take "tobacco in leaf, powder, in smoke, by mouth or nostrils in any of the churches of Seville."[44]

From the middle of the seventeenth century, nasal snuff provided the main way in which Spaniards enjoyed tobacco—to the disapproval of others besides the Roman popes. Throughout the century, satires of and attacks on tobacco generally are directed against snuff, and powdered tobacco also is used in or referred to by several plays during this Golden Age of Spanish drama. According to these sources, snuffing initially was a practice of slaves and drunks *(cosa de esclavos y bebedores de taverna)*. Soon, however, it was adopted throughout the kingdom by men and women, monks, nuns, ecclesiastics, lords, and princes, none of whom felt they could do without it.[45] Its popularity remained high among all classes until the last decades of the eighteenth century, when some, especially in the cities, opted instead for the cigar, the cigarette, and the pipe. The state manufactories continued to produce snuffs of many types, but Spanish literature now treated the habit as confined mainly to the elderly, to priests, and to the inhabitants of rural villages, especially in Galicia, a mountainous province along the Atlantic coast north of Portugal.[46]

From Portugal and Spain, snuff and other forms of tobacco were soon brought to the Italian peninsula. An old legend has it that the papal nuncio to Lisbon, Cardinal Prospero de Santa Croce, introduced both the tobacco plant (in 1561) and nasal snuff (about 1585) to Rome when he returned to the papal court from his diplomatic missions. Other aristocratic patrons have received credit for bringing tobacco from Iberia to Florence and the other Italian states.[47] While this aristocratic patronage may have occurred, humble sailors must also have brought snuff to such ports as Genoa, Naples, and Venice. Extensive trade linked southern Italy to Catalonia; and the kingdoms of Naples and Sicily and the duchy of Milan formed part of the Spanish realm starting in 1559.

As is almost always the case in tracing the early history of tobacco, the first dated references are found in prohibitions of and fulminations against the new product. Innocent X interdicted any use of tobacco in St Peter's because "We have been greatly pained to learn that there are certain persons, clergy as well as laity, so unmindful of the reverence due to consecrated places that they do not hesitate to smoke or snuff up the herb commonly known as tobacco even in the church of the Prince of the Apostles." According to an attack on tobacco published the same year, such prohibitions were sorely needed. While saying mass some years earlier, this source states, a priest in Naples took snuff just after receiving holy Communion; the fit of sneezing that followed caused him to vomit up the Sacrament in full view of the congregation.[48]

Judging by the censure of the practice, snuff was first taken in most parts of the Italian peninsula not later than 1700. A Sicilian satire published in 1665 states that chewing, snuffing, and smoking all were commonplace in that region. In 1668, the Venetian Senate, which had levied heavy taxes on tobacco, prosecuted an English captain who had clandestinely smuggled in some Milanese snuff. During the eighteenth century, snuffing was nearly universal: As the middling and lower classes continued to enjoy the aromatic powder, snuff also became the fashion at the secular as well as at the ecclesiastical courts of Italy.[49]

At least in some regions, moreover, large numbers of Italians continued to enjoy snuff into the twentieth century. In the northern provinces of Lombardy and Venetia, for example, snuff formed more than half of all tobacco sales in 1821. Consumers in the Italian kingdom, which was created in 1870, bought more than seven million pounds of snuff in that year, about 20 percent of all sales by the new state monopoly. As late as 1950, more than one and a half million pounds were used—although snuff by now represented only 2 percent of the total market.[50]

Snuffing apparently was taken up in France somewhat later than in Spain or Italy. By the 1640s, snuff was common enough in Seville and Rome that several popes felt constrained to forbid its use during mass. By the following decade it also was taken at the court of Louis XIV in Paris. Only from the 1680s on, however, can its use by the common folk be documented. Credit for bringing snuff to France has been given both to Jean Nicot and to the younger brother of the Duke of Lorraine. Nicot, who was ambassador to Portugal from 1559 to 1561, is said to have given a box of powdered tobacco to Queen Catherine de Medicis on his return to France in the latter year; both the queen mother and two of her sons, Francis II and Charles IX, are described as having been enthusiastic snuffers, partly to cure their tendency to headaches.[51] However, Jean Liebault, in a book published in 1567, attributes the introduction of snuff at the French court to François de Lorraine, Grand Prior of the Order of Malta (and not to his older brother, the Cardinal-Duke of Lorraine, as some recent versions of the legend have it).[52] According to Liebault, François ordered that tobacco be grown in his garden and personally took three ounces of snuff a day.

Although the veracity of both these legends has been attacked, neither is inherently impossible.[53] In the 1560s, snuff was available in Spain and Italy, where both purported patrons had close ties—Catherine as a native Florentine and François de Lorraine as a client of the Spanish crown. However, if the queen did use snuff, few people initially followed her example. The practice seems to have been reintroduced into France during the 1620s, when the French government made a concerted effort to colonize islands of the Caribbean whose natives took snuff.[54] By the 1650s, it must have been noticeable at the court of Louis XIV, who unsuccessfully tried to eliminate it through both prohibition and persuasion.[55] Physical artifacts also bear witness to the growing popularity of powdered tobacco. A silver snuffbox exists with the date of 1655, and these utensils of courtly elegance become numerous starting in the 1670s.[56]

Because of the influence of Louis's court, it is plausible that the use of snuff spread downward, first to the wealthy bourgeoisie of Paris and subsequently to the country gentry. In Molière's *Don Juan,* first presented in 1665, Sganarelle's opening speech praises tobacco and describes snuff as the "passion of gentlemen" *(honnêtes gens)*—a reference that presumably was intelligible to his Parisian audience. Not later than the 1690s, consumers in the provinces also began to use snuff in significant amounts. In a book published in 1700, Jean Brunet claimed that snuff taking was still an exotic practice outside Paris in the 1670s and 1680s. During the following decade, however, it became common enough to provide a handsome profit to some of the companies that subleased (from the national monopoly) the right to sell snuff in specific regions.[57]

There can be no question that the eighteenth century was the high point of snuff taking as an aristocratic art form at the French court—and also in the courts of London, Berlin, and Vienna, which copied Paris. We have fewer anecdotes about the less fashionable classes in France, many of whom had to make do with snuffboxes made out of perishable wood.[58] Nonetheless, ordinary folk also seem to have preferred nasal snuff to any other form of tobacco. In 1789, according to the oldest extant accounts, fully 85 percent of all sales took the form either of prepared snuff or hard pressed tobacco *(tabac ficelé)*, which usually was ground at home to make snuff.[59] Literary evidence suggests that snuffing became less fashionable among the aristocracy during the nineteenth century. As was also the case in Spain, however, snuff remained popular among the people even after it lost its aristocratic cachet. Indeed, snuff sales in France did not reach their all-time high—about 28 million pounds a year—until 1861. From the 1870s on, the use of snuff began to fall each year, but the decline was slow. As recently as 1949, almost 2 million pounds were purchased throughout France at the retail stores of the tobacco monopoly, now a department of the state.[60]

Literary sources suggest that Spanish and Portuguese sailors brought tobacco from the New World by 1600. In these countries and in Italy, snuff probably was preferred to smoking tobacco until at least 1800. Its spread to Central Europe was made easier by the political and economic connections uniting Spain and the eastern states. During the sixteenth and seventeenth centuries, much of Europe was ruled by the House of Habsburg. In addition to southern Italy, Spain, and the Spanish possessions in the New World, the empire of Charles V (1500–1558) thus included Austria, Bohemia, and Hungary as well as what are today the Netherlands and Belgium. On Charles's death, his son Philip II became ruler of Spain, Italy, and the Netherlands, while his uncle Ferdinand received Austria, Bohemia, and Hungary. However, the two branches of the family maintained close ties and cooperated diplomatically until the extinction of the Spanish Habsburgs in 1700. Given these military, diplomatic, and economic ties, it is likely that snuff was present both in the Netherlands and in Central Europe by 1600. Soldiers who used snuff in Spain presumably continued to do so while on duty in Holland or Bohemia, and there thus is some logic to the old story that Spanish soldiers fostered the use of tobacco in the Germanies during the Thirty Years War (1618–1648).[61]

The city of Cologne became the center for tobacco manufacturing and wholesaling in the western half of the Germanies, and legend has it that the powdered form of tobacco was brought to that city by French Huguenots fleeing the persecution of Louis XIV in 1661. French families did dominate the tobacco trade in Cologne at the beginning of the eighteenth century, but snuff may well have been present in Germany before 1661 since a book published in 1658 attacks the practice.[62] Grimmelshausen's *Simplicissimus* of 1667 also assailed tobacco, which, he says, was used by nine out of ten workers.

Some of them drink [smoke] their tobacco, some eat it, others sniff it up through the nostrils—indeed, I am surprised that I have not yet found anyone plugging his ears with it. But the other methods I have myself seen practiced by persons of all classes, from prince to bishop, from bishop to barber; and each of them is prepared to explain why he does it and how it benefits him.[63]

French fashions were everywhere imitated during the eighteenth century, and snuff was the favored way to taking tobacco at the courts of Vienna and Berlin as well as the courts of the lesser German princes. In Prussia, Frederick the Great (1740–1786) was very fond of snuff, which often soiled his clothes and face. His example was widely imitated, and many exquisite snuffboxes were created for the German and Austrian courts.[64] As in France, the habit was maintained among the aristocracy well into the nineteenth century. Thus Prince Metternich, Habsburg foreign minister from 1809 to 1848, both took snuff and looked down on smokers.

If the aristocracy and middle classes preferred snuff, aromatic powders were also inhaled, according to a satire appearing in 1720, by the less fashionable classes in Germany

from the highest to the lowest. I have sometimes wondered to see how lords and lackeys, High Society and the mob, woodchoppers and handy men, broom-squires and beadles, take out their snuff-boxes with an air and dip into them. Both sexes snuff, for the fashion has spread to women; the ladies began it and are now imitated by the washer women.[65]

Snuffers probably never formed a majority among the working classes in the Germanies, the Netherlands, and the Habsburg empire, but many continued to use powdered tobacco well into the nineteenth century. The sales records of the Habsburg tobacco monopoly begin in 1784, at the height of the passion for snuff. In that year, manufactured snuff represented about one-third of total sales—somewhat less than in France or in Italy, but still a large share of the overall market. In subsequent years, snuff sales tended to fall in proportion to total sales, but at a slow rate. Indeed, the Habsburg monopoly sold more snuff in 1882 than it had a hundred years earlier.[66]

While the Spanish were occupying Central and South America, English adventurers were bringing their flag to Virginia, where the natives smoked *Nicotiana rustica*. English fleets also raided Spanish possessions in Central America, Florida, and the Caribbean, where *Nicotiana tabacum* was both smoked and taken as snuff. It is not certain which of these English captains was the first to introduce tobacco to polite society in England—early sources can be interpreted to support the case for Sir John Hawkins about 1565, Sir Francis Drake in 1573, or Sir Walter Raleigh in 1577 and 1586.[67] By the 1590s, tobacco must have been used in significant and noticeable amounts, since the crown levied the first in a long series of import duties, and contemporary plays refer to it as a familiar sight. In 1604, probably because of his hatred of Raleigh, King James I anonymously published *A Counterblaste to Tobacco,* his vitriolic attack on the practice.[68]

In England, in contrast to the Continent, these early literary sources most frequently mention smoking. However, they also provide evidence that nasal snuff was one of the forms in which tobacco first was introduced into England. As early as 1589, John Lyly, in an attack on Puritan practices, may have referred to snuff in a metaphor: "What will be powder of *Martins* wit be good for? Marie blowe vp a dram of it into the nostrels of a good Protestant, it will make him giddie; but if you minister it like *Tobacco* to a Puritane, it will make him as mad as a *Martin.*" [69]

Although the hyperbole of Lyly's prose is somewhat ambiguous, other references make it certain that snuff was not foreign to the Elizabethan age. In 1599 Henry Buttes describes tobacco as

Translated out of India in the seed roote; Native or sative in our own fruitfullest soiles: Dried in the shade, and compiled very close: of a tawny colour, somewhat inclining to red: most perspicuous and cleare: Which the Nose soonest taketh in snuffe.

And Thomas Dekker in 1602 similarly describes the fashionable gallant with his "ladle for the cold snuff into the nostril" fashioned out of gold or silver. [70]

While snuff has been taken in England since the reign of Elizabeth I, it did not become a royal and aristocratic passion until the eighteenth century. During the 1600s, literary sources do not treat snuff as exotic or strange, and it was taken by several famous writers, including John Dryden and Samuel Pepys, the latter using it as a prophylactic against the plague of 1665. [71] However, the eighteenth century unquestionably was the golden age of snuffing among the aristocracy and those that copied their habits. Although smoking did not entirely disappear, it was considered coarse; snuff was virtually the sole socially acceptable way of using tobacco until well into the nineteenth century.

From Queen Anne (1702–1714) through George IV (1799–1820), most British rulers were devoted to snuff, and courtiers and gentry followed their example. An elaborate etiquette governed how snuff was to be taken, exquisite and costly snuffboxes were created in gold and silver, and high prices were paid for certain fashionable tobacco blends. During this era, the wealthy everywhere in Europe attempted to copy the practices of the French court. Those setting themselves up as professors of snuff etiquette thus used French names and advertised themselves as familiar with the practices of the French court. However, the word *snuff* is itself Dutch, suggesting that the practice was initially taken from that nation rather than from France or Spain.

Among the English gentry, smoking began to return to favor during the 1820s and 1830s. As Chapters 5 and 6 show, a mature individual rarely changes her or his tobacco preferences, and snuffers did not suddenly become smokers. More and more, however, those taking up tobacco for the first time now began to choose other forms. Apparently the generation coming of age during the Romantic era of the 1820s began to consider snuff old-fashioned and out of date. Contributing to this attitude was the availability of new ways of smoking that could be seen as heroic or at least elegant. The cigar first appeared in England about 1800 and sold in some quantity from the 1830s, and the handsome briar began to replace the humble clay during the 1860s.[72] Judging by the account books of Theyer and Fribourg, a retailer that supplied tobacco to the court and nobility, a change away from snuff first became noticeable in the 1830s. Until 1830, the firm sold only insignificant amounts of tobacco and cigars, and snuff still predominated as late as 1845. From 1850, cigars and pipe tobacco began to equal snuff in sales, with snuff falling below 50 percent of total sales starting in 1859.[73]

Because their authors are interested in the London world of the fashionable and the aristocratic, these literary references tell little about tobacco preferences in the provinces or among the working classes. Memoirs and novels of the period often portray country squires and gentry as smoking clay pipes. But many individuals also took snuff both because they wished to copy courtly practices and also because snuffing was somewhat less expensive than smoking.[74] Of the working class in Britain itself, we know even less. Some travelers to Ireland and Scotland noted the fondness for snuff among all classes, including the most humble.[75] Too much has sometimes been read into these comments, but they tend to suggest that working-class snuffers were no less frequently encountered in Britain.

At the end of the eighteenth century, an aristocratic house like Theyer and Fribourg sold almost nothing but snuff. In contrast, Lilly and Wills, which catered to humbler consumers in Northern England, seems to have sold roughly equal amounts of smoking tobacco and snuff. Each was only one of thousands of firms, however, most of which had a limited and regional market. By 1850, according to witnesses before a parliamentary committee investigating the tobacco trade, about 90 percent of all tobacco was smoked in pipes. Similar estimates were made by those studying the living conditions of the poorer classes.[76] In 1907, when the British government first collected exact statistics, snuff represented 1 percent of total sales in the United Kingdom, and consumption has held relatively steady in subsequent years.[77] The earlier sources indicate that its share of the overall market was much higher during the nineteenth century, but no precise estimate is possible. In contrast to Scandinavia and the United States, where most snuff is taken orally, many (though not all) purchasers in the United Kingdom continue to use powdered tobacco as a nasal product, particularly in the country towns of the north.[78]

In England, as in Spain, France, and Italy, snuff was the dominant form of tobacco at least during the eighteenth century. In contrast, the British colonists in North America always seem to have preferred pipes and chewing tobacco. Some nasal snuff was imported for the mercantile and landowning groups, which were most directly influenced by the habits of the British aristocracy. While a small amount also reached the interior, much of the tobacco consumed in the

American colonies was homegrown. Only a limited number of small manufacturing plants were built, and most of their output took the form of pressed
plug.[79] After the revolution, the U.S. preference for chewing tobacco seems,
if anything, to have increased. While tobacco manufacturing grew in importance, few mills were devoted solely to snuff.[80] By 1880, when accurate governmental data become available, chewing tobacco thus represented more than
half of all tobacco products manufactured in the United States, and snuff formed
only 2 percent. With the new wave of immigration from Europe, snuff consumption significantly increased between 1880 and 1925, reaching an all-time
record of 41 million pounds in 1929.[81] Since then, while consumption of pressed
plug has fallen sharply, snuff sales generally have been stable. From the second
third of the nineteenth century, most of this U.S. production has taken the form
of moist oral snuff rather than nasal snuff.[82]

3.4 MOIST ORAL SNUFF

In current U.S. usage, the word snuff refers to manufactured products that
consumers use in two different ways. As summarized in the previous section,
nasal snuff, which is inhaled or sniffed up into the nostrils, is one of the original forms in which tobacco always has been taken. Since at least the first third
of the nineteenth century, snuff also has been consumed orally, with this practice being most frequently found in the United States and the Scandinavian
countries.[83] Rather than inhaling it into the nose, consumers place moist snuff
between the lip and the gums—with Americans traditionally placing it behind
the lower and Swedes behind the upper lip. In the Southern states, where the
practice has been called *dipping,* most users of oral snuff simply allow it to sit
in place while they absorb its flavors. Others have maneuvered the tobacco by
"rubbing and chewing" it—rubbing the snuff throughout the mouth and moving it around with the tongue.

Like nasal snuffs, those intended for oral use generally have been made from
air- or fire-cured dark leaf. After being aged and conditioned for handling, the
leaf is chopped or cut, often into short ribbons or strips. The chopped leaf is
then packed in hogsheads or other containers to undergo aging or sweating for
up to three years. In this process, the temperature rises, and at intervals the
tobacco may be removed and returned to equalize conditions throughout the
container. Some products or brands are flavored, and all contain a relatively
high moisture content when they are packed into retail containers.[84]

Oral snuff represents a development of snuff intended for nasal use, some of
which were sold in a coarse-cut and moistened form during the eighteenth century. Thus, we cannot establish precisely when snuff first came to be used as
an oral product in the United States. Literary evidence shows that it has been
used in this way at least from the beginning of the nineteenth and perhaps
already during the eighteenth century. Several of the products currently sold
have been made in the same way since the 1830s, but farmers and planters may

have moistened store-bought snuff or even made their own oral snuffs for several decades before specific products were created to meet their needs.

Charles Gage, perhaps the leading authority before World War II on tobacco usage, states that "relatively few people now living" have seen anyone take powdered snuff into his nostrils. Writing in 1933, Gage suggests that the use of moist snuff as an oral product "is probably largely confined to laboring classes in the South, particularly Negroes, and to the Scandinavian population in Wisconsin and Minnesota."[85] An antislavery writer before the Civil War also attributed dipping primarily to women of the "poor White" class, 98 percent of whom he described as using snuff in this way. Although it clearly is overstated, this writer's description provides a catalogue of the various techniques of dipping used in his day.

The female snuff-dipper takes a short stick, and wetting it with her saliva, dips it into her snuff-box, and then rubs the gathered dust all about her mouth, and into the interstices of her teeth, where she allows it to remain until its strength has been fully absorbed. Others hold the stick thus loaded with snuff in the cheek, *a la quid* of tobacco, and suck it with a decided relish, while engaged in their ordinary avocations; while others simply fill the mouth with the snuff, and imitate, to all intents and purposes, the chewing propensities of the men.[86]

By the 1930s, when Gage conducted his study of tobacco habits, oral snuff probably was taken mainly by the working classes. However, it is not certain that this always was the case. A. L. Adams, who traveled throughout the South in the 1860s, found dipping to be widespread in many areas—particularly in Virginia, West Virginia, the Carolinas, and Georgia—among white persons of all classes and particularly among young ladies (and their mothers) of some standing in society.[87] Given the relative tenacity of tobacco habits, it is likely that oral snuff also had been used by others of the gentry when it first appeared. Indeed, homemade oral snuff may well have been one of the original forms used in rural areas before manufactured plug became available in the 1820s.[88] As Adams indicates, Southern farm-owners—including many wealthy planters—often carried around their own homegrown tobacco. They first may have learned to enjoy orally their own coarsely cut leaf and then switched to prepared oral snuff when this became available during the 1820s or 1830s.

Although no evidence of any direct connection has been found, it is curious that oral snuff also became widespread in Sweden during precisely the same decades of the 1820s and 1830s. At first oral snuff seems to have been substituted for pressed chewing tobacco. By the 1840s, however, snuff had established itself as the most popular tobacco product in Sweden, where it consistently outsold both smoking tobacco and pressed plug for almost a century.[89] Oral snuff also has been highly popular in Iceland, where it took more than a third of the total sales in 1932 (when records begin).[90] In these countries, snuff is thus a dominant product. In Norway and Denmark, sales of pressed chewing tobacco initially were larger than those of oral snuff. However, the latter has represented a significant and—in the case of Denmark—growing portion of the national market.[91]

3.5 SMOKING TOBACCO

Just as they have used powdered snuff from the very beginning, so Europeans also have smoked cut tobacco ever since they first found the American Indians using it in this form. To cut into small cubes or strips tobacco that has been first cured and spun is so obvious a way of preparing it for smoking that it would be pointless as well as impossible to try to identify where this was first done. In describing the evolution of spun and pressed products, tobacco was at first sold in a braided and later in a pressed form from which the users might prepare their own snuff, cut off a chunk for chewing, or slice off smaller pieces for smoking. Along with spun products, cut tobacco, ready for the pipe, was offered for sale in Holland and Germany from the time of the seventeenth century. As part of its never-ending war against smugglers, however, the company that farmed the state monopoly in France until 1793 sold only twisted or "rolled" tobacco impressed with its seal and did not offer ready-cut leaf for sale.[92] The new state monopoly that was erected in 1810 did offer cut tobacco, but some smokers continued to purchase twist, spun, or pressed tobacco down to the 1870s because these forms retained moisture longer than fine-cut.

Today few smokers cut up plug tobacco, and we may safely assume that almost all plug is purchased for chewing. The demise of the smoker's plug is coincidental with the replacement of clay pipes by briar, and it also may be connected to the introduction of better types of packaging beginning about 1850. Until the middle of the nineteenth century, cut tobacco generally was sold loose or packed in cloth bags. Although the latter were sealed (for example with candle wax) by the maker, they were difficult to reseal once opened.[93] The use of cans to preserve tobacco became possible only after about 1860, when paper packets also became less expensive with the development of new techniques for making paper directly from wood pulp.[94] The use of tin (later aluminum) foil, plastic sheets, or film to keep tobacco moist and fresh are even more recent phenomena; the cellophane wrapper around cigarette packages, for example, was added at the end of the 1930s.[95]

According to the accounts of the French state monopoly, sales of twist and plug products declined dramatically as a percentage of all sales during the 1850s and 1860s, while sales of powdered snuff and ready-cut smoking tobacco almost doubled. By 1885, the monopoly no longer intended hard carottes and pressed rôles for the smokers' market; from that year on, its accounts unequivocally refer to all twisted or pressed products as "chewing tobacco."[96] We can not ask the buyers of 1880 why they bought cut tobaccos rather than plug; but it is reasonable to assume that improved packaging, which kept cut tobacco moister and more flavorful, may have played some part in their decision. Ready-cut long continued to be pressed after being stemmed and moistened, but the cutting was now done at the factory by the manufacturer's machines rather than at home by the individual smoker.[97]

Whether sold in a pressed form or already sliced or flaked, tobacco intended for smoking seems always to have been made of air-, sun-, or fire-cured dark leaf—which comprised, after all, the overwhelming majority of all tobaccos produced before 1850. Since its discovery in 1864, the heavier grades of flue-cured Burley are also used, particularly in the United States.[98] And most cut tobacco typically seems to have been made of one type of leaf, with the modern blends or mixtures that combine two or more different types becoming usual only during the second half of the nineteenth century.[99] Many Europeans smoking mixtures are still unflavored, and this also seems to have been the case in earlier centuries.[100] Industry studies prior to the first half of the nineteenth century do not mention the addition of flavorings, and the earliest accounts of the tobacco monopolies do not distinguish between various brands of smoking tobacco (as they do in the case of snuffs).[101] U.S. companies apparently began to add sweetening agents to cut tobacco in the 1850s when they also introduced flavoring into plug intended for chewing. For most U.S. companies, cut tobacco was distinctly second to chewing tobacco in sales,[102] and their success with their more important plug products probably suggested that they should also add sweeteners to their smoking mixtures.[103]

In sum, from the time of its introduction to Europe about 1550, cut tobacco for smoking has not radically changed; today, as in earlier centuries, most cut tobacco is made from the heavier dark types and is cut into small plugs, slices, or fine ribbons from tobacco leaves that have first been cured, moistened, and pressed. Greater changes have taken place over the years in the materials forming the container or pipe in which cut tobacco must be placed before it is set afire. For a full three centuries—from the 1570s to the 1870s—clay provided the only pipe material available to most Europeans. Wealthy aristocrats and royalty sometimes boasted of silver pipes, but these were mainly for show.[104] Some gentlemen and burghers owned porcelain pipes ornamented with paintings or pipes carved out of fragrant woods. However, since porcelain is fragile and wood burns up quickly with steady use, these were too costly for most consumers. Meerschaum, a soft mineral that looks like white clay, also is fragile as well as expensive; moreover, because the main source in Asia Minor was controlled by a cartel for almost a century, supplies were severely limited. Although it became available in Central Europe in the 1750s or earlier, meerschaum was rare in England before 1850, was found as a costly luxury in France only toward 1850, and reached the United States somewhat later.[105]

Although it is less than a perfect medium for smoking tobacco, the overwhelming majority of pipes were thus made of clay. In England clay pipes were made in the 1590s and possibly in the 1570s. Early in the seventeenth century, English masters founded workshops in Denmark, Switzerland, and the Netherlands, where the town of Gouda became the most important early center of this art.[106] For the next three centuries, strong dark tobacco was smoked in cheap clay pipes throughout England, France, the Germanies, and Central Europe; in America, which still possessed forests, cherry and other aromatic woods were common, as was the corncob.

An ideal medium for smoking tobacco is briar, the root of a shrub found all around the shores of the Mediterranean. Although the local peasantry probably had carved it into pipes earlier, the commercial possibilities of this wood were only realized in the 1840s by artisans in the southern French city of Saint Claude, which became the center of a thriving industry supporting hundreds of workers and producing 30 million pipes a year around 1900.[107] A pipe manufactory was opened in Germany about 1848, and briar pipes were imported into England by 1853. Although they at first were almost as expensive as meerschaum,[108] the expansion of the industry soon reduced their price, and briar pipes became common in the 1870s.[109] Not only did briar soon make clay largely a curiosity, but it also substantially increased the number of pipe smokers. In France, the detailed records of the state monopoly show that sales of cut tobacco rose significantly after 1845,[110] and pipe smoking also increased in the United States[111] and in England, where the more felicitous aromas of tobacco smoked in a briar may have contributed to a greater acceptance of smoking after 1865.

3.6 CIGARS

At first glance cigars may appear to be a straightforward and "natural" product. But their manufacture and distribution is both complicated and labor-intensive. Strictly speaking, what the Spanish call a true or pure cigar (*cigarro puro*) is a cylindrical roll composed solely of tobacco leaves in three different forms— the filler, the binder, and the wrapper. In the manufacturing process, the filler is formed into the shape of the cigar and wrapped in the binder to create a bundle called a bunch. The latter is then covered with the wrapper, which is wound on spirally (clockwise or counterclockwise) starting at the fire end and ending at the head. Until the late 1920s, all this was done by hand; today in Europe and the United States, the making of the filler bunch usually is mechanized, but the wrapper leaf still is applied manually to the best grades.[112]

Before they are rolled into cigars, the leaves are cured and sweated through the application of heat and humidity. The dried leaves are then remoistened so as to be pliable, and the stems are removed either by hand or mechanically, in the case of the less expensive fillers.[113] The leaves usually have not been sweetened or sauced before rolling, but a flavoring sometimes is added during the process of assembly.[114] In order to preserve its even-burning and aromatic qualities, the cigar must be kept moist until it is used, and the more expensive brands are individually encased in aromatic woods.

Although these proportions have changed somewhat since the advent of machine manufacturing in the 1930s, an older rule had it that a cigar is about 85 percent filler, 10 percent binder, and 5 percent wrapper. These three layers need not be made from the same leaf, but all three must be compatible in taste and aroma. Until the end of the nineteenth century, manufacturers primarily used *long filler,* pieces of leaf about as long as the cigar itself; more recently, the cheaper brands are made of smaller pieces of leaf or even scrap tobacco, the latter now renamed *short filler.*[115] Almost any air- or sun-cured dark tobacco may be used for cigar filler provided that it burns evenly without charring, gives off a pleasant aroma, and possesses a flavor appropriate to cigars.

The requirements for binder and wrapper leaves are more stringent. They must be fairly large, relatively thin, and capable of being stretched without tearing; a silky texture and pleasant color are preferred for the more expensive products. Wrapper leaves with these desirable qualities traditionally have been those grown in fairly rich organic or volcanic soils that are well drained; high humidity and frequent rainfall are also needed.[116] It is because these conditions are present that the most sought-after leaf has come from tropical islands in the Caribbean (Cuba) or in the Far East (the Philippines). However, wrapper types also have been grown successfully under shade both in northern Florida and southern Georgia and even along the Connecticut River valley in the Northeastern United States.[117]

These environmental requirements as well as difficulties in transportation may help to explain why cigars were adopted by Europeans much later than either cut smoking tobacco or snuff. As described in Chapter 4, most of the European states both forbade tobacco production in their own lands and also erected state or farmed monopolies that controlled the tobacco market. Among the tobaccos available for import from the Americas, the most desirable cigar leaf came from colonies of Spain which required them to ship it only to the royal factories in the motherland. Rather than purchasing manufactured cigars from the Spanish, the French and Habsburg monopolies preferred to increase their profits by making their own products from the less expensive leaf grown in Virginia and Hungary. While the English crown did not establish a monopoly, it taxed Spanish products at a higher rate than Virginia tobacco, and it did not allow its colonies to purchase Spanish goods.

Even if a free market had permitted their import, the extremely slow transportation system made it difficult to distribute cigars widely prior to the nineteenth century. As with the evolution of pressed plug and smoking tobaccos, the available means of packaging could not keep cigars moist during the long months that would have been needed to take them from the West Indies to, say, rural Suffolk, Normandy, or Transylvania. Because of these distribution difficulties, the most common products prior to 1800 were powdered snuff and a kind of multipurpose twist or plug that the consumer cut up only as needed.

Although governmental regulations undoubtedly contributed to the late adoption of cigars, consumer tastes were also at work. When the state monopolies did put them on sale during the nineteenth century, consumers were slow to accept this new product, and the cigar rarely formed more than one-fifth of total sales in any European country. Moreover, the Portuguese and Spanish and their colonists in the Americas, with access to the best cigar leaf, at first probably made greater use of snuff, pipes, and (at least among the Spanish) *papelates,* a form of cigarette wrapped in paper or corn silk.[118] When the Spanish reached the Americas, they found their inhabitants using tobacco in many forms. Something like the modern cigar was found in parts of what are today the West Indies, Mexico, and Brazil, as were large and small cigarettes consisting of a sheath of vegetable matter filled with tobacco.[119] In many cases the early accounts do not make it clear which of these two forms the colonists were using; only after 1600 is there sure evidence that cigars were common in parts of Spanish America.[120] By 1676, the taste had spread to Spain itself, where the royal factories at Seville and Cadiz made true cigars as well as cigarillos and papelates. However, snuff and even the pipe probably remained more popular among the Spanish, who did not make frequent use of cigars until after 1750 or even 1800.[121]

In Europe, cigars were not present outside Spain until just before 1800—more than 250 years after the adoption of snuff and the pipe. At first, they were smoked only by a few individuals and generally were held in low repute until the 1840s. A number of writers attribute the spread of cigars throughout Europe to Napoleon's Peninsular Campaigns in Spain (1808–1812). Unfortunately, this explanation does not square with the fact that cigars were sold in England in 1800, eight years before Napoleon invaded Spain. Judging by their rarity in England and France after 1812, moreover, if any soldiers did learn to smoke cigars in Spain, few kept up the habit after their return.

The precise year in which cigars first were sold outside Spain cannot be established. The rare sources that do mention cigars before about 1800 treat them as an exotic curiosity. In France, for example, they are not described in the famous *Encyclopédie* (1751–1772), which does discuss snuff, pipes, and chewing tobacco. The French state monopoly, which was reestablished in 1810, may have sold imported cigars by 1812.[122] As Chapter 5 shows, however, few smokers purchased this expensive luxury in the 1820s or 1830s, and the monopoly did not manufacture its own cigar until the 1840s.[123] German entrepreneurs possibly established cigar factories in Rome and Hamburg by the 1790s. If so, neither seems to have been a great success, and cigars were still treated as a novelty in a German grammar of 1809.[124] Cigars *(Zigarri)* were slow to catch on even among the enthusiastic smokers who were subject to the Habsburg empire. Although they may be present in a retail price list of 1818, the Austrian state monopoly no longer sold them by the 1820s, and it did not establish a cigar factory until 1848.[125] In the Netherlands, which was later second only to Germany in the consumption of cigars, the first factory was erected in 1826, but the industry began to grow only from the middle of the 1840s.[126] No leaf suitable for wrapper was grown in Europe until the twentieth century; factories therefore used binders and wrappers from Java and Sumatra to contain fillers made either from the local air- or fire-cured dark tobacco or from milder Virginia, Brazilian, or Java leaf.[127]

In England cigars also were unknown until the very end of the nineteenth century.[128] According to the account books of Fribourg and Treyer, this purveyor of snuff to the aristocracy first carried Spanish cigars—at a very high price—in 1800.[129] Perhaps because of their cost, few smokers took up cigars; and for at least another twenty years they remained a novelty enjoyed only in private and only by individuals who were both wealthy and daring. Only fifteen thousand pounds of cigars were imported in 1824, and fewer than ten thousand pounds were imported in 1825.[130] Sales began to rise when the tariff on imported cigars was halved in 1829 (from eighteen to nine shillings a pound), but any form of smoking in public, whether pipe or cigar, continued to be held in low repute by Victorian moralists.[131]

Although it is also difficult to know precisely when Americans first smoked them, cigars clearly were brought from the Caribbean to North America at least thirty years before they were carried from Spain to the rest of Europe. Prior to the American Revolution, British law forbade the import of goods from the Spanish colonies; like other products, however, cigars may have been smuggled into New England. According to legend, a Colonel Israel Putnam, who had served with the British expedition against Havana in 1762, brought home three donkey loads of cigars that he distributed at his tavern in Pomfret, Connecticut. Cigars are also mentioned as present in New York in 1765, and factories are said to have been established in that city and in Philadelphia in the 1770s.[132]

Like their European counterparts, smokers in the United States took up cigars with enthusiasm only during the decade of the 1840s even though the tariff on imported cigars had already been cut in 1816.[133] Even with low tariffs, it remained costly to import cigars from Havana, and the rise in demand after 1840 thus encouraged the establishment of factories that used both Cuban and U.S. leaf. While the filler supplies much of the flavor, a cigar also needs a flexible and attractive wrapper leaf. Small amounts of tobacco had been grown in Connecticut for home use in cigars as well as in twist, and a number of small manufacturing enterprises were founded shortly after 1800. From 1830 on, the sweating or curing process was improved, and experiments with Maryland seed led to the development of Connecticut Broadleaf, which is of smooth texture and nearly tasteless, allowing the Cuban filler to dominate.[134] Henceforth, in addition to imported cigars, smokers in the United States had available a domestic product composed of a filler blending smaller or larger amounts of Cuban with Pennsylvania, New York, or Ohio leaf; a Havana binder; and a wrapper made of shade-grown Connecticut Broadleaf. As demand grew, factories making cigars by hand were erected in New England, New York, and throughout the nation.[135]

3.7 CIGARETTES

The history of cigarette consumption generally repeats that of the cigar—only occurring forty years later. During the first three centuries of its use, tobacco was either smoked in a pipe, chewed, or taken as nasal snuff. The true cigar—tobacco tightly rolled and wrapped in tobacco—was carried from Spain and its colonies to Europe and the United States about 1800 but was not widely used until after 1840. The true cigarette—tobacco tightly rolled and wrapped in paper—was adopted even more slowly by European and U.S. smokers. Like the cigar, the cigarette was developed in Spain during the 1600s and is frequently mentioned in Spanish sources during the following century. However, cigarettes were manufactured outside Spain only after 1840, were only taken up by smokers in the 1880s, and only experienced rapid sales growth toward the end of the nineteenth or the beginning of the twentieth century. The English, who began to smoke them before World War I, were among the first to become fans of the cigarette, which became ubiquitous in most countries only after 1925.[136]

The native peoples in Brazil, Mexico, and the Caribbean Islands sometimes smoked tobacco loosely contained in sheaths of vegetable matter, including reeds, sugar cane, banana leaves, and corn silk.[137] However, the Europeans were quicker to copy the Indians' other ways of using tobacco—chewing, snuff, and the pipe—because of the inherent problems posed by these primitive prototypes of the cigarette. Perhaps the most serious of these is the tendency for the taste of the vegetable matter to be incompatible with that of tobacco. Vegetable matter also tends to be either too stiff or too weak to roll tightly, so that the tobacco burns too rapidly or even falls out into the mouth. Most European smokers would not even consider cigarettes until these problems (inherent in any home-rolled product) were overcome at the end of the nineteenth century through the development of special papers and the mechanization of manufacturing.[138]

The rather meager evidence about tobacco use in Spanish America suggests that the white population smoked tobacco wrapped in corn silk (sometimes called cigarillos) as well as pipes and possibly cigars by the end of the sixteenth century.[139] Sometime after 1600, it became apparent, possibly in Spain, that a fine paper wrapper was preferable, and the papelate came into existence.[140] Although the maize cigarette also continued to exist, papelates slowly gained popularity; by the end of the eighteenth century cigarette smokers were common in Spain and are frequently portrayed by the painter Goya.[141] And papelates also seem to have been widely used in Mexico by 1765, when the newly erected state monopoly seized large quantities of cigarette papers.[142]

Because some tobacco manufacturers used Oriental tobaccos at the end of the nineteenth century, antiquarians have assumed that this product was carried along the trade routes from Spain to Italy and the Levant. And they have additionally asserted that it was brought to Western Europe from the Near East by soldiers who were taught to smoke cigarettes by the Russians and the Turks during the Crimean War (1854–1856). However, the evidence suggests that paper cigarettes were little used in the Ottoman Empire or in Russia prior to 1850.[143] Cigarettes also were not common in the parts of Italy visited by English or French tourists; they were not sold at all in Lombardy and Venetia during the years these were under the Habsburg state monopoly (1815–1866)— although the latter usually tried to provide its clients with the products they preferred.[144] Given the existing evidence, it is likely, if less romantic, that it was the French who introduced the Russians and the Turks to cigarettes during the Crimean War and thus carried this way of smoking tobacco from the West to the East.

After the Spanish, the French would seem to be the first Europeans to have smoked cigarettes. About 1830, during a fad for all things Spanish, the pape-late (as well as maize cigarettes) became briefly fashionable, especially among young men and women who wished to present a Bohemian appearance.[145] They presumably rolled their own since the state monopoly did not sell cigarettes until 1843 or 1844.[146] Apparently the fashion for hand-rolled cigarettes died as quickly as it arose; sales of the monopoly's products also languished as the majority of the French continued to use either snuff or the pipe. In 1868, the state monopoly sold only 26 thousand pounds of its cigarettes, and although sales began to increase during the 1870s, this product still represented only 2 percent of the monopoly's total sales in 1885, forty years after it was first offered for sale.[147]

In England, where foreign visitors must have smoked them in the larger cities, cigarettes may have been made in small quantities by the 1840s. The earliest known record of their sale (noted as made-to-order) dates from 1852,[148] and the first cigarette factory was opened by Robert Cloag about 1860.[149] Sales of these early cigarettes, rolled by hand from Oriental and Russian tobaccos, seem to have been slow.[150] They apparently increased in the 1880s when manufacturers began offering lower prices as well as cigarettes made from milder Burley and flue-cured Bright. (These tobaccos, which first became available in Britain in the late 1860s, are called Virginia tobacco by the English, although they are mainly grown in other states.)[151] Greater acceptance of smoking by the middling classes—typified by the introduction in 1868 of the first smoking cars on the railroads—may also have played a role in popularizing cigarettes.[152]

Throughout Europe, the 1880s saw the first real acceptance of the cigarette. Perhaps discouraged by the tepid sales of cigarettes in France, other state monopolies (the best source for early sales statistics) waited several decades before introducing this product. In the Habsburg realm, the state monopoly offered its first paper cigarettes in 1865; called *double cigarettes,* these were about three times as long as the standard cigarette, had a mouthpiece at either end, and were cut in two before use.[153] They enjoyed some success, and a greater variety of brands became available. Like the English and the French, the subjects of the Habsburgs were pipe smokers and snuffers, and they did not immediately take to cigarettes; sales began to increase significantly only after 1880, primarily cutting into the demand for cigars.[154] In Italy, the state monopoly created in 1868 was even slower to provide its clients with cigarettes, which were not offered for sale until 1884.[155]

It was also not until the 1880s that cigarettes began to be used in regions with a free market in tobacco, such as the Germanies and the Netherlands. Although factories making cigarettes as well as small cigars existed by the 1860s in Germany, their output apparently was minute, and it is not broken out separately in the summaries of tobacco manufacturing published by the Imperial German government during the 1870s. By 1913, while cigarette sales had risen, cigars still took almost half of total tobacco sales. In the Netherlands, judging by artistic and literary sources, smokers also continued to prefer the established products throughout the nineteenth century, and even considered cigarettes to be somewhat silly and unmanly.[156]

Among the European peoples, the Scandinavians were the last to take up the cigarette. Their reluctance was perhaps due to their unusually high consumption of smokeless products; thus, in order to adopt the cigarette habit, they first had to learn to smoke. Cigarettes were introduced in these states only toward 1900. The Swedes began to buy them in significant quantities toward the end of the 1920s, considerably later than in England, Italy, or the United States.[157] Cigarettes came to constitute 50 percent of tobacco sales in Denmark and Norway later than in any other European countries except the Netherlands and Belgium.[158]

At the end of the nineteenth century, the United States (and probably Canada) were, after Scandinavia, the main regions in which consumers preferred smokeless tobacco instead of the pipe.[159] Cigarettes became popular in the United States almost as slowly as in Scandinavia. Although it is not certain when cigarettes were first manufactured in this country, they are mentioned before 1860 only by travelers to Cuba or France. At first the industry apparently was confined to New York; not until the early 1880s did several plug or smoking tobacco manufacturers begin to make this product in the Virginia–North Carolina area. Among these the most influential perhaps was James Duke, whose company apparently was the first to introduce automated production with the introduction of the Bonsack machine in 1883 or 1884.[160]

Companies such as Duke's marketed cigarettes much more aggressively than the lethargic state monopolies in France, Italy, or the Habsburg empire. However, advertising and promotion apparently do not determine tobacco preferences, for American smokers were even slower to take up this new product than those in Europe. Between 1880 and 1910, American consumers who had overwhelmingly preferred plug chewing tobacco, began to use increasing amounts of smoking tobacco and cigars. Although cigarette production also rose, the increase largely reflected rapid population growth. In 1910, cigarettes represented only 2 percent of the U.S. market, a smaller share than in any European country outside Scandinavia.[161]

Cigarettes really did not become a mass habit in the United States until the decade of the 1910s, when several companies introduced cigarettes primarily made of sweetened Burley and Bright tobaccos in a blend much like that used in plug chewing tobacco.[162] U.S. manufacturers thus created a distinctive new product. Until the 1930s, most of the cigarettes produced outside the United States were *straight* or unblended, and the American blended cigarette thus is different both from European Turkish or Virginia brands and also from the black cigarettes (made of fire-cured dark tobaccos) that were provided by the state monopolies in France, Spain, Italy, and Central Europe. But tobacco preferences change slowly, and U.S. consumers did not immediately desert other products. While cigarette sales continued to grow after 1920, consumption of cigars and pipe tobacco declined at a relatively slow rate, and sales of snuff remained stable. Not until 1941, some eighty years after their introduction, did cigarettes finally take more than half of the total U.S. market.[163]

NOTES

1. Brongers, *Nicotiana Tabacum*, 26–27

2. Consumers using this oral method sometimes moved the tobacco around in the mouth, but they rarely chewed the leaf as violently as, for example, users of bubble gum. Few have actually eaten or swallowed it—or at least not very much of it. This somewhat erroneous name is also found in other languages, such as German *(Kautabak)*. Like the English *chew*, the particular French word *chiquer* for this way of using tobacco similarly is derived from the Germanic root. (French sources also use *mâcher*, the general word for chewing derived from Latin.) Perhaps the word *chew* is onomatopoetic, resembling the sound made by users, even if not totally accurate.

3. According to an estimate cited by Brooks, *(Mighty Leaf*, 235), as late as 1883, 28 million pounds of tobacco in the United States escaped the manufacturing process and were directly consumed by the grower.

4. Garner, *Production*, 30; Robert, *Tobacco Kingdom*, 161–71. As Robert notes (p. 161), "The extent of manufacture and domestic consumption of the leaf in the Colonial and Early National period is purely a matter of conjecture."

5. Tilley *(Bright Tobacco*, 490) gently corrects Robert, *Tobacco Kingdom*, 211.

6. Tilley, *Bright Tobacco*, 490–93; Robert, *Tobacco Kingdom*, 211–16; Robert, *Story of Tobacco*, 74–78; Heimann, *Tobacco and Americans*, 117–19, 152–55.

7. Tilley, *Bright Tobacco*, 513; Robert, *Story of Tobacco*, 75; Robert, *Tobacco Kingdom*, 215.

8. Ibid., 213–14.

9. Quoting ibid., 215. Compare Tilley, *Bright Tobacco*, 513; Heimann, *Tobacco and Americans*, 132–35.

10. Price, *France and the Chesapeake*, 422.

11. Ibid.; see Chapter 4, Note 53, concerning smuggling into England.

12. Price, *France and the Chesapeake*, 383; Compare Nash, "English and Scottish Tobacco Trades," 356.

13. Hanauer, *Études économiques*, II:597.

14. Barbour, *Capitalism in Amsterdam*, 62–63, 71; Bloom, *Economic Activities of the Jews*, 61.

15. Hanauer, *Études économiques*, II:587–98.

16. Brongers, *Nicotiana Tabacum*, 84–86.

17. Price, *France and the Chesapeake*, 424–26.

18. Price, *France and the Chesapeake*, 468–69.

19. Quoting Brongers, *Nicotiana Tabacum,* 89; Compare Price, *France and the Chesapeake,* 422–23.

20. Brongers, *Nicotiana Tabacum,* 86–87; Price, *France and the Chesapeake,* 423–34.

21. Dickson, *Panacea or Precious Bane,* Ch. 4, passim; Brooks, *Tobacco in Arents,* I:106; Perez-Vidal, *Espana en la historia del tabaco,* 129; Corti, *History of Smoking,* 108–9.

22. Brooks, *Mighty Leaf,* 109.

23. See Tables 6.1 through 6.3.

24. McCausland, *Snuff and Snuff-Boxes,* 13–32, 213; Tenant, *American Cigarette Industry,* 128–29; Perez-Vidal, *España,* 130–32; Price, *France and the Chesapeake,* 176, 193, 406; Pierre Julien, "La Chique et le Marin," 25–27; Hitier and Sabourin, *Le Tabac,* 97–98.

25. Fairholt, *Tobacco,* 280–82; Billings, *Tobacco,* 243; McCausland, *Snuff,* 82–83; Mackenzie, *Sublime Tobacco,* 296–97. The older studies of Fairholt (1859) and Billings (1875) are especially useful when they speak of their firsthand experiences; Fairholt, who spent many years working in the tobacco industry, can in certain instances be considered a primary source.

26. France, Direction générale de manufactures de l'État, *Rapport concernant la fabrication . . . pour l'année 1819,* 60; France, Direction générale de manufactures de l'État, *Rapport . . . pour l'annee 1845,* 122. According to Price, (*France and the Chesapeake,* 420) relatively small amounts of Latakia were imported to make snuff during the eighteenth century.

27. At least that was the composition in 1845 according to Joubert, *Nouveau Manuel complet,* 113–22; compare Bouant, *Le Tabac, culture et industrie,* 178–79.

28. Brongers, *Nicotiana Tabacum,* 84. As late as 1752, a French snuff factory at Marloix still used huge stone mortars that required four men to operate: Price, *France and the Chesapeake,* 426.

29. Billings, *Tobacco,* 223–25; McCausland, *Snuff,* 80, 92; Beckett, *Coal and Tobacco,* 146.

30. Billings, *Tobacco.*

31. Fairholt, *Tobacco,* 283; Billings, *Tobacco;* McCausland, *Snuff,* 89–90.

32. Garner, *Production,* 477–78.

33. Tobacco ferments for about two months in the United States, according to Garner, *Production* (1945); compare Brennan, *Tobacco Leaves* (1915), 145–46. It is allowed to ferment for four months in France according to the *Encyclopédie Larousse,* vol. 19 (1976), p. 11,612.

34. Garner, *Production;* Heimann, *Tobacco and Americans,* 65; McCausland, *Snuff,* 88. Since the nineteenth century, legal copyright has covered some of the names of geographical regions—such as Copenhagen—when they are assigned to specific brands of snuff.

35. McCausland, *Snuff,* 84.

36. Scented snuffs were fermented for three weeks according to the eighteenth-century sources cited by Brongers, *Nicotiana Tabacum,* 86.

37. McCausland, *Snuff,* 88.

38. This was the case with Fribourg and Treyer, whose clients also purchased sieves, brushes, and parchment to moisten snuff after purchase: Evans, *Old Snuff House,* 16.

According to Price (*France and the Chesapeake*, 471), eighteenth-century French manufactories also moistened prepared snuff after grinding it.

39. Fairholt, *Tobacco*, 268–70; McCausland, *Snuff*, 86–87; Mackenzie, *Sublime Tobacco*, 165–166.

40. Evans, *Old Snuff House*, 14; McCausland, *Snuff*, 85; Perez-Vidal, *España*, 75–76.

41. See note 27.

42. Brongers, *Nicotiana Tabacum*, 175; Fairholt, *Tobacco*, 235–41.

43. Dickson, *Panacea or Precious Bane*, 147–50; Ortiz, *Cuban Counterpoint*, 74; Corti, *History of Smoking*, 106–8; Curtis, *Story of Snuff*, 63.

44. Dickson, *Panacea or Precious Bane*, 150–54; Corti, *History of Smoking*, 129.

45. Perez-Vidal, *España*, 73–74; Ortiz, *Cuban Counterpoint*, 211.

46. Perez-Vidal, *España*, 85–86.

47. Ortiz, *Cuban Counterpoint*, 241; Dickson, 152–53; Comes, *Histoire*, 82.

48. Comes, 85; Corti, *History of Smoking*, 130–32.

49. Ibid., 187; Comes, *History of Smoking*, 93–96.

50. See Tables 5.10 through 5.12.

51. Comes, *History of Smoking*, 69; Laufer, *Introduction of Tobacco*, 49–52; Curtis, *Story of Snuff*, 39–40; Brooks, *Mighty Leaf*, 125.

52. *L'Agriculture et la maison rustique*. Compare Fermond, *Monographie du tabac*, 14; Comes, *History of Smoking*, 70; Laufer, *Introduction of Tobacco*, 53; Corti, *History of Smoking*, 59–60; Brooks, *Mighty Leaf*; Curtis, *Story of Snuff*.

53. Dickson, *Panacea or Precious Bane*, 92, 151–52.

54. Ibid., 92–93; Price, *France and the Chesapeake*, 73–77.

55. Fairholt, *Tobacco*, 243; Curtis, *Story of Snuff*, 61–62; Brooks, *Tobacco in Arents*, I:158.

56. Curtis, *Story of Snuff*, 82; Fairholt, *Tobacco*, 244.

57. Price, *France and the Chesapeake*, 47, 160.

58. Rival, *Tabac, miroir du temps*, 97.

59. See Table 5.7.

60. See Table 5.9.

61. Corti, *History of Smoking*, 97–102; Brongers, *Nicotiana Tabacum*, 157; Mackenzie, *Sublime Tobacco*, 148.

62. Brooks, *Tobacco in Arents*, 158; Corti, *History of Smoking*, 118–20, 188.

63. Ibid., 108–9.

64. Ibid., 200–1.

65. Cohausen, *Satyrische Dedancken*. See McCausland, *Snuff*, 29; Corti, *History of Smoking*, 197.

66. See Tables 5.1 and 5.5.

67. Laufer, *Introduction of Tobacco*, 3–16; Dickson, *Panacea or Precious Bane*, 132–38; Mackenzie, *Sublime Tobacco*, 76–87; Corti, *History of Smoking*, 67–72.

68. Mackenzie, *Sublime Tobacco*, 88–108; Dickson, *Panacea or Precious Bane*, 167–74; see Section 4.9.

69. Dickson, *Panacea or Precious Bane*, 179.

70. For Buttes's *Diets Dry Dinner* and Dekker's *Gull's Hornbook*, see Laufer, *Introduction of Tobacco*, 39–40; Curtis, *Story of Snuff*, 46; Dickson, *Panacea or Precious Bane*, 185–89.

71. McCausland, *Snuff and Snuff-Boxes*, 14–15; Brooks, *Tobacco in Arents*, 160–61; Curtis, *Story of Snuff*, 45; Mackenzie, *Sublime Tobacco*, 164–65.

72. See Notes 109 and 131; McCausland, *Snuff and Snuff-Boxes*, 71.

73. Evans, *Old Snuff House*, 39.

74. Apperson, *Social History of Smoking*, 131.

75. McCausland, *Snuff and Snuff-Boxes*, 36–37; Laufer, *Introduction of Tobacco*, 40; Mackenzie, *Sublime Tobacco*, 163; Brooks, *Tobacco in Arents*, I:160.

76. Alford, *W. D. & H. O. Wills*, 27, 110; Walker, *Under Fire*, 25.

77. See Table 6.14.

78. McCausland, *Snuff and Snuff-Boxes*, 77–78.

79. Robert, *Story*, 75–77, 104; Gottsegen, *Tobacco, a Study*, 2–3; Heimann, *Tobacco and Americans*, 65, 82, 193.

80. Robert, *Tobacco Kingdom*, 175.

81. See Table 6.10.

82. See Section 3.4.

83. Robert, *Story*, 102.

84. Garner, *Production*, 477–78.

85. Gage, *American Tobacco Types*, 94, 72.

86. John H. Aughey, quoted in Robert, *Story*, 102.

87. Billings, *Tobacco*, 244–47.

88. For the development of tobacco manufacturing in the United States during the late eighteenth and early nineteenth centuries, see Notes 4 and 5.

89. See Table 5.13.

90. See Table 6.7.

91. Tables 6.6, 6.8, and 6.9.

92. Table 5.8.

93. Brongers, *Nicotiana Tabacum*, 86. In England most tobacco was sold loose until the second third of the nineteenth century according to Penn, *Soverane Herbe*, 131.

94. Although a Frenchman, Nicholas Appert, received a prize in 1810 for developing a method by which cans could be used to preserve food and other products, handmade cans were expensive, and the industry did not assume importance until the invention of machines to produce stamped (1847) and soldered (1876) cans.

95. Tilley, *R. J. Reynolds*, 363. See pp. 154–71 for Reynolds's development of machinery to package Prince Albert (introduced in 1907) in tin cans and George Washington (introduced in 1910) in foil inserted in cloth bags.

96. See Table 5.8.

97. Garner, *Production*, 475–77; Akehurst, *Tobacco*, 479. With improvements in machinery, tobacco for smoking and cigarettes now can be cut under pressure without first being pressed: Hitier and Sabourin, *Le tabac*, 72–77.

98. Akehurst, *Tobacco*.

99. Penn, *Soverane Herbe*, 125–26.

100. Hitier and Sabourin, *Le Tabac*, 72–77.

101. Brongers, *Nicotiana Tabacum*, 86 (citing a source from 1745); Fermond, *Monographie du Tabac* (1857), 204.

102. Thus Robert (*Tobacco Kingdom*, 170–71); "By 1860 ninety-eight per cent of the tobacco factories of Virginia and North Carolina were engaged in the manufacture of plug and twist, two per cent in the making of smoking tobacco. Accordingly, in the

ante-bellum period, the term manufactured tobacco was virtually synonymous with chewing tobacco.''

103. Tilley (*Bright Tobacco*, 511) gives a somewhat earlier date for the introduction of flavored smoking tobaccos. She attributes the preserving of tobacco (before about 1839) by sprinkling it with licorice water to ''a man named Cavendish of Norfolk, Virginia.'' However, in England the Customs Office uses the term Cavendish for any sweetened tobacco in a cut form; when pressed, flavored tobacco is called Negrohead. Furthermore, the British say that the name refers instead to the Cavendish who was an admiral of Elizabeth I and the ancestor of the dukes of Devonshire: Penn, *Soverane Herbe*, 130.

104. Mathieu-Dairnvaell, *Le Tabac vengé*, 24.

105. Brongers, *Nicotiana Tabacum*, 166; Rival, *Tabac, miroir du temps*, 155–59; Mackenzie, *Sublime Tobacco*, 252; Penn, *Souverane Herbe*, 152–53; Fairholt, *Tobacco*, 194–95.

106. Brongers, Nicotiana Tabacum, 31; Libert, *Tobacco*, 37.

107. Rival, *Tabac, miroir*, 160–61; Libert, *Tobacco*, 41.

108. Fairholt, *Tobacco*, 198.

109. Libert, *Tobacco*, 41; Mackenzie, *Sublime Tobacco* 253–55; Apperson, *Social History*, 176.

110. Table 5.7.

111. Table 6.10.

112. Billings, *Tobacco*, 259; Akehurst, *Tobacco*, 478; Hitier and Sabourin, *Le Tabac*, 88–95.

113. Heimann, *Tobacco and Americans*, 98; Akehurst, *Tobacco*, 478; Hitier and Sabourin, *Le Tabac*, 72–80.

114. Garner, *Production*, 472.

115. Akehurst, *Tobacco*, 477.

116. Ibid., 31; Gage, *American Tobacco Types*, 38–40.

117. Ibid., 46–47.

118. Brooks, *Tobacco in Arents*, I:79, 166, 216; Fairholt, *Tobacco*, 218; Billings, *Tobacco*, 266.

119. Brooks, *Tobacco in Arents*, I:15; Heimann, *Tobacco and Americans*, 7–14; Dickson, *Panacea or Precious Bane*, 106–7.

120. Perez-Vidal, *España*, 87–88. Compare Fairholt, *Tobacco*, 216; Corti, *History of Smoking*, 206.

121. Perez-Vidal, *España*, 90–95.

122. According to Corti (*History of Smoking*, 222) cigars were sold in 1812 in the Illyrian provinces occupied by the French. Sales are recorded in the published accounts of the French state monopoly from 1818.

123. See Table 5.8.

124. Fairholt, *Tobacco*, 219; Corti, *History of Smoking*, 207, 221–22.

125. Ibid., 222; Hitz and Huber, *Geschichte der Österreichischen Tabakregie*, 174.

126. Brongers, *Nicotiana Tabacum*, 221.

127. Corti, *History of Smoking*, 246; Hutson, *Consumption*, 8.

128. Apperson, *Social History*, 138; Perez-Vidal, *España*, 95.

129. Evans, *Old Snuff House*, 34–36.

130. Fairholt, *Tobacco*, 220; Penn, *Souverane Herbe*, 88–89.

131. Apperson, *Social History*, 140–56; Mackenzie, *Sublime Tobacco*, 229–33.

132. Ramsey, *History of Tobacco Production in the Connecticut Valley*, 125–126; Heimann, *Tobacco and Americans*, 86–87.

133. Garner et al., "History and Status," 457.

134. Ramsey, *History of Tobacco Production*, 128–30.

135. Heimann, *Tobacco and Americans*, 88–101.

136. See Tables 6.2 through 6.4 below.

137. See note 118 and the sources cited by Brooks, *Tobacco in Arents*, I:168.

138. Efforts to mechanize cigarette manufacture began in Europe in the 1870s; the first fully automatic device was the Bonsack machine introduced in the United States in 1883 or 1884. See Brongers, *Nicotiana Tabacum*, 230; and Chapter 6, Note 3.

139. Perez-Vidal, *España*, 97–100.

140. Ibid., 100–101; Brooks, *Tobacco in Arents*, I:170. According to Mackenzie (*Sublime Tobacco*, 264), the head of the Dominican order criticized the clergy in Saragossa for taking snuff and smoking papelates during ecclesiastical meetings.

141. Perez-Vidal, *España*, 102–5.

142. Tilley, *Bright Tobacco*, 504.

143. The most comprehensive collection of references to tobacco in travelers' accounts remains that of Comes, *Histoire*, 117–26 (the Balkans), 165–68 (Egypt), 227–47 (Mesopotamia, Arabia, Syria, and Palestine). The only mention of cigarettes I can find among these accounts dates from 1865 (p. 235). Fairholt (*Tobacco*, 204–11), whose book was published in 1859, describes the pipe as widely used in the Turkish Empire by smokers of both genders and all ages. Billings (*Tobacco*, 146; published in 1875) quotes (but does not identify) a traveler in Turkey who spoke of the fondness for the pipe among Turkish men and women but who also mentioned the use of cigarettes by young girls. For Russia, see Brongers, *Nicotiana Tabacum*, 228; Tilley, *Bright Tobacco*, 505. Although it all is referred to as Turkish, much of the Oriental leaf used in cigarettes came from Greece or the Caucasian provinces of Russia.

144. Tables 5.10 and 5.11 below.

145. Perez-Vidal, *España*, 112. The description of cigarette smokers is that published in 1845 by Mathieu-Dairnvaell, *Le Tabac vengé*, 114–17. Mathieu-Dairnvaell states that the French borrowed the cigarette habit from the Spanish after 1800 but especially after 1830; however, he also mentions that maize cigarettes were smoked by the less fashionable classes along the Mediterranean coast, and sailors or travelers may well have imported this habit into the French Midi during the eighteenth century.

146. Tilley, *Bright Tobacco*, 505; Penn, *Souverane Herbe*, 197. According to the accounts of the state tobacco monopoly, it sold only seven thousand pounds of cigarettes in 1845; see Table 5.8.

147. Table 5.8.

148. Evans, *Old Snuff House*, 37.

149. Gloag later claimed to have opened his factory in 1856, but 1860 is more likely: Alford, *W. D. & H. O. Wills*, 123–25. For the early history of cigarettes in England, see also Akehurst, *Tobacco*, 25; Apperson, *Social History*, 179–85; Penn, *Souverane Herbe*, 196–97; Mackenzie, *Sublime Tobacco*, 265.

150. In his study published in 1859 *(Tobacco)*, Fairholt mentions cigarettes only in connection with Latin America and makes no reference to their use in England.

151. See Section 2.3 for the development of Bright and Burley.

152. See Tables 6.2 and 6.14.

153. Corti, *History of Smoking*, 253.

154. See Table 5.5.

155. Table 5.12.

156. Brongers, *Nicotiana Tabacum,* 228–30; Corti, *History of Smoking,* 259; Tables 6.16 and 6.3.

157. Table 5.13.

158. Table 6.4

159. Table 6.5

160. Tilley, *Bright Tobacco,* 506–10; Robert, *Story of Tobacco,* 140–45; Chapter 6, Note 3.

161. Table 6.10; Table 6.2.

162. Chapter 6, Note 13. See also Tilley, *Bright Tobacco.* Heimann, *Tobacco and Americans,* 206–11; Robert, *Story of Tobacco,* 230–35.

163. Tables 6.10 through 6.12.

Chapter 4

Governmental Policies toward Cultivation and Marketing

4.1 SUMMARY

Since there was no mass press in Europe during the sixteenth century, the first treatises on tobacco were written by scholars and physicians; these savants mainly were interested in the plant as an ornamental or in investigating its possible use as a beneficial drug that potentially might cure many diseases.[1] Toward the beginning of the seventeenth century, the leaves of the plant also came to be regarded as a source of pleasure or diversion, and some rulers reacted to tobacco's more frequent use by prohibiting its cultivation or consumption. These edicts, the phrasing of which today often arouses amusement, have been recounted at length.[2] For our purposes, they are of interest as our first evidence that the ruler's subjects had begun to make use of tobacco.

It was not possible to enforce these prohibitions, and the few surviving sources show that they had no effect. Tobacco grows rapidly, and it can be grown throughout Europe; once processed into powder or twisted into a braid, it is easily carried in small packages. Because it is easy to raise and transport, ancien regime rulers could not prevent the use of tobacco—especially since they lacked many of the technologies, including guns, roads, and accounting systems, available to modern governments. Thus, these early prohibitions were a dead letter, and their barbarous enforcement in nations such as Russia was as ineffectual as most of the sumptuary laws passed during the seventeenth century.[3]

Once they realized that they could not halt tobacco's diffusion throughout the populace, European governments almost uniformly attempted to gain as much revenue as possible from its consumers. Almost as soon as the plant was introduced into Europe from the Americas, governments thus began to tax its use and also to regulate its production, manufacture, and sale in order to facilitate taxation. Ancien regime finance is a complex and arcane subject, but it is safe to say that, with the possible exception of the Swiss and Dutch, all governments during the seventeenth and eighteenth centuries were chronically short of the revenues needed to obtain their goals.

Given the economic and administrative technology of the time, governments had few sources of revenues. Agriculture remained the largest economic sector and the main source of wealth. However, there were limits to the taxes governments could levy on farm workers or owners; if a government raised taxes beyond these limits, the former would die and cease to produce foodstuffs, and the latter would have no capital with which to keep up the land. Although trade and finance formed a much smaller segment of the economy, some wholesale merchants and bankers did have large incomes, especially if they were involved in international trade. Despite computerized records, however, even today's governments find it extraordinarily difficult to tap finance capital; during the eighteenth century, most could neither measure nor tax commercial dealings.

Thus, all governments derived a large part of their revenues from taxes on consumption—either through import and export duties or through higher prices for such necessities as salt, tea, and alcohol. With tobacco, they quickly came to see that this particular commodity and the products made from it can bear an especially heavy burden of taxes. Since it is an agricultural product that is more or less refined before consumption, governments can tax and regulate tobacco at one or more of the several stages through which it travels from the farmer to the user—when it is grown, when the leaf is processed into manufactured products, when it is transported either as leaf or as product, or when it is sold. In their efforts to maximize revenues, various governments have attempted to tax tobacco at one or more of these stages; to enforce these taxes and prevent smuggling, they have had to erect elaborate regulatory schemes.

Table 4.1 summarizes how governments regulated these various stages of the tobacco industry from about 1650 to 1914. As it indicates, tobacco was treated as a governmental monopoly by states that—until 1776—ruled over all of the Americas and most of Europe as well as over as many as 80 percent of their peoples. Until the end of the nineteenth century, most of these governments were not capable of administering this monopoly as a department of the state. Thus, they farmed these monopoly rights to one or more corporations; that is, for cash up front they auctioned off the sole right for a set period of years to manufacture and sell tobacco products. The concessionaire groups enforced these rights both by employing their own police powers and by calling on those of the state.

Only one of these tobacco farms, that in France, has been the subject of analysis. All of them were unpopular, and all routinely were accused of abusing their powers, particularly those of police. Certainly, neither these farms nor the state itself could control or even monitor agricultural production. Since they could not prevent farmers from keeping back some of their crop and selling it at a market price, they thus decided not to permit any domestic cultivation.

Table 4.1

Governmental Regulation of the Tobacco Industry, Mid-Seventeenth through Nineteenth Centuries

	Cultivation	Imports	Manufacture	Sale
Britain	prohibited	high duties	private	private
Sweden	encouraged (18th century)	prohibited (18th Century)	mixed	private
Switzerland	---------------------{private}---------------------			
Netherlands	---------------------{private}---------------------			
Alsace	---------------------{private}---------------------			
Spain	prohibited	-------------{farmed}----------------		
Portugal	pwhitech	-------------{farmed}----------------		
France	controlled	---{farmed to 1791; state in 1810}----		
Italy	prohibited	------{farmed; state since 1882}------		
Austria	prohibited	-----{farmed to 1784; then state}-----		
Prussia	regulated	----{state 1765-1787, then private}---		
Bavaria	------------------{private since 1717}--------------			
Russia	-----------------{state but ineffectual}------------			
Poland	-------------{private to Partitions 1776-1795}------			
U.S.	------------------{private after 1776}-------------			

Note: State means public administration of a monopoly; *farmed* indicates that the government granted
its monopoly powers to a private concessionaire; *private* means that the tobacco industry was
not subject to particular regulations (although it was under the general laws regulating trade).
Both Britain and Spain permitted their colonies in the Americas to export only to the mother
country; both left the industry within the colonies in private hands until 1764, when the
Spanish government ordained a state monopoly over all phases of the industry.

Russia

Hence, all the monopoly states except Sweden prohibited tobacco growing within
their realms and instead largely depended on leaf imported from the British
and, to a lesser extent, the Spanish colonies in the Americas. During the eighteenth century, a great tobacco-producing zone—second only to that in Virginia
and Maryland—stretched along the Rhine River from Utrecht in the Netherlands to Lower Alsace, thus taking in the small states of the Palatinate, the
Hanau district on the Main, and Cleves, as well as the provinces of Gelderland
and Overyssel in the United Provinces of the Netherlands.[4] And significant
amounts were also grown in Pomerania, Brandenburg, and Hungary. (Much
leaf also was produced for local consumption in the Ukraine and in other provinces of Poland, but little of this was suitable for the international market.)[5]

Throughout most of the Continent, however, tobacco was grown only clandestinely and in relatively limited quantities.

Ancien regime governments normally adopted *mercantilist* policies; they sought, erroneously, to avoid trade deficits by prohibiting imports and fostering exports. In this particular case, however, their need for immediate cash from sale of the tobacco farm outweighed any concern they may have felt either over impoverishing their peasantry or over the future balance of payments. None of the monopolists could totally stamp out smuggling either by land or, especially in the United Kingdom, by sea. But they may well have succeeded in maximizing profits in the near term. The demand for tobacco is relatively inelastic. Thus, even if it had reduced smuggling, a reduction in the government's retail price or (in England) in import duties probably would not have increased sales sufficiently to yield the monopolist the same amount of revenue it gained by collecting punitive prices for two-thirds of the tobacco consumed within its jurisdiction.[6] Moreover, precisely because demand is inelastic, tobacco revenues have been highly predictable; for this reason, the French and Polish governments could pledge or alienate these revenues after World War I to secure loans foreign bankers otherwise might not have granted.

Certainly the regimes with tobacco monopolies have been loath to relinquish the revenues these produce. With the creation of the modern nation-state during the nineteenth century, most governments ceased to farm the tobacco monopoly and erected it into a state department, which usually reported directly to the finance minister. In thus nationalizing and perhaps rationalizing these monopolies, Joseph II of Austria (1784) and Napoleon of France (1810) were early leaders. Their example was followed by the new kingdom of Italy, which replaced the various farmed monopolies on the peninsula with one national state administration in 1882. Similarly, all six of the successor regimes to the Hapsburg Empire after World War I immediately took over for their own use the apparatus and facilities of the Austrian *regie*. Between the wars, therefore, only Sweden and the nations of the Iberian peninsula maintained a farmed monopoly.

As Table 4.2 shows, however, most of these monopoly regimes did sharply reverse their policy toward domestic cultivation after World War I. Rather than prohibiting domestic production, they now attempted to supply all their own needs while importing as little foreign leaf as possible. To this end they encouraged or forced local farmers to improve their crop, which was virtually confiscated at a price fixed by the state tobacco administration. Gross production dramatically increased in virtually all these states, including some (such as Italy and Spain) where little tobacco had been grown before the war. The quality of the leaf produced was sometimes less impressive, but consumers without an alternative choice did purchase the state products.

Table 4.2
Governmental Regulation of the Tobacco Industry, 1918–1945

	Cultivation	Imports	Manufacture	Sale
Britain	nil	high duties	private	private
Switzerland	--------------------{private}----------------------			
Netherlands	--------------------{private}----------------------			
Sweden	permitted; state	-----------{farmed}----------------		
France	encouraged; state	-----------{state}----------------		
Greece	encouraged; state	-----------{state}----------------		
Italy	encouraged; state	-----------{state}----------------		
Spain	regulated	-----------{farmed}----------------		
Portugal		-----------{farmed}----------------		
Austria	none	-----------{state}----------------		
Germany	private	-----------{private}--------------		
E. Europe	encouraged; state	-----------{state}----------------		
Russia	--------------------{state but ineffectual}---------			
U.S.	regulated	-----------{private}--------------		

Note: E. (Eastern) Europe refers to Czechoslovakia, Hungary, Poland, Rumania, and Yugoslavia.
State means public administration of a monopoly; *farmed* indicates that the monopoly rights
were granted to a private concessionaire; *private* means that the tobacco industry was not
subject to particular regulations (although it was under the general laws regulating trade.)

4.2 FRANCE

France provides an example of both continuous and complete regulation of
every stage of the industry that lasted—despite periods of criticism—for more
than three hundred years and under all the various forms of government essayed
by the French nation. In 1621 the crown ordained import and export duties,
and after 1674 the state abrogated to itself total control both over tobacco cultivation and also over the fabrication and sale of tobacco products. Rather than
attempting to establish a state department, it sold or farmed a monopoly to a
private company, whose powers were, however, enforced by the royal courts.
With the exception of a few months in the early 1720s, this tobacco farm
remained in existence under various names from 1674 to 1791, paying the state
increasingly larger sums for its privileges.[7]

So lucrative was the monopoly of tobacco that Napoleon reestablished it in
December 1810—although this time as a department of the state rather than as
a farm. Under different names and in various administrative guises, the state
has retained control until the present day over the production of tobacco in
France as well as the manufacture and sale of tobacco products. From 1810
until 1926, successive governments placed the monopoly (from 1831 the Régie
Française des Tabacs) under various tax departments. In the latter year, a con-
stitutional law renamed and reorganized it as the Service National d'Exploitation
Industrielle des Tabacs et Allumettes (SEITA).

This 1926 law both granted to SEITA a large measure of autonomy (includ-

Table 4.3

Tobacco Production in France (in thousands of U.S. pounds)

1840	19,621
1860	55,556
1875	28,439
1900	48,501
1925	69,225
1950	112,215

Source: France, Institut National de la Statistique, *Annuaire statistique de la France*, 1955, p. 75*.

ing the right to advertise its products) and also centralized within it control of every aspect of the tobacco industry—except for the politically sensitive choice of retailers *(débitants)*. The treaty of Rome (1971) creating the European Economic Community (EEC) legally opened cultivation to citizens of other member states, and the monopoly over the import and wholesale trade was abolished in 1976. In practice, however, SEITA—now a société or nationalized company rather than an administrative service—retains an effective monopoly over the production and processing of French tobacco and the manufacture and distribution of products for the French market.[8]

The soil and climate in parts of France are distinctly favorable to the cultivation of certain kinds of tobacco—although consumers during many periods have preferred other types than these. Thus, the extent of production in France has always been more or less determined by governmental policies. Under the system of farmed monopoly from 1674 to 1791, the state auctioned off to a private company the right to control all aspects of the industry for some number of years; since bids for these monopoly rights were based on anticipated profits, the state—as well as the current concessionaire—was interested solely in maximizing current cash revenues. However, the monopoly found it virtually impossible to force domestic producers to deliver all of their crop, and smuggling of illegal tobacco products was common by land and by sea.[9]

For these reasons—and even though the policy was contrary to contemporary mercantilist theories that condemned imports—the monopoly company and the government deliberately sought to prevent the consumption of domestic or even European tobacco. While the monopoly company did import, for example, some expensive luxury snuffs from Spain, it preferred to make products for the mass market with leaf imported by sea from the British colonies in North America. Cultivation in France itself was prohibited except in a few limited areas. Similarly, the monopoly would not procure leaf from neighboring Alsace, lest consumers acquire a taste for this easily smuggled product.[10]

In contrast, the state monopoly since 1810 has generally sought to encourage domestic production and limit foreign purchases. Since the monopoly must purchase all that is produced, cultivation has remained under strict control. Production has been permitted only in some *départements,* and each individual grower must obtain an annual license that indicates the number of square feet to be devoted to the tobacco crop.[11] Throughout the nineteenth century, and particularly since the formation of SEITA in 1926, the state tobacco administration has sponsored research aimed at improving both the plant itself and methods of cultivation. As Table 4.3 indicates, these efforts helped to increase production from about 69 million pounds per year in 1925 to about 112 million in 1950.[12]

4.3 THE ITALIAN PENINSULA

As in France, a governmental monopoly has existed in Italy virtually since the introduction of tobacco. From the seventeenth century onward, the various states governing the Italian peninsula established monopolies—usually in the form of a farm to a private company—that lasted, often continuously, until the formation of modern Italy in the 1860s. During the seventeenth century, monopolies were thus granted by the rulers of Mantua (1627), Lombardy (1637), Piedmont (1647), Naples and Sicily (1650), Ferrara and the Papal States (1657), Venice (1659), and Bologna (1660).[13]

When some of these states changed hands at the Congress of Vienna in 1815, their new rulers—although sometimes reorganizing the legal status and organizational structure of the tobacco monopoly—retained the principle of government monopoly. Lombardy and Venetia, for example, were united to the Habsburg domains, and they henceforth came under and were supplied with tobacco products by the Austrian state monopoly.[14]

Most of these farms or state bodies came under criticism both by consumers and by economists, but the revenues they produced were so large that the new Italian monarchy adopted a similar but centralized system in 1869—granting a monopoly to a private farm in 1869 and taking over direct management of cultivation, production, and sales in 1882.[15] As in France, the monopoly was modernized as an industrial concern in the 1920s under the name MonItal. With the formation of the EEC, its legal monopoly technically ended in 1979, and it in fact has lost market share to imported brands.[16]

4.4 THE IBERIAN PENINSULA

The Spanish Empire included regions producing large amounts of tobacco as well as leaf that could be turned into products that were highly esteemed and sought after during the seventeenth and eighteenth centuries. Thus, the Varinas leaf cultivated in Venezuela always sold at a premium on the Amsterdam market, while the snuff produced from Cuban leaf in Seville was widely sold throughout Europe as *tabac de'Espagne*. Since the Spanish government was almost continuously bankrupt, its regulations sought primarily to maximize governmental revenues by renting the right to import and sell this colonial leaf as dearly as possible. From the early 1600s, the growing of tobacco in Spain itself was forbidden; however, despite severe and harsh penalties, some clandestine production and extensive smuggling of contraband could never be halted.[17]

Even though its colonies of the Philippines and Cuba were lost in 1898, this prohibition was not lifted until 1919; the country today produces fairly substantial amounts of tobacco for internal consumption.[18]

As early as 1611, a high duty was placed on imports; with collection of this duty from 1630 on being leased or farmed to the highest bidder.[19] The rights to import, to manufacture products from, and to sell colonial leaf were also leased, and the industry came to be centralized in Seville. From 1614 on, all tobacco not consumed in Cuba had to be shipped to Seville.[20] Hence, the city naturally became the center of production for the *Renta de Tabacos*, which was accorded a monopoly over manufacturing in 1684. The Renta continued to add facilities, culminating in an enormous new plant constructed in 1757 primarily for the manufacture of the highly profitable snuff formed from Cuban tobacco.[21]

Throughout the eighteenth century, the crown continued to seek ways to increase its revenues from these tobacco monopolies. From 1701 onward, existing restrictions in the mother country were made even more punitive with the reorganization of the Renta,[22] and a government monopoly from seed to consumption was ordained for Spain's American colonies in 1764 and extended to the Philippines two years later.[23] Despite Spain's loss of its colonies, administrative difficulties, and criticism by agricultural interests during the nineteenth century, the principle of a farmed monopoly over manufacturing and sales has been retained. Monopoly rights were auctioned off to the first of a series of private companies in 1887; they are today held by the Compania Gestora del Monopolio Español de Tabacos—or Tabacalera.[24]

4.5 THE HABSBURG EMPIRE

Governmental control also was established almost as soon as tobacco was introduced into the Habsburg realms—although at first as a complex web of individual monopolies in various regions consistent with the heterogeneous and decentralized nature of Habsburg rule. According to legend, Habsburg soldiers learned the use of tobacco in the 1630s while fighting in the Germanies during the Thirty Years War, and tobacco was cultivated in Hungary from the 1660s.[25] In 1662, the first government monopoly or *appalto* seems to have been granted for the Tyrol, and the exclusive privilege of establishing a tobacco factory at Enns was similarly sold in 1676 to the merchant Johannes Geiger.[26]

In 1670, Count Christopher Klevenhiller, the royal master of the hunt, received the exclusive right to import tobacco into the Austrian realms. In subsequent years, however, the government reverted to selling the rights to import and manufacture in various regions to the highest bidder. The imperial treasury also established some of its own manufactory plants; offices to sell the products from these state factories were set up in various provinces, and agents with contracts in other provinces had to pay for authorization to sell it at retail.[27]

Until 1735, however, individual subjects were permitted to grow and sell their own tobacco.

In 1701 the Emperor Leopold I restated his sovereign rights throughout the Austrian realms, and Charles VI attempted between 1723 and 1726 to change this system of contracts with individuals into a state regie. From 1725 on the price of tobacco was regulated, and its cultivation was prohibited in Bohemia and Austria.[28] This first attempt to create a state tobacco administration was not thought a success. The crown went back to the previous system of farming out the monopoly to private contractors, and additional restrictions were placed on cultivation and sale. This return to the appalto system was not popular, and the farmers were widely believed to misuse their privileges in an oppressive manner.[29]

Consonant with his other efforts as an enlightened despot to centralize authority and improve governmental finances, Joseph II did succeed in 1784 in establishing a regie under a special state administration with its headquarters in Vienna. Although the laws on which it is based were modified in 1835, the present Tabakregie in the Republic of Austria thus effectively is a continuation of the organization set up in 1784. The regie primarily sought to make its monopoly yield the highest possible revenue rather than to maximize sales. Crown officials purchased leaf, controlled the manufacture and wholesale distribution of tobacco products, and supervised sales by private contractors; in principle, they conferred the privilege of selling at retail on those agents who were willing to take a smaller percentage of the retail price fixed by the state administration.[30]

The Vienna regie that was established in 1784 controlled all aspects of manufacture and sale in the Austrian Duchies, the Tyrol, Bohemia, Moravia, Silesia, Galicia, Dalmatia and (from 1815) Lombardy and Venetia.[31] The crown did not, however, extend state control over manufacturing and sales to the Hungarian lands until 1850. Henceforth, a second and separate administration was established with its headquarters in Budapest. (A third administration was erected for Bosnia and Herzegovina when those lands were attached to the crown in 1878). In contrast to the Austrian lands, cultivation of tobacco remained free in Hungary and Transylvania, whose producers sometimes exported more of the harvest than they delivered to the state warehouses.[32] In return, the Vienna regie, while depending heavily on Hungarian supplies, was not limited to these; it often supplemented them with foreign leaf either to obtain a lower cost or to respond to consumer tastes.

4.6 CENTRAL EUROPE BETWEEN THE WARS

Three separate state monopolies existed side by side in the Habsburg realms in 1918—an Austrian, a Hungarian, and a Bosnian monopoly. Consumers and economists may not have been entirely happy with the regie system. But none of the successor states created out of the former Habsburg realms was willing to renounce this secure source of funds, and the new governments took over the factories and distribution system of the former empire. State tobacco administrations were thus created for Czechoslovakia (1918), Poland (1922), Rumania (1920), and Yugoslavia (1919), in addition to those already existing in Austria and Hungary.[33] Since World War II all these countries continue to be supplied by the same state monopolies—although, except in Austria, their legal basis was modified to correspond to a Communist system of jurisprudence.

In all six of these countries, the state exercised total control over the production or purchase of tobacco leaf and the manufacture and distribution of tobacco products; indeed, except in Austria, governmental control was perhaps more rigid than it had been under the Habsburgs. In Austria, the only country not growing its own crop, the government continued to be the sole buyer of foreign leaf. The governments of the other five countries, while strongly encouraging domestic production, generally controlled the price paid to farmers. In most of the five, including in Hungary, production and export were permitted only by license—a more restrictive policy than under the Habsburg regime, which allowed sales to foreign buyers. In Yugoslavia the state required farmers to turn over their entire crop and did not even permit them to keep leaf for their own private consumption.[34]

While all the Central European states continued and strengthened state monopolies, they broke sharply with earlier policy regarding domestic production. The Habsburg regie primarily had sought monopoly profits and had followed a policy most likely to achieve that goal—that is, it sold each purchaser the most expensive tobacco he or she was willing to pay for, whether foreign or domestic. Between the wars, in contrast, the state monopolies, which often were directly subordinate to the minister of finance, primarily sought a favorable balance of payments by encouraging domestic production and exports while keeping out imports of foreign leaf. Given that tobacco will grow almost anywhere, all succeeded in increasing gross production. In Rumania, for example, gross production tripled from a prewar total of 15 to 18 million pounds to 48 million pounds in 1925. In Czechoslovakia, production of leaf increased almost 1,300 percent—from about 2 million pounds in 1920 to almost 28 million pounds in 1935. As Table 4.4 indicates, similar records were also set, at least for a time, in Poland and Hungary.[35]

Although gross production increased, the type of crop produced sometimes

Table 4.4
Tobacco Production in Four European Countries (in thousands of U.S. pounds)

	1925	1930	1935
Czechoslovakia	12,720	22,095	27,811
Hungary	33,780	75,354	40,314
Poland	4,875	13,080	18,064
Yugoslavia	26,560	24,885	29,589

Source: Hutson, *Consumption and Production of Tobacco in Europe.*

was less impressive. The Oriental leaf of Macedonia and Herzegovina and some dark tobaccos from Hungary have been esteemed, but the leaf in Poland and Czechoslovakia was often of low quality. It is impossible to prove the case, but it is highly likely that at least some of the individuals who were forced to consume the tobacco offered by these Central European monopolies would have preferred different or foreign products had they been permitted to buy them at a market price.

4.7 THE GERMANIES

Unlike the Habsburgs, the rulers in the Germanies taxed but did not establish monopolies over the production, manufacture, and sale of tobacco. In sharp contrast to their southern and eastern neighbors, the Germanies enjoyed a relatively free market until the Communist occupation after World War II. Until 1815, those German-speaking regions not ruled by the House of Habsburg were governed by some three hundred more or less sovereign princes, some of whom erected state monopolies that were farmed to private contractors. For example, in Wurttemberg, the right to import and collect excise taxes on tobacco was farmed out in 1687, and a total monopoly over production and sales existed from 1700 to 1770 and again from 1808 to 1821.[36]

Except during brief periods, however, no monopoly was created either in Prussia or in Bavaria, the two states with the most extensive territories and the largest populations. In Bavaria, while import duties were levied from 1646, the monopoly established in 1691 was abolished in 1717. And in Prussia, where a monopoly was present from 1719 to 1724, Frederick the Great at first granted monopoly rights to private contractors and then attempted—as did Joseph II in Austria-Hungary—to establish an ambitious state monopoly from 1765 to 1787. After Frederick's death in 1787, his successors gave up the scheme, and Prussia remained a region of free trade until 1945.[37]

A century later, Otto von Bismarck, the powerful chancellor of Prussia and, after 1871, of the new German Empire, strongly favored a state monopoly after the model of that in Austria-Hungary. After lengthy study, however, the Reichstag (the legislature of the German Empire) turned down the suggestion in 1882. Opponents argued that, because many Germans preferred hand-crafted cigars, production could not be centralized in a few factories and the industry would be difficult to rationalize. Public awareness of the high prices charged by the Vienna regie probably also played a role in defeating the proposal.[38] The tobacco market was freer at some periods than in others. At the end of the nineteenth century, a cartel was created in the new German Empire that worked closely with government and financial institutions. And no industry could escape governmental and party guidelines under the National-Socialist regime of 1933 to 1945.[39] Unlike those living under the Habsburgs, however, German consumers during the nineteenth century did have a choice among numerous suppliers providing differing products.

4.8 THE SCANDINAVIAN STATES

Political sovereignty in Scandinavia today is divided among five separate states—including the three contiguous kingdoms of Sweden, Norway, and Denmark, to which are usually added the republics of Finland and Iceland. A sense of separate nationality is fairly recent in most of these states, which often were united under one crown in earlier centuries. Thus, Norway was joined first with Denmark from 1397 to 1814 and then with Sweden from 1814 until it achieved independence in 1905. Similarly, Finland, conquered by the Swedish crown in the thirteenth century, became an autonomous region under the Russian czars from 1808 to 1917. These small and sparsely inhabited states have always been characterized by close cooperation between the government and commercial interests.

Although it was not unified into one state-chartered monopoly until 1915, the tobacco industry in Sweden was from the early 1700s on a mix of state and private enterprises often subordinated to mercantilist laws and guidelines. During the eighteenth century, most European states restricted imports of manufactured tobacco. As we have seen, however, state factories in France, Spain, Austria, and the Italian states depended on imported leaf tobacco; to maximize profits by controlling supply, these countries actually banned or strictly limited domestic production. In contrast, the Swedish crown kept out both foreign leaf and foreign manufactured products. Instead, from the 1720s on, it sought—with some success—to build up rather than to restrict domestic cultivation of tobacco.

From the middle of the sixteenth century, Swedish governments made a concentrated effort to acquire manufacturing skills. Particularly during the rule of the *Hats* party (1738–1765), the state sought through direct intervention and subsidies to achieve self-sufficiency in such essential industries as tobacco, textiles, salt, and iron.[40] To achieve these goals, it first totally prohibited all imports of manufactured tobacco, and then in 1719 it permitted foreign products under very high duties. In the 1730s, decrees again prohibited the importation of snuff (1734) and spun (roll or twist) tobacco (1739), and every form of manufactured tobacco had been banned (except under expensive special licenses) by the 1770s.[41]

Unlike most of the other ancien regime states, the Swedish government apparently was able to enforce these restrictions; by the 1750s, all foreign products had disappeared except for minute quantities of cut Cavendish (Virginia) tobacco. Given this encouragement, the Swedish tobacco industry grew very rapidly, by 1764 employing more than two thousand workers divided fairly evenly between private and state-owned establishments. To curb imports even of unmanufactured tobacco, from the 1720s the government also sponsored the production of domestic leaf, issuing pamphlets that described how to raise tobacco in a cold northern climate. These efforts also enjoyed some success: By the 1770s, domestic production may have accounted for as much as half of all leaf used in the manufacture of tobacco products.[42]

Because of the limited domestic market, however, Swedish private or state companies could not produce sufficient qualities to ensure low prices, and they continued to require substantial governmental subsidies. In 1765–1766, the party of the Hats was replaced by that of the *Caps,* which was more moderate in applying mercantilist theories. Toward the end of the eighteenth century, the government limited subsidies to domestic industry, lowered tariff rates, and abolished many import restrictions. Thereafter, governmental policies remained moderately protectionist, allowing a number of private firms to manufacture tobacco products, including snuff. In 1795, Samuel Fiedler established a snuff mill in Gothenburg and began a small business, which later developed into three separate companies. At the end of the nineteenth century, the firm of Jacob Ljunglof in Stockholm became the leading producer of snuff, producing the brand Ettan, which was exported throughout Europe. Domestic cultivation of tobacco also continued, although at a reduced rate without tariff protection and governmental encouragement.[43]

Swedish governments continued to permit multiple producers throughout the nineteenth century. From June 1, 1915, until January 1, 1967, the tobacco industry became a state monopoly, which was operated by a concessionaire company (Aktiebolaget Svenska Tabaksmonopolets) in partnership with the state. Only the concessionaire company could purchase or import leaf and manufacture tobacco products. However, cultivation remained in private hands, and other companies were permitted, under certain restrictions, to import and sell foreign products. The monopoly again concentrated snuff production in Gothenburg, where it built a large factory about 1920 to manufacture snuff and chewing tobacco.[44]

In contrast to Sweden, the kingdoms of Denmark and Norway—the latter united with Denmark until 1814 and then with Sweden until 1915—generally have left all stages of the tobacco industry to private individuals. A fairly heavy duty was placed on the import of foreign tobacco in the 1650s, collection of which was farmed by 1669. However, the state monopoly was abrogated in 1778. The governments of Denmark have subsequently permitted private firms both to manufacture and to import tobacco products—as have the governments of Norway since it regained its independence in 1915. Although domestic cultivation has been permitted, only small amounts of tobacco have been grown due to the unfavorable terrain, soil, and climate.[45]

4.9 THE UNITED KINGDOM AND BRITISH AMERICA

During the seventeenth and eighteenth centuries, the regulations decreed by the British crown had a significant effect on tobacco consumption because its colonies in Virginia and Maryland produced a large percentage of the leaf used throughout Europe as well as in Britain itself. Prior to occupying North America, the British had already conquered Ireland, which remained under British rule until 1922. In 1707, Scotland was joined to Britain and Ireland to form the United Kingdom; this union was of particular interest to American planters since Glasgow became the main port for American tobacco exports until the revolution.

Because of the importance of tobacco to several states in the American South, an enormous literature on this industry has described with minute attention every aspect of British regulation. Nevertheless, while the ways in which they attempted to carry out these policies may have varied, the succeeding governments, at least from 1660 to the present, do seem to have followed consistent policies that can be succinctly outlined. (1) As have most governments, the British crown primarily sought to raise as much revenue as possible from the tobacco habit. In contrast to many other states, however, the crown never attempted to establish a monopoly over manufacturing or retail sales.[46] Taking advantage of the fact that the United Kingdom occupied two islands, it has instead levied very high duties on the imported leaf from which private companies manufacture tobacco products. (2) To protect this source of revenue, cultivation of tobacco was prohibited throughout the United Kingdom until the early 1900s. (3) Until the revolution in 1776, tobacco grown in the North American colonies had to be shipped to England, and the government sought to keep out tobacco grown elsewhere.

The British crown was one of the first to impose a duty on imported tobacco leaf (shortly after 1590), and it has always levied this tax at a very high rate.[47] Throughout the eighteenth and nineteenth centuries, the duty more than trebled or quadrupled the price to the consumer;[48] put another way, the tax during these centuries—as the American producers complained—was as much as eight or nine times the price received by the producer.[49] It is crucial to understand that this tax in principle always has been levied at a uniform rate on each pound of tobacco leaf imported into the United Kingdom without regard to the purpose for which the leaf was later used. In addition, manufactured products from other countries—such as cigars—have been taxed at even higher rates than leaf, which has had the effect of making the retail cost of these products prohibitive except to the wealthy.

In sum, even though the United Kingdom did not establish a state monopoly, retail prices to the consumer consistently have been among the highest in the world.[50] Comparisons are imperfect because per capita incomes and the cost of competing products vary. It is nevertheless true that British consumers during, for example, the 1920s paid higher prices than those in any other European country for smoking tobacco, cigarettes, cigars, and snuff.[51] Import duties at so punitive a rate provided an obvious incentive to smuggling, against which English governments waged a long struggle. Since about 1850 smuggling has supplied only a small part of consumption;[52] during the seventeenth century,

however, one-third and more of the tobacco consumed in Britain and Scotland
escaped governmental taxes.[53]

Although the crown found it somewhat easier to end local cultivation than
to control smuggling, tobacco grown by local farmers also threatened governmental revenues. Nothing in the soil or climate precludes the cultivation of
tobacco in England, where it was extensively grown from the early 1600s. It
is true that these early crops were described as pungent and strong; had the
government not suppressed domestic production, however, advances in the sci-
ence of agriculture might well have given us English, Scotch, and Irish tobacco
at least equal to that produced across the channel in France.[54] The crown first
prohibited tobacco cultivation in 1619, ordering that existing stocks be destroyed. This prohibition was frequently repeated until 1660 and as frequently
ignored or violently contravened.[55] Tobacco production in the United Kingdom
seems to have ended during the first quarter of the eighteenth century, partly
because the price of American leaf fell and partly because smugglers became
more effective.[56] Laws forbidding the growing of tobacco also were extended
to Ireland (where the crown allowed some cultivation from 1778 to 1831) and
to Scotland (after 1782). Although they were finally repealed in 1910, virtually
no tobacco is grown today in the United Kingdom.[57]

While its primary objective has been to collect these punitive taxes on imported leaf, the crown also has given preference to tobacco grown in British
colonies. Prior to the American Revolution, the importation of leaf from other
empires was either forbidden or subject to higher duties.[58] In return, the colonists were required to ship their crop only to British ports or (after 1707) Scottish ports; the import duties were rebated on tobacco not landed in England but
reexported to the continent.[59] Since 1919, under the Imperial Preference scheme,
the rate of duty has been lower on tobacco grown in British colonies as well
as on that grown in the homeland itself.[60] Partly because adulteration decreased
its revenues, as well as for reasons of public health, the government also has
attempted to prevent the addition of other substances to the tobacco sold in the
United Kingdom. Adulteration, sometimes with disgusting materials, was frequent throughout the eighteenth century. It was forbidden by acts of 1821 and
1843 that permitted only water or colored water to be used in the manufacturing
process.[61]

4.10 THE UNITED STATES

The American Revolution of 1776 was fought largely to free local governments from acts—such as the Navigation acts regulating the shipping of tobacco and other American products—imposed by the central government. Perhaps as a result, until recently the tobacco industry and consumers in the United
States were subject to less governmental regulation than those of almost any
other nation. Indeed, until the 1860s, all regulation of the industry was carried

out by the state governments. These neither established monopolies on the French model nor levied taxes on the raw material in the English manner. Rather, state laws regulating quality, transportation, and wholesale auctions were intended to procure a degree of honest dealing among farmers and manufacturers.[62] For its part, the federal government limited itself to levying a tariff—which was reduced to a relatively low rate from 1816 to 1861—on imported tobacco products such as cigars.[63]

The national government has taxed tobacco products continuously since 1862, as have many state governments beginning in 1923. The federal tax is somewhat unusual, and it is important to understand its exact mechanism. Unlike a sales tax, the federal tax is not collected from the consumer through the retailer. It is imposed instead on manufacturers, who have been required to place a stamp on the various products they produce. In administering the tax, the Internal Revenue Service receives detailed reports from manufacturers showing the amount of tobacco each has purchased, the amount on hand, and the quantity of cigarettes, cigars, or other products each has manufactured. However, the tax is not due from the manufacturer until the articles produced are withdrawn or removed from the factory for wholesale and retail distribution.

Since it was imposed in July 1862, the tax has been applied at varying rates in two different ways. (1) In the case of products such as cigars or cigarettes that are sold by the piece, the manufacturer pays a set tax of so many cents or dollars for every thousand that are withdrawn from the factory for consumption. During some periods, a somewhat higher rate has been levied on cigars and cigarettes weighing more than three pounds per thousand; at other times, a higher tax per thousand has been imposed on those that were intended to sell at a higher retail price. (2) In the case of products that are sold by weight— such as snuff, cut smoking tobacco, and plug and twist chewing tobacco—the tax also is levied by weight at a rate of so many cents or dollars per pound.

At first, the government attempted to differentiate between the various types of manufactured tobacco. However, from 1872 on there were only two rates of taxation—one on snuff and a second on all other products. Since 1890, all types except cigars and cigarettes have been lumped together as "manufactured tobacco and snuff" and taxed at the same rate.[64] In part this uniform rate is simply an admission that the end use of tobacco products cannot be determined with any exactitude. In advocating a uniform rate in 1865, the commissioner of internal revenue pointed out, for example, that an individual consumer of plug tobacco might sometimes chew it and at other times cut it up for smoking.[65]

In addition to the federal tax, since 1923 many states (and some cities) have levied a second (or third) tax on cigarettes and sometimes also on manufactured tobacco. In most cases these are collected from the wholesaler or the retailer at a rate of so many cents on each package of cigarettes sold.[66] Finally, together with most other agricultural products, tobacco cultivation has been controlled by the federal government beginning with the imposition of the Agricultural

Adjustment Act of 1933, and the inspection and grading of tobacco before sale became mandatory with the Tobacco Inspection Act of 1935.[67]

NOTES

1. In *Panacea or Precious Bane,* Sarah Dickson meticulously analyzes these early treatises that describe, advocate, or attack the use of tobacco. Dickson was the curator of the Arents tobacco collection at the New York Public Library. Thus she was able to study in a leisurely manner these rare books and manuscripts in several languages. Her analysis appears to be definitive and final. However, she sometimes assumes too rigidly that tobacco or a particular type of product was not present until it is mentioned in these literary sources. For example, sailors returning from Cuba or other members of the lower classes may well have used snuff for some years before the intelligentsia became interested in tobacco. Thus, her chronology provides us with unimpeachable proof for the latest possible dates that tobacco was introduced into some European states.

2. Although Dickson's history (ibid.) offers a more balanced statement of the evidence, colorful accounts of these early prohibitions are provided by Corti, *History of Smoking,* Chapters 4 through 6; Penn, *Soverane Herbe,* Chapter 2; Mackenzie, *Sublime Tobacco,* Chapters 4 and 5. While the diatribes of James I and Sultan Murad are amusing, they probably did not prevent anyone from using tobacco.

3. Price, *Tobacco Adventure,* 16–20, provides a sound summary of the Russian government's efforts (which again were ineffective) to prohibit tobacco during the seventeenth century.

4. Price, *France and the Chesapeake,* 485; Price, *Tobacco Adventure,* 88. For the rise and decline of production in the Netherlands, see Slicher van Bath, "Agriculture in the Low Countries," 184–85; Roessingh, *Inlandse tabak,* 498–503.

5. French consumers bitterly complained when the trade disruptions caused by the American Revolution forced the French monopoly to import Ukrainian tobacco: Price, *France and the Chesapeake,* 719–20.

6. Nash, "English and Scottish Tobacco Trades," 371–72.

7. Although his discussion is organized in a manner that sometimes makes it unnecessarily difficult to follow, Price appears to have investigated the sources relating to all aspects of the tobacco farm in his twelve-hundred-page study, *France and the Chesapeake.* It is difficult to see how anything more can be said about the subject, and Price's study thus supersedes earlier works such as that of Gondolff, *Le tabac sous l'ancienne Monarchie.*

8. There is no history of the state monopoly since 1810 comparable to Price's detailed and comprehensive study of the ancien regime (ibid.). The manuals give brief outlines of the administrative changes; thus, Israel, *Le Tabac en France,* 131–36; Tucker, *Tobacco: An International Perspective,* 101–10. Compare also Rival, *Tabac, miroir du temps,* 224–30.

9. Price, *France and the Chesapeake,* 137–40.

10. Ibid., 143–60, 376–92.

11. Hitier and Sabourin, *Le Tabac,* 38.

12. France: Institut National de la Statistique; *Annuaire statistique de la France, 1954* (1955), 181–82, 75*.

13. See the sources cited by Comes, *Histoire,* 85–97.

14. For the purposes of the tobacco monopoly, Lombardy and Venetia were effectively treated as provinces of Austria; thus, in Austria, Statistische central-commission, *Tafeln zur Statistik des Österreichischen Monarchie* (1821–1859), and Note 31. Corti, *History of Smoking,* 238–46, provides an amusing account of the "cigar revolution" that preceded more serious disturbances in 1848; patriots in Lombardy and Venetia sought to boycott the products, and especially the highly profitable cigars, of the Austrian monopoly.

15. Comes (*Histoire.* p, 98) gives the profits of the various monopolies in 1858 (not including those in Venetia or the Papal States) at some 53 million lire.

16. Tucker, *Tobacco: An International Perspective,* 110.

17. Comes, *Histoire,*68; Perez-Vidal, *España,* 184–86. The prohibition of domestic production dates from 1606 according to Perez-Vidal.

18. Legal cultivation began in 1921; by 1934, domestic production furnished some 16 of the 55 million pounds consumed in Spain: Hutson, *Consumption in Europe,* 88–89.

19. Comes, *Histoire,* 65; Brooks, *Tobacco in Arents,* I:143.

20. Comes, *Histoire,* 8.

21. Perez-Vidal, *España,* 228–37.

22. Ibid., 186.

23. Comes, *Histoire,* 65; Ortiz, *Cuban Counterpoint.* Although the state monopoly for the Philippines was decreed in 1766, the decree was not implemented until 1782; see de Jesus, *Tobacco Monopoly in the Philippines,* 26–34.

24. Comes, *Histoire,* 60; Hutson, *Consumption in Europe,* 88; Tucker, *Tobacco: An International Perspective,* 111–12.

25. Comes, *Histoire,* 112. Corti, *History of Smoking,* 100–02, 112–13 (and others) similarly attribute to the Thirty Years War the spread of tobacco into the Germanies, Central Europe, and Scandinavia; according to this view, soldiers from these regions learned how to use tobacco from Spanish, Dutch, and English mercenaries and brought the habit back to their homelands. Although some anecdotal evidence does support this hypothesis, the data from more recent periods suggests both that tobacco habits change very slowly and that they are little affected by social fads—or even by deliberate advertising.

26. Benesch, *150 Jahre Österreichischen Tabakregie,*11–12.

27. Hess, *American Tobacco and Central European Policy,* 122.

28. The crown continued to permit but controlled the growing of tobacco in Galicia and in the Tyrol; both areas produced only limited quantities in comparison to the large harvests in Hungary: Hess, *American Tobacco,* 126.

29. Benesch, *150 Jahre,* 12–13; Hess, *American Tobacco,* 127; Corti, *History of Smoking,* 195.

30. The Tabakregie's manufacturing facilities, administrative methods, personnel, and finances are analyzed at length by Hitz and Huber, *Geschichte der Österreichischen Tabakregie 1784–1835.*

31. Ibid., 191.

32. Comes, *Histoire,* 113. Given that the retail prices charged by the Austrian regie were quite high, there clearly was extensive smuggling from Hungary and Croatia into the Austrian lands. As with all illegal commerce, this cannot be precisely quantified, but it does distort to some extent our estimates of consumption based on the Tabakregie's record of sales.

33. Hutson, *Consumption in Europe*, 54, 80–87, 96–107; Benesch, *150 Jahre*, 20–24.

34. Hutson, *Consumption in Europe;* for the tobacco import policies of these state monopolies during the 1930s, see Beltchev, *Tobacco in Bulgaria,* Chapter 7.

35. Hutson, *Consumption in Europe.*

36. Comes, *Histoire,* 109. Compare Gray and Vertrees, "International Tobacco Trade," 6.

37. Comes, *Histoire,* 109; Corti, *History of Smoking,* 203–4.

38. Corti, *History of Smoking,* 220; some of the discussion is printed in the *Bericht der Taback-Enquete-Commission* (Germany).

39. Hutson, *Consumption in Europe,* 73.

40. Hovde, *Scandinavian Countries,* I:21–25.

41. Price, *Tobacco Adventure,* 95–98.

42. Hovde, *Scandinavian Countries,* I:73; Price, *Tobacco Adventure,* 97–98.

43. Hovde, *Scandinavian Countries,* I:25; World Health Organization, (WHO), *Tobacco Habits Other than Smoking,* 41.

44. Hutson, *Consumption in Europe,* 47; WHO, *Tobacco Habits,* 41.

45. Gray and Vertrees, "International Tobacco Trade," 11; Comes, *Histoire,* 111; Hutson, *Consumption in Europe,* 44, 50.

46. Like his peers on the continent, James I, who declared a royal monopoly over tobacco imports in 1624, tried to raise ready cash by farming import duties; his successors after 1660 did not reestablish this monopoly. See MacInnes, *Early English Tobacco Trade,* 52; Brooks, *Tobacco in Arents,*I:89.

47. MacInnes, *Early English Tobacco Trade,* 35.

48. See Rive, "Consumption of Tobacco," 72–74, for the import duties on and wholesale prices of leaf tobacco from 1786 to 1924; United States Department of Agriculture, *First Annual Report,* 123–35, for foreign rates on imports from the United States from 1923 to 1936. The U.S. Department of Agriculture's *Annual Report 1951,* 67–70, lists foreign duties for sixteen countries as of August 1951. In that year, the United Kingdom levied a duty of more than $8.00 on every pound of unmanufactured tobacco; in none of the other European countries cited was the tax more than $1.30 per pound.

49. Thus, Gray (*History of Agriculture in the Southern States,* 244): "Between 1685 and 1703 the duties on colonial tobacco were increased from 2 to 6½ pence per pound, an amount more than six times the price usually received by the planter." Since tobacco prices fell, the import tax became even more onerous during the first half of the nineteenth century, when it was, according to Robert (*Story of Tobacco,* 72) "equivalent to an ad valorem duty of 800 or 900 percent."

50. See *Staatkundig en Staathuishoudkundig Jaarboekje voor 1884* for a comparison of retail prices and consumption from 1870 through 1883 in the United States, the United Kingdom, and six European states.

51. Hutson, *Consumption in Europe,* 12–19.

52. Rive, "Consumption of Tobacco," 71; Rive, "Tobacco Smuggling," 568.

53. Economic historians find smuggling of some importance because it reduces the usefulness of the official trade statistics in analyzing economic trends. Common sense would seem to support Cole's argument ("Trends in Eighteenth-Century Smuggling," 406–9) that smuggling increases when the rate of duty is raised and decreases when the rate of duty is lowered. Cole thus suggests that smuggling reached a peak in the 1730s

and 1740s, declined during the later half of George II's reign, and sharply increased in the late 1770s. Given this assumption, Cole concludes that just before 1784, smuggling provided perhaps half the tea consumed in Britain; in the same way, as much as half the tobacco used there also was smuggled during some periods, such as the 1730s. According to Nash ("English and Scottish Tobacco Trades," 372), governmental efforts to control smuggling improved by 1750, so that only about one-third of the tobacco consumed in Britain and Scotland escaped duty in that year.

54. Brooks, *Tobacco in Arents,* I:113–14.

55. Ibid., I:114–18; MacInnes, *Early English Tobacco Trade,* Chs. 4 and 5.

56. Brooks, *Tobacco in Arents,* I:118; Nash, "English and Scottish Tobacco Trades," 369.

57. Mackenzie, *Sublime Tobacco,* 145–146.

58. Brooks, *Tobacco in Arents,* I:92–93; Gray, *History of Agriculture in the Southern States,* 243.

59. Brooks, *Tobacco in Arents,* I:120; Gray, *History of Agriculture,* 244–52; MacInnes, *Early English Tobacco Trade,* 144–46; Nash, "English and Scottish Tobacco Trades," 358–63. For a classic discussion of the Navigation Acts, which are tangential to the main thrust of this study, see Beer, *Commercial Policy of England;* Beer, *Origins of the British Colonial System;* and Beer, *The Old Colonial System.*

60. Hutson, *Consumption in Europe,* 34, 38–39; Mackenzie, *Sublime Tobacco,* 146.

61. Rive, "Consumption of Tobacco," 70; Mackenzie, *Sublime Tobacco,* 220–24. An 1863 revision of the act permitted the manufacture in bond of sweetened Cavendish and Negrohead; for the meaning of the latter terms, see Chapter 3, Note 103.

62. For the inspection and auction systems during the nineteenth century, see Gray, *History of Agriculture,* 771–74; Robert, *Tobacco Kingdom,* 121; Robert, *Story of Tobacco,* 68–72; Herndon, *William Tatham,* 435–36. For the twentieth century, see Robert, *Story of Tobacco,* 212–13; Gage, *American Tobacco Types,* 61–74; Garner, *Production of Tobacco,* 17–19.

63. Garner et al., "History and Status," 457.

64. For the rates imposed by the Internal Revenue Acts of 1862 through 1926, see U.S. Dept. of Agriculture, *First Annual Report,* 135–37; for the rates imposed by the acts of 1942 and 1951, see U.S. Dept. of Agriculture, *Annual Report 1951,* 51.

65. United States; Internal Revenue Service, *Report of the Commissioner of Internal Revenue . . . for the year ending July 30, 1865,* p. 9.

66. By 1950, forty-three of the forty-nine states and the District of Columbia were taxing cigarettes: U.S. Dept. of Agriculture: *Annual Report 1951,* 56–58. The practicability of these taxes is analyzed by White, *Operation of Tennessee Tobacco Taxes.*

67. Gage, *American Tobacco Types,* 68; Herndon, *William Tatham,* 422–26. There have been studies of the New Deal. For an overview of the federal tobacco programs, see Badger, *Prosperity Road,* 195–235; Mann, *Tobacco: The Ants and the Elephants.*

Chapter 5

Tobacco Consumption in Countries with State Supervision, 1780–1950

5.1 SUMMARY

Taken together, the French and Habsburg monopolies and the Swedish tobacco industry supplied tobacco products to consumers in every region of the European Peninsula—from the Arctic Circle in the north to the Mediterranean in the south, from the Atlantic Ocean in the west to the Carpathian Mountains in the east. These consumers spoke many different languages, earned their living in economies that varied from neolithic to industrialized, practiced every type of Judaism and Christianity and several forms of Islam, and cherished dissimilar and often contrasting customs. Throughout the two centuries under review, the tobacco industries in these states largely reacted to consumer demands rather than leading them, and they did not use advertising or promotion either to increase total sales or to boost specific products. Partly to keep out imported products, the industry in each case did seek to provide consumers with the goods they requested; the Habsburg and French monopolies in particular consistently provided products at every price range from the cheapest cut and pressed tobacco to the most exquisite snuffs. Since few if any factors were constant throughout so large and diverse an area over two centuries, it is striking that tobacco habits in these nations evolved in remarkably similar ways. The relative uniformity in the patterns of consumer demands throughout Europe suggests that choices between tobacco products—and possibly between other consumer products—respond to common, deep-seated preferences that are independent of social, economic, political, and cultural circumstances.

Tables 5.1 and 5.2 summarize these changes during the century from 1780 to 1880 at approximately twenty-year intervals. (With the exception of Sweden, which added Norway to its domain in 1814, the political boundaries of each state did not change substantially during these years; the tables list separately the Italian lands governed by the Habsburgs from 1815 to 1861.) As Table 5.1 shows, per capita tobacco consumption was relatively low throughout Europe when the records begin about 1780. Among the available products (which did not as yet include cigars or cigarettes), snuff was definitely the favored way of enjoying tobacco in France and Northern Italy, where it represented at least two-thirds of all sales to the local populace. In the Habsburg realms, smoking was more popular, but a large minority (representing at least one-third of sales) took snuff. The Swedes had then, as they do now, unusual preferences, over-whelmingly opting for pressed or plug chewing tobacco rather than for either powdered snuff or cut smoking tobacco.

In all these regions, tobacco preferences were substantially modified about the middle of the nineteenth century (or a little earlier in Sweden), and the new habits established at this time lasted over more than three generations until the 1920s. Perhaps the most profound of these changes was the demise of the multipurpose plug, which the user might cut up in large pieces for chewing, cut into smaller pieces for smoking, or grind for snuff. This pressed product, which was perhaps the most popular way of purchasing tobacco during the eighteenth century, continued to be sold until the 1860s. During the 1870s, however, the records of the Habsburg and French monopolies clearly recog-nized that pressed tobacco was intended solely (or at least primarily) for use as chewing tobacco. During these years, both monopolies and the Swedish indus-try also began to offer cigars—the French from 1819, the Swedes at the end of the 1820s, and the Austrians about 1845. The French tobacco regime also pi-oneered in providing paper cigarettes (about 1845), followed by the Austrians (about 1875) and the Swedes (prior to World War I). By the 1870s, all five of the products with distinctive purposes—snuff, chewing tobacco, smoking to-bacco, cigars, and cigarettes—thus were available in something like the forms that are used today.

In choosing between the products available to them, consumers show strong and lasting preferences. Perhaps one of the most significant findings of this study is the reluctance of individuals to change their tobacco habits. With rare exceptions, most consumers tend to be fixed strongly not only in choosing a product—for example, in choosing between cigars and snuff—but also in choosing a specific quantity and quality of the product type they prefer. Tobacco pref-erences are thus relatively fixed in the near term; changes take place almost solely as new consumers enter into the market, and the latter often emulate the habits of their neighbors. At the same time, tobacco is not absolutely necessary to life. In the longer run, therefore, tobacco preferences can be highly volatile as these small changes accumulate from generation to generation.

Throughout the Western world, significant changes in tobacco habits seem to have occurred first during the 1850s and again during the 1920s. In neither case, however, does the evidence suggest that consumers made a sudden and

Table 5.1
Use of Tobacco Products circa 1785, 1820, 1840, and 1860

1. Use of Tobacco Products about 1785 [1]

	Total 1,000 pounds	Per Head[3]	Snuff	Hard[4]	Plug[5]	Cut	Cigars[6]
Austria[7]	14,288	--	31%	-----{69%}----			--%
France[7]	15,050	.58	57	29	15	--	--
Sweden[8]	1,286	.61	10	--{73}--		17	--

Percent of Total[2]

==

2. Use of Tobacco Products about 1820 [9]

	Total 1,000 pounds	Per Head	Snuff	Hard	Plug	Cut	Cigars
Austria[7]	18,198	1.32	22%	-----{78%}----			--%
France[7]	23,160	.76	58	--{11}--		28	3
North Italy[7,10]	3,349	1.43	56	--	--	45	--
Sweden[7]	2,393	.93	38	--{24}--		38	--

==

3. Use of Tobacco Products about 1840 [11]

	Total 1,000 pounds	Per Head	Snuff	Hard	Plug	Cut	Cigars
Austria[7]	32,347	2.00	13%	--{11%}--		76%	--%
France[7]	39,649	1.17	37	2	2	55	3
North Italy[7]	3,299	.94[12] .77[14]	64[13]	--	--	37[13]	--
Sweden[8]	3,441	1.10	57	--{18}--		24	1

==

4. Use of Tobacco Products about 1860 [15]

	Total 1,000 pounds	Per Head	Snuff	Hard	Plug	Cut	Cigars
Austria[7]	63,347	2.72	7%	-----{78%}----			16%
France[7]	72,880	1.68	38	1	1	50	9
Italy[7]	33,246	1.24	22	--	--	48	30
Sweden[8]	6,204	1.61	61	--{15}--		27	7

[1] The reported data refer to the following years: Austria (Habsburg empire, excluding Italy and Hungary), 1784; France, 1789; Sweden, 1780.

[2] Percentages may not sum to 100 percent due to rounding into whole numbers.

[3] *Per capita* manufacture/sales in pounds per inhabitant.

[4] "Tabac ficelé" (1789); "carottes" (1819–1860).

[5] Includes twist ("menu filé") and pressed tobacco ("gros rôles" and "rôles").

[6] Includes cigarillos.

[7] Sales.

[8] Manufacture.

[9] 1820 except for France (1819) and northern Italy (1821).

[10] Total of sales in Lombardy and Venetia.

[11] 1840 except for France (1845).

[12] Lombardy.

[13] Average of sales in Lombardy and Venetia.

[14] Venetia.

[15] The reported data refer to the following years: Austria, 1861; France, 1861; Italy, 1868; Sweden, 1860.

Table 5.2
Use of Tobacco Products circa 1880[1]

			Percent of Total[2]				
	Total	Per head[3]	Snuff	Chewing	Cut	Cigars[4]	Cigar-ettes
Austria[5,6]	71,245	3.15	7%	3%	69%	18%	1%
France[7]	79,977	2.11	18	3	66	10	2
Germany[6]	154,972	3.60	8	1	63	27	--
Hungary[6]	9,515	--	1	--	88	11	--
Italy[7]	35,228	1.32	21	--	40	39	--
Sweden[6]	11,410	2.65	62	18	10	10	--
U.S.[6]	194,204	3.87	2	55	28	24	1

[1] Data for 1880 except for Austria (1882), France (1885), and Germany (average 1871–1879).
[2] Percentages may not sum to 100 percent due to rounding into whole numbers.
[3] Per capita manufacture/sales in pounds per inhabitant.
[4] Includes cigarillos.
[5] Habsburg empire, excluding Hungary.
[6] Manufacture.
[7] Sales.

dramatic switch from one type of product to another. What changed was the relative likelihood that new consumers would tend to take up one product rather than another. (In mathematics, one might call this a modification in the second derivative: What changed was the rate of change of the rate of change.) In France—as an examination of Table 5.1 indicates—the 1850s witnessed a sharp increase in sales both of cut smoking tobacco (called *scaferlati*) and also of cigars, which were accepted for the first time since their introduction more than thirty years earlier. The popularity of cigars proved to be short-lived, and their sales have fallen in every subsequent year since 1885. But pipe smoking retained its popularity and became the most common way of consuming tobacco in France for almost a century. Moreover, once they had opted for the pipe, smokers were slow too take up the cigarette. Although the French tobacco monopoly introduced cigarettes in 1845, for many years its customers preferred either pipe tobacco or snuff. After forty years, cigarettes comprised only 2 percent of the monopoly's sales in 1885 (Table 5.2); and they did not outsell scaferlati until 1943 (Table 5.9).

The rise of pipe smoking during the 1850s is tied to an equally sharp increase in per capita consumption of all types of tobacco, which reflects the greater prosperity and more equitable distribution of income under Napoleon III. In the shorter term, therefore, the French definitely were not smoking more because they were snuffing less; as Table 5.1 indicates, sales of snuff rose along with and even more rapidly than those of cut tobacco during the 1850s. Indeed, sales of snuff, which is often inaccurately associated with the ancien regime, began to decline only during the 1860s, and they then dropped only at a very slow rate (about 1 percent a year) until the 1920s. In the same way, the demand for chewing tobacco also proved remarkably stable under the Third Republic and even grew in proportion to the increase in population (Table 5.10).

The history of tobacco consumption in France may serve as a model in tracing the evolution of tobacco habits throughout Europe and North America. Certainly the story is much the same in the Italian and the Central European regions served by the Habsburg monopoly. In contrast to those under the French crown (who preferred snuff by as wide a margin), the German and Slavic subjects of the Habsburgs already favored the pipe in 1784. However, with one-third of total sales, snuff was a strong second in popularity (Table 5.1). The 1850s would again seem to represent a turning point in the rate of change from smokeless tobacco, with cigars in this case showing the most rapid growth (Table 5.1). Although both cigars and cigarettes initially were adopted more rapidly than in France, their sales soon slowed, and the pipe remained the most common way of smoking in the Austrian empire. After choosing a form (or forms) of tobacco that suited their tastes, consumers apparently remained with that preference—whether for snuff, chewing tobacco, the pipe, cigars, or cigarettes.

If the subjects of the Habsburgs traditionally tended to be smokers, the minority who preferred smokeless products was equally tenacious. After a significant drop during the 1850s, snuff sales fell only very slowly in subsequent years, and snuff long remained a profitable part of the monopoly's business. Indeed, so gradually did per capita consumption decline that the largest sales of snuff in terms of quantity were recorded by the Austrian state monopoly as late as 1882. And, although comparisons between consumption under the Empire and under the tiny republic erected in 1918 are somewhat tenuous, chewing tobacco sales between the wars show the same stability exhibited in France (Table 5.5).

Although we have no evidence from other regions prior to the creation of the Kingdom of Italy, the Habsburg monopoly recorded sales in Lombardy and Venetia from 1821. These again suggest that new tobacco habits were established about 1850 and endured until the 1920s. Unlike their Austrian overlords, the inhabitants of these regions, which were among the more economically and culturally advanced parts of the peninsula, long continued to prefer snuff to the pipe. Smoking became more common with the introduction of the cigar about 1845. As in France, however, the increase in smoking during the 1850s at first led to an expansion of the total market rather than to a decline in snuff sales (Table 5.1). Indeed, the Italians remained fond of snuff longer than any other Europeans except the French, and snuff sales in the Kingdom of Italy were at their highest as late as the 1880s. Ultimately, the cigarette did become the favorite product of Italian tobacco consumers, who adopted it somewhat earlier than those in other countries. Nevertheless, snuff continued to represent a comparatively high portion of tobacco sales until World War II (Table 5.3).

Sweden also provides continuous (or virtually continuous) records of tobacco consumption over more than two centuries, and these records suggest that the evolution of tobacco habits among the Swedes followed the same rhythms as in Austria, Italy, and France. In all countries, a decisive change took place with the shift from multipurpose plug to products intended for specific uses; once established, the patterns set during the first half of the nineteenth century endured until the 1920s. However, the Swedes, and possibly the other Scandinavian peoples, ended with preferences that are anomalous when compared to those of other Europeans. In Austria, France, and Italy, the nineteenth century witnessed the growing dominance of pipe smoking and the slow eclipse of smokeless tobacco. In Sweden, precisely the opposite happened: The Swedes increasingly came to adopt oral snuff, and sales of pipe tobacco steadily dropped in proportion to sales of smokeless tobacco between 1820 (Table 5.1) and 1870 (Tables 5.2 and 5.4).

For about a century, from about 1825 to 1925, oral snuff was by far the most popular way of using tobacco among the Swedes. However, much as a loyal minority continued to use snuff in lands where smoking became the majority taste, so also in Sweden sales of cut tobacco and cigars remained relatively stable after 1870—with each product representing about 10 percent of the overall market. Pressed chewing tobacco, although also eclipsed by snuff, similarly retained a loyal following until World War I. Only cigarettes were absent from the Swedish market; perhaps because consumers did not request them, the tobacco industry did not produce cigarettes until the twentieth century, almost fifty years after their introduction in France. Although they were thus relatively slow to become popular, cigarette sales suddenly began to climb at the end of the 1920s. By 1951, as Table 5.3 shows, cigarettes thus had become the most widely used tobacco product. Oral snuff retained about a third of the market, and pipe tobacco held its position in third place.

The evidence from these very different cultures demonstrates that per capita consumption normally is as stable as tobacco habits. Not only do consumers tend to favor certain products, but many seem to use the same amount of their preferred product each day. Thus, fluctuations in per capita consumption primarily are due to changes in product preferences. In particular, a change from smokeless products to smoking tobacco is accompanied by an increase in total usage. In Austria, this change was complete by about 1860, and per capita consumption then leveled off and remained stable at about three pounds a year. In France, higher tobacco sales can be precisely dated to the fifteen years between 1845 and 1861, which saw both total consumption and per capita usage almost double. And it is during these same years that the pipe was established as the most popular way of using tobacco; following 1861, as sales of pipe tobacco and cigars slowed, so also did total consumption.

Throughout Europe, the decisive decade for the adoption of the tobacco habit would seem to be that of the 1850s. In Sweden also, following forty years of stability, per capita consumption suddenly increased by more than 50 percent between 1850 and 1860 before again leveling off. This rise again was coincidental with a sharp (if short-term) increase in smoking, in this case of cigars. In any era, different consumers will use varying amounts of snuff, cigars, or chewing tobacco. These individual variations cannot be captured by aggregated sales data, and no one explanation for this connection between smoking and higher usage is totally persuasive. Whatever the reason, however, consumers of smokeless tobacco products clearly do tend, on average, to use less each day than do those that smoke a pipe, cigars, or cigarettes.

5.2 THE HABSBURG EMPIRE

The second oldest series of tobacco production and sales statistics is that of the Austrian state tobacco monopoly—the Swedish records are older by only four years. This state monopoly, which has preserved and published its records (in part and during some years) since 1784, was created in that year as a department of the Habsburg imperial bureaucracy. Following World War I, it was taken over virtually intact in 1918 as a department of the Austrian Republic. Since the Habsburg regie thus served regions in what are today Czechoslovakia, Poland, Italy, and Yugoslavia, comparisons between the administration's sales before and after world War I are suggestive but inexact.

Although early census data is of doubtful accuracy, overall tobacco consumption in the empire apparently did increase during the first half of the nineteenth century.[1] In contrast to the case in several other regions, however, Table 5.3 shows that per capita consumption has not grown significantly since 1850. During the sixty-odd years between 1850 and 1913, for example, sales by the monopoly held steady at about three pounds per inhabitant. In marketing terms, the tobacco industry thus was comparatively mature by 1850, with the fairly substantial increase in total sales during subsequent years being largely a function of general population growth. In part, slow growth of sales may have resulted from the regie's policy of keeping prices high. However, it is also true that other regions were simply catching up to the Austrians in their enjoyment of tobacco, since in 1850 the latter already consumed twice as much tobacco each year as the French, Italians, or Swedes.

Prior to 1840, consumption of chewing tobacco cannot be precisely estimated because it is not singled out in the published records; these make a distinction only between prepared snuff and all other forms of manufactured tobacco—the latter being very loosely designated as "smoking tobacco" (Rauchtabak). However, we do know that the regie's factories from the beginning produced twist and pressed products as well as ready-cut. When records become more precise in 1840 (Table 5.4), production of cut smoking mixtures (at 24,450,000 pounds) greatly exceeded that of spun products (3,554,000 pounds). Earlier in the nineteenth century, however, judging by contemporaneous records from France and Sweden, rôles and carottes probably enjoyed greater popularity and thus formed a larger part of the Austrian regie's production.

Table 5.3
Sales by the Austrian State Tobacco Monopoly, 1784–1913[1]

	Total (1,000 lbs)	Per Head	Percent of Total Sales Snuff	Other Forms
1784	14,288		31%	69%
1790	15,403		32	68
1800	21,527		24	76
1810	22,505		20	80
1815	16,128		27	73
1820	18,198	1.32	22	78
1830	26,331	1.70	13	87
1840	33,847	2.00	13	87
1850	37,347	2.10	12	88
1861	51,588	2.72	9	91
1870	56,712	2.78	7	93
1882	70,193	3.15	7	93
1890	67,827	2.84	6	94
1900	78,820	3.02	4	96
1910	85 848	3.04	3	97
1913	83,914	2.91	3	97

[1] Excluding sales by the state tobacco monopolies for the Habsburg lands in Hungary and Italy.

Sources: Hitz and Huber, *Geschicte der Österreichischen Tabakregie* (1784–1830); Austria, Statistische Central-Commission, *Tafeln zur Statistik der Österreichischen Monarchie* (1840–1850); Austria, Central-Direction der Tabakfabriken und Einlosügsämter, *Tabellen zur Statistik des Österreichischen Tabak-Monopols* (1861–1870); Austria, Statistische Central-Commission, *Österreichisches statistiches Handbuch* (1882–1913).

Although it did not use advertising or other marketing strategies to boost sales, the state monopoly did try, albeit sometimes in a lethargic manner, to meet consumer demands. Since tobacco growing was prohibited throughout the Austrian realm, the monopoly also was content to import specific products that it was not yet capable of manufacturing. Beginning about 1845, it thus offered for sale imported cigars, adding cigars of its own manufacture by 1861. It was peculiarly slow to offer either imported or domestic paper cigarettes, which were not put on sale until about 1875, a full thirty years after they were introduced in France. At about the same time, the tobacco administration also came to realize that spun and pressed products were no longer cut up by pipe smokers but were consumed orally; these smokeless products were now forthrightly labeled *chewing tobacco (Kau-und Kübeltabak)*. By the middle of the 1870s, the monopoly thus offered to customers the five major products—snuff, chewing tobacco, pipe tobacco, cigars, and cigarettes—in something like their modern forms.

In choosing between the products offered to them by the state monopoly, Austrian tobacco consumers were characteristically slow to change their preferences. Taken as a group, the diverse peoples of the empire preferred the pipe:

Table 5.4
Products Manufactured by the Austrian State Tobacco Monopoly,[1] 1840–1913

	Thousands of U.S Pounds						Percent of Total Products[3]				
	Snuff	Spun	Cut	Cigars[2]	Cigarettes	Total	Snuff	Spun	Cut	Cigars[2]	Cigarettes
1840	4,343	3,554	24,450	---	---	32,347	13	11%	76%	--%	--%
1850	4,860	5,378	28,690	---	---	38,928	13	16	74	--	--
1861	4,396	----{49,605}---		9,957	---	63,958	7	--{78}--		16	--
1870	4,294	----{47,860}---		8,210	---	60,364	7	--{79}--		14	--
1882	5,102	4,159	49,044	12,469	450	71,224	7	6	69	18	1
1890	4,142	2,873	46,158	12,700	2,854	68,727	6	4	67	19	4
1900	2,982	3,273	52,179	12,981	6,933	78,348	4	5	67	17	9
1910	2,684	2,738	53,944	12,895	15,421	87,682	3	3	62	15	18
1913	2,554	2,860	55,116	15,907	14,355	90,792	3	3	61	18	16

[1] Excluding the production of the tobacco monopolies for the Habsburg lands in Hungary and Italy.
[2] Includes cigarillos.
[3] Percentages may not sum to 100 percent due to rounding into whole numbers.

Sources: Austria, Statistische Central-Commission, *Tafeln zur Statistik der Österreichischen Monarchie* (1840–1850); Austria, Central-Direction der Tabakfabriken und Einlosungsämter, *Tabellen zur Statistik des Österreichischen Tabak-Monopols* (1861–1870); Austria, Statistische Central-Commission, *Österreichisches statistiches Handbuch* (1882–1913).

Table 5.5
Sales by the Austrian State Tobacco Monopoly, 1850–1950[1]

Thousands of U.S Pounds

	Snuff	Spun	Cut	Cigars[2]	Cigar-ettes	Total	Per Head
1850	4,539	3,209[3]	27,488	2,111	---	37,347	2.10
1861	4,670	--{41,546}---		5,372	---	51,588	2.72
1870	4,129	--{47,925}---		---{8,787}----		60,841	2.78
1876	4,682	--{53,428}[4]--		10,671	172	68,953	3.16
1882	4,829	--{52,738}---		12,284	340	70,191	3.15
1890	3,954	--{48,790}---		12,302	2,780	67,826	2.84
1900	2,866	--{55,455}---		13,738	6,697	78,756	3.02
1910	2,520	2,816	53,877	12,546	13,910	85,669	2.84
1913	2,411	2,703	54,327	11,383	13,090	83,914	2.91
=== ======							
1920	379	---{5,076}---		1,528	5,586	12,569	1.92
							3.61
1930	265	773	10,183	1,944	10,046	23,211	3.51
1940	200	700	9,700	1,500	17,200	29,300	---
1950	100	300	3,200	600	13,100	17,300	2.50

Percent of Total Sales[5]

	Snuff	Spun	Cut	Cigars[2]	Cigar-ettes
1850	12%	9%[6]	60%	6%	--%
1861	9	--{81}-		10	--
1870	7	--{79}-		---{14}--	
1876	7	--{77}-[7]		15	--[8]
1882	7	--{75}-		18	1
1890	6	--{72}-		18	4
1900	4	--{70}-		17	9
1910	3	3	63	15	16
1913	3	3	65	14	16
==					
1920	3	--{40}-		12	44
	1	3	49	10	37
1930	1	3	44	8	43
1940	1	2	33	5	59
1950	1	2	19	4	76

For more than a century between 1784 and World War I, the regie could antic-ipate that fully two-thirds to three-fourths of its sales would consist of cut smoking tobacco. For many years, prepared snuff was the second most popular product, with cigars beginning to outsell snuff only in 1861.

The continuing popularity of snuff into the second half of the nineteenth century is particularly striking. As indicated in Table 5.3, manufactured snuff represented more than a third of all the tobacco sold by the Habsburg monopoly prior to the French Revolution.[2] Virtually every history of tobacco assumes that snuff consumption fell off rapidly during the early nineteenth century. In fact, as Table 5.5 shows, the Austrian state monopoly sold more snuff in 1882 (about 5 million pounds) than it had sold about a century earlier in 1784 (about 4.5 million pounds). Over the years, sales of prepared snuff did decline in proportion to total sales—but at a comparatively slow rate. During the some sixty years between 1850 and 1913, for example, snuff consumption as a per-centage of all usage fell at a rate of only 2 percent per year (Table 5.5). Given the relative tenacity of snuff users, the state regie was willing throughout the nineteenth century to budget funds to maintain or even to improve its snuff manufactories.

Since overall tobacco consumption in the Austrian Empire grew along with and only about as rapidly as the adult population, it is reasonable to assume that increased sales of cut tobacco and other products after 1861 represented the presence of new purchasers rather than a drastic change in preference by existing snuff consumers. Overall, a majority of Habsburg subjects probably always were smokers. However, some smokers now took up cigars or, more slowly, cigarettes rather than opting for the pipe. Cigars, which were first of-fered for sale about 1845, were rather quickly accepted, with sales doubling each decade between 1850 and 1876 (Table 5.5). After 1880, however, cigar

---

Notes to Table 5.5

[1] For 1850 through 1913, excludes sales by the state tobacco monopolies for the Habsburg lands in Hungary and Italy.

[2] Includes cigarillos.

[3] For 1850, the category "gespunste" includes Rollen (1,959) and Kau-und Kübeltabak (1,250).

[4] For 1876, Kau-und Kübeltabak (2,770) are included under the general category "Rauchtabak."

[5] Percentages may not sum to 100 percent due to rounding into whole numbers.

[6] For 1850, the category "gespunste" includes Rollen (5.3 percent of all sales) and Kau-und Kü-beltabak (3.4 percent of all sales).

[7] For 1876, Kau-und Kübeltabak (listed under the general category "Rauchtabak") comprised 4.0 percent of all sales.

[8] Less than 0.5 percent.

Sources: Austria, Statistische Control-Commission, *Tafeln zur Statistik der Österreichischen Mon-archie* (1850); Austria, Central-Direction der Tabakfabriken und Einlösungsämter, *Tabel-len zur Statistik des Österreichischen Tabak-Monopols* (1861–1870); Krükl, *Das Tabak-Monopol in Oesterreich und Frankreich* (1876); Austria, Statistische Central-Commis-sion, *Österreichisches statistiches Handbuch* (1882–1913); Hutson, *Consumption and Production of Tobacco in Europe* (1920–1930); Lee, *Tobacco Consumption in Various Countries* (1940–1950).

consumption ceased to grow and even began to decline as those smokers that did not use pipes increasingly took to cigarettes rather than to cigars. As had been the case twenty years earlier with cigars, cigarette sales also increased rapidly when the product was first offered in the 1890s but then began to level off.

By 1913, a kind of stasis was reached, with most tobacco consumers apparently having firm preferences. In that year, the last year of peacetime tobacco consumption for almost ten years, pipe tobacco constituted about two-thirds of total sales, and cigars and cigarettes together comprised less than one-third (Table 5.5). Nevertheless, after a century and a half, smokeless products continued to retain the allegiance of a small but loyal minority. With both enjoying sales of more than two million pounds a year, manufactured snuff and chewing tobacco each represented about 3 percent of tobacco sales throughout the empire.

In an empire as polyglot as that of the Habsburgs, these national sales data conceal some significant variations between provinces in consumer preferences. By 1913, for example, manufactured snuff—which as late as 1850 had been widely sold throughout the empire—primarily was consumed in the mountainous regions along the Adriatic Coast in provinces that later became part of the kingdoms of Italy (the Tyrol and Istria) and Yugoslavia (Dalmatia and Carniola). Since consumers in these same regions also were likely to use chewing tobacco, the Adriatic provinces formed—along with Galicia in southern Poland—a stronghold of smokeless tobacco, both nasal and oral. Throughout the empire as a whole (Table 5.6), smokeless forms comprised about 6 percent of all sales in 1913. In contrast, smokeless products represented from 10 to 30 percent of sales in Galicia (11 percent), Dalmatia (11 percent), Carniola (17 percent), Istria (15 percent), and the Tyrol (29 percent). It would be tempting to see in these data a preference for smokeless products on the part of hardy mountaineers. However, since the Habsburg records do not distinguish by social class, this hypothesis can not be substantiated; it might be that these smokeless products were in fact purchased by residents of Tyrolean towns.

5.3 FRANCE

The Habsburg empire, whose rulers erected a state tobacco monopoly in 1784, enjoys the distinction of preserving the oldest continuing series of tobacco consumption data. The records of the French government, which established its monopoly in 1810, are continuous only since 1818. However, they are in some years more precise and clearly organized, allowing the historian to pinpoint more nearly the years during which major changes in tobacco habits took place. Overall, per capita consumption of tobacco was relatively low under the ancien regime and during the first half of the nineteenth century. Judging by the records of the tobacco monopoly summarized in Table 5.7, consumption increased very rapidly between about 1845 and 1860,[3] held relatively

Table 5.6
Sales by the Austrian State Tobacco Monopoly, 1913

| | Thousands of Pounds | Percent of Total Sales[1] | | | | |
		Snuff	Chewing	Cut	Cigars[2]	Cigarettes
Entire Empire	83,914	3%	3%	65%	14%	16%
Austria[3]	26,537	1	--[4]	59	23	17
Czechoslovakia						
Bohemia	23,251	2	--[4]	62	16	20
Moravia	6,607	1	--[4]	68	14	17
Italy						
Tyrol	4,982	7	22	54	10	8
Istria	3,504	13	2	56	9	21
Poland						
Galicia	13,802	6	5	79	4	6
Silesia	2,654	1	--	61	20	18
Yugoslavia						
Carniola	1,395	2	15	61	10	12
Dalmatia	1,005	1	10	72	5	12

[1] Percentages may not sum to 100 percent due to rounding into whole numbers.
[2] Includes cigarillos.
[3] The historical provinces existing in 1913 have been assigned to the state that administered them after 1918.
[4] Less than 0.5 percent.

Source: Austria, Statistisches Central-Commission, *Österreichisches statistisches Handbuch.*

steady between 1860 and 1890, and has again risen since 1900—but at a much slower rate compared to the dramatic increase during the years around 1850.[4]

Historians have advanced several explanations for the relatively restrained use of tobacco in France during the two centuries between 1650 and 1850. Many have attributed low per capita use to the relatively high prices charged by the companies farming the monopoly.[5] These prices made tobacco truly a luxury item, available only to those individuals—priests, governmental officials, and aristocrats—with much higher than average incomes. Others see a correlation between low per capita usage and the French people's widespread preference for nasal snuff. Snuff takers tend to use less tobacco each day than smokers.[6] And because snuff users do not share tobacco aromas with bystanders, they may not make converts to tobacco as quickly as smokers.[7] Judging by the more than two hundred years of precise information offered by the records of the French monopoly, both of these hypotheses have some validity,

Table 5.7

Sales by the French State Tobacco Monopoly, 1789–1949 (per capita and percentages)

	Per Head	Percent of Total Sales [1]		
		Snuff	Hard [2]	Rôles
1789	.58	57%	29%	15%

	Per Head	Snuff	Hard [2]	Plug [3]	Cut [4]	Cigars [5]	Cigar-ettes
1819	.76	58%	-{11%}-		28%	3%	--%
1830	.76	50	----{48}----			2	--
1835	.84	46	----{52}----			2	--
1845	1.12	37	2	2	55	3	--[6]
1861	1.95	38	1	1	50	9	--[6]
1868	1.82	25	--{4}--		61	10	--[6]
1878	1.93	22	--{4}--		62	10	2

	Per Head	Snuff	Chewing [3]	Cut [4]	Cigars [5]	Cigarettes
1885 [7]	2.11	18	3	66	10	2
1892	2.08	15	3	70	9	3
1900	2.38	13	3	72	8	5
1910	2.34	12	3	72	6	8
1913	2.45	11	3	72	6	9

1920	2.63	7	2	74	5	12
1925	2.60	7	2	68	3	20
1930	3.01	5	2	60	2	32
1938	2.72	3	2	58	1	36
1949	2.83	2	1	44	1	53

[1] Percentages may not sum to 100 percent due to rounding into whole numbers.
[2] "Tabac ficelé" (1789); "carottes" (1819–78).
[3] From 1819 through 1885 includes "menu filé," "gros rôles," and "rôles"; from 1885 through 1949 includes "carottes" and "rôles."
[4] "Scaferlati."
[5] Includes cigarillos.
[6] Less than 0.5 percent.
[7] From 1885 through 1913 this excludes Alsace and Lorraine, which were administered as part of the German Empire during those years.

Sources: Price, *France and the Chesapeake,* p. 426 (1789); France, Direction générale des manufactures de l'État, *Rapport concernant la fabrication et la vente exclusives du tabac* (1819–1861); Bouant, *Le Tabac,* p. 290 (1868–1878). France, Institut National de la Statistique, *Annuaire Statistique de la France* (1885–1920, 1938–1949); Hutson, *Consumption and Production of Tobacco in Europe* (1930).

but neither can be fully proved. One difficulty in evaluating changes in consumption is obvious: The French monopoly recorded only legal sales and could not measure smuggling, which in some rural regions near the frontiers may have accounted for more than one sale in three.[8] While smuggling apparently declined in importance during the nineteenth century, no accurate estimate of its importance in any era is possible.

The rise in tobacco sales between 1845 and 1861 cannot be attributed solely to a shift in preferences from snuff to smoking products. Furthermore, the increase did not respond to lower prices, since the state monopoly charged exactly the same range of prices for tobacco products (during years of generally stable currencies) both in 1845 and in 1861. It is certainly true that sales of cut pipe tobacco (called *scaferlati* in French) did rise during these years coincidentally with the increase in total consumption. Cigar sales also increased 413 percent in sixteen years as this tobacco product became popular with the French for the first time since its introduction to the market thirty years earlier. As Table 5.8 indicates, however, the French were not smoking more because they were snuffing less. Indeed, snuff sales reached their all-time high of about 28 million pounds in 1861. And the growth in snuff sales between 1845 and 1861 (86 percent) actually was greater than the increase in sales of scaferlati (67 percent) during the same years.

One factor contributing to higher tobacco sales is the long period of economic growth that began in France during the 1830s and continued with some pauses until the 1870s. While it did not immediately benefit the French people with rigid uniformity, industrialization over the course of these forty years reduced differences between classes while substantially increasing the purchasing power of poorer groups.[9] The French people were still comparatively poor in the 1850s—compared, say, to the poorest 10 percent of the populace in the United States today. However, they no longer had to spend all their income for bread, as they had a century earlier. Almost all individuals now had some discretionary income that could be spent on previously unobtainable pleasures, such as snuff or pipe tobacco. It was always the policy of the French monopoly (as it was that of the Austrian) to sell products at a wide range of prices. But even the cheapest tobacco was beyond the reach of many persons until the middle of the nineteenth century. Perhaps the most plausible explanation of increased tobacco sales after 1845 is simply that their relatively higher incomes now allowed more French citizens to try and to adopt tobacco products of all kinds.

As was also the case in the Habsburg empire after the middle of the nineteenth century, this larger pool of tobacco users tended to turn away from the multipurpose rôles and carottes, which could be smoked, ground, or chewed as the user wished. Most now preferred products already prepared for use, including manufactured snuff as well as ready-cut pipe tobacco and cigars. Among pressed products, a decline in sales is particularly noticeable in the case of the hard, string-wrapped carottes, which were grated at home to produce nasal

Table 5.8

Sales by the French State Tobacco Monopoly, 1789–1878 (in thousands of U.S. pounds)

	Snuff	Twist[1]	Hard[2]	Plug[3]	Cut[4]	Cigars	Cigar-ettes	Total
1789	8,515	---	4,321	2,214	---	---	---	15,050
1819	13,532	130	---{2,478}--		6,453	569	---	23,162
1830	12,236	86	-------{11,689}------				547	---	24,528
1835	12,922	80	-------{14,432}------				636	---	28,070
1845	14,806	97	963	595	21,852	1,329	7	39,649
1861	27,512	216	966	772	36,579	6,819	15	72,879
1868	17,520	------{2,698}------			41,986	6,884	26	69,114
1878	15,393	------{2,592}------			44,154	7,410	1,516	71,065

[1] "Menu filé."

[2] "Tabac ficelé" (1789); "carottes" (other years).

[3] "Gros rôles" and "rôles."

[4] "Scaferlati."

Sources: Price, *France and the Chesapeake*, p. 426 (1789); France, Direction générale des manufactures de l'État, *Rapport concernant la fabrication et la vente exclusives du tabac* (1819–1861); Bouant, *Le Tabac*, p. 290 (1868–1878).

snuff. As Table 5.8 indicates, although demand for prepared snuff and all other products increased, sales of carottes stagnated and were virtually the same (at about a million pounds a year) in 1861 as in 1845. As discussed in Chapter 3, improved packaging that kept tobacco more moist and fresher may have induced snuff takers to purchase prepared snuff rather than cutting up plug.

In contrast, although it rose more slowly than sales of snuff, pipe tobacco, and cigars, demand for the softer pressed plug did increase after 1845. This shift from harder to softer plug indicates that pressed products were now being purchased primarily by chewers. Recognizing this change in use, the French state monopoly began by 1885 (and almost certainly a decade earlier) to characterize its remaining pressed products as "chewing tobacco" *(tabac à chiquer).* It will be remembered that plug intended mainly for chewing also took the place of multipurpose products in the Austrian empire during precisely the same decade of the 1870s.

Not later than 1885, therefore (as in the Austrian empire), the French tobacco consumer had available the five main types of products found today— snuff, chewing tobacco, pipe tobacco, cigars, and cigarettes. In choosing among these five types of products, the French established habits or preferences that changed little over the next sixty years. Whereas most of the tobacco sold by the state monopoly until 1830 took the form of snuff (whether prepared or made at home by grinding carottes), pipe smoking now replaced snuff as the primary way of consuming tobacco. As shown in Table 5.9, scaferlati, which is intended for use in pipes (although it can be used to roll a kind of very

Table 5.9
Sales by the French State Tobacco Monopoly, 1885–1950[1]

	Thousands of U.S Pounds						Percent of Total Sales				
	Snuff	Chewing[2]	Cut[3]	Cigars[4]	Cigar-ettes	Total	Snuff	Chewing[2]	Cut[3]	Cigars[4]	Cigar-ettes
1885	14,519	2,701	52,811	7,993	1,952	79,977	18%	3%	66%	10%	2%
1892	12,076	2,717	55,612	7,209	2,367	79,981	15	3	70	9	3
1900	10,843	2,504	61,148	6,350	3,971	84,814	13	3	72	8	5
1910	10,557	2,537	66,050	5,220	7,166	91,529	12	3	72	6	8
1913	10,395	2,530	69,561	5,717	8,926	97,128	11	3	72	6	9
1920	7,366	2,407	74,752	5,410	12,004	101,928	7	2	74	5	12
1925	8,502	2,318	80,609	3,440	23,368	118,297	7	2	68	3	20
1930	6,205	2,254	73,370	2,955	39,382	124,166	5	2	60	2	32
1938	3,473	1,720	65,291	735	40,742	111,962	3	2	58	1	36
1949	1,729	1,419	50,976	949	62,109	117,139	2	1	44	1	53

[1] From 1885 through 1913 this excludes Alsace and Lorraine, which were administered as part of the German Empire during those years.

[2] From 1885, the reports of the French government include both carottes and rôles under "tabac à chiquer."

[3] "Scaferlati."

[4] Includes cigarillos.

Sources: Hutson, *Consumption and Production of Tobacco in Europe* (1925–1930); France, Institut National de la Statistique. *Annuaire Statistique de la France* (all other years).

strong cigarette), henceforth represented more than 60 percent of sales in every year between 1868 and 1935. Demand rose each year, with an all-time high in sales (about 81 million pounds) being reached in 1925.

Those French persons that smoked thus preferred the pipe. Compared to consumers in some other major nations—such as Austria, Germany, or Italy—the French showed little taste for cigars and were slow to adopt the cigarette. Of the eleven countries for which there is sales data for 1900, France ranked next to last in the consumption of cigars and cigarettes, with these products representing only 13 percent of sales (see Table 6.2). Indeed, cigar consumption actually peaked as early as 1885 and declined in every following year. And cigarette sales, which grew slowly until the 1920s, increased almost entirely at the expense of cigars. Only after World War II did a majority prefer the cigarette—several decades after it had become the favored tobacco product in many other European nations (Table 6.4).

But not everyone took up the pipe. And the French, who perfected the use of snuff during the Eighteenth Century, remained loyal to powdered tobacco after it had become something of a rarity in several other countries. When records began in the 1780s, the French were the most assiduous users of snuff in the Western world. Tables 5.7 and 5.8 show that powdered snuff represented at least three out of every four pounds of tobacco sold in 1789. Although consumption was low compared to more recent years, the French also used more snuff per capita than those in other nations. Moreover, snuff sales in absolute terms continued to increase until 1861, when they began to decline both in terms of physical volume and in proportion to sales of other products. But if the use of snuff became less common after the 1860s, it did not quickly disappear from France, where it continues to be enjoyed today. During the forty years between 1885 and 1925, as Table 5.9 indicates, demand for snuff dropped slightly more than 1 percent a year. As in Austria, the French tobacco monopoly could look forward each year to relatively stable sales of prepared snuff, and it thus took pains to satisfy this profitable market.

Just as pipe smokers and snuff takers were tenacious in their preferences, also tenacious was the smaller group that preferred chewing tobacco. Demand for plug or rôles remained stable and grew in proportion to the increase in population. From 1870 to 1939, under the Third Republic chewing tobacco thus comprised a steady 2 to 3 percent of sales each year (Table 5.9). These data cannot tell us whether this group used only chewing tobacco. Since some consumers use smokeless products in circumstances when a fire would be dangerous, it is likely that at least some among those purchasing chewing tobacco also smoked on some occasions.

5.4 THE ITALIAN PENINSULA

Judging by the published records of the state monopoly (Table 5.10), since 1870 the inhabitants of the Italian peninsula consistently have consumed less

Table 5.10
Per Capita Sales in Lombardy and Venetia, 1840–1850, and by the Italian State Tobacco Monopoly, 1870–1950 (in U.S. pounds per resident)

LOMBARDY AND VENETIA

1840	.94	.77
1850	1.04	.84

ITALIAN STATE TOBACCO MONOPOLY

1870	1.22
1880	1.24
1890	1.21
1900	1.10
1910	1.31
1920	1.61
1925	1.54
1930	1.45
1940	1.97
1950	1.85

Sources: Austria, Statistische Central-Commission, *Tafeln zur Statistik der Österreichischen Monarchie* (1840–1850); Italy, Instituto centrale di statistica, *Sommario di statistiche storiche italiano* (1870–1950).

tobacco per person than have the residents of other nations in Europe. Several explanations for this low per capita consumption have been suggested. Italians may simply have used large amounts of tobacco that is not captured by official records since these do not measure smuggling, which is known to have been significant in some years. However, although they may not accurately measure total consumption, the monopoly's records do suggest what types of products were popular with Italians. Smugglers presumably brought in the same range of products as the official stores—it is not likely, that is, that they carried in only snuff or only cigarettes. Thus, the government's data may be taken as describing overall trends in product preferences.

Since the nineteenth century, observers also have attributed Italy's low per capita consumption to the high prices charged by the state monopoly; since the Italians were among the poorest people in Europe until the 1960s, many simply could not afford tobacco. And a third explanation may lie in the comparatively high consumption of nasal snuff. Italians were among the first Europeans to use snuff, and they long remained loyal to this type of product. As Table 5.11 indicates, sales of nasal snuff in proportion to other products long have been higher than those in any other country except France. (Scandinavians purchase more of a powdered tobacco also called snuff, but they consume this product orally rather than inhaling it.) If, as some analysts believe, consumers of smokeless tobacco use less each day than smokers, then low per capita con-

Table 5.11
Sales by the Austrian State Tobacco Monopoly in Lombardy and Venetia, 1821–1855

Lombardy

	Thousands of U.S Pounds				Percent of Total Sales[1]		
	Snuff	Cut[2]	Cigars	Total	Snuff	Cut	Cigars
1821	1,044	835	---	1,879	56%	44%	--%
1825	992	640	---	1,632	61	39	--
1830	981	760	---	1,741	56	44	--
1840	954	1,009	---	1,963	49	51	--
1845	951	937	280	2,168	44	43	13
1850	910	990	531	2,431	37	41	22
1855	914	1,299	743	2,956	31	44	25

Venetia

	Thousands of U.S Pounds				Percent of Total Sales[1]		
	Snuff	Cut[3]	Cigars	Total	Snuff	Cut	Cigars
1821	814	656	---	1,470	55%	45%	--%
1830	808	461	---	1,269	64	36	--
1840	1,039	297	---	1,336	78	22	--
1845	981	263	177	1,421	69	19	13
1850	1,005	188	410	1,603	63	12	26
1855	1,312	241	692	2,244	59	11	31

[1] Percentages may not sum to 100 percent due to rounding into whole numbers.

[2] Does not include the following amounts of cut tobacco sold at reduced prices or "Limito-Preise" to the military (sales of "Limitotabak" were not reported for the earlier years): 562 (1840), 490 (1845), 601 (1850), and 440 (1855).

[3] Does not include the following amounts of cut tobacco sold at reduced prices or "Limito-Preise" to the military (sales of "Limitotabak" were not reported for the earlier years): 481 (1840), 430 (1845), 605 (1850), and 615 (1855).

Source: Austria, Statistische Central-Commission, *Tafeln zur Statistik der Österreichischen Monarchie.*

sumption in Italy is fully consistent with a higher than average preference for nasal snuff.

Although little evidence is available from the central regions or from Sicily prior to the creation of the Kingdom of Italy in 1861, the Habsburg tobacco monopoly published accounts for the areas it served—Lombardy (1815–1861) and Venetia (1815–1866). These show that nasal snuff continued to be preferred to smoking products into the 1850s. As summarized in Tables 5.10 and 5.11, in 1855 snuff thus comprised one-third of all sales in Lombardy and two-thirds of those in Venetia—a level of snuff consumption equalled only in France. The preference for snuff in these regions is significant because Lombardy (with its capital at Milan) and the Venice region are among the more economically

Table 5.12
Sales by the Italian State Tobacco Monopoly, 1868–1950

| | Thousands of U.S Pounds | | | | Percent of Total Sales[1] | | | |
	Snuff	Cut	Cigars[2]	Cigar-ettes	Total	Snuff	Cut	Cigars[2]	Cigar-ettes
1868	7,244	15,923	10,068	---	33,235	22%	48%	30%	--%
1870	6,909	16,890	8,790	---	32,589	21	52	27	--
1880	7,445	13,933	13,849	---	35,227	21	40	39	--
1890	7,344	14,974	14,376	130	36,824	20	41	39	--[3]
1900	5,692	14,147	13,993	1,900	35,732	16	40	39	5
1910	4,495	13,272	21,202	6,349	45,318	10	29	47	14
1920	5,860	16,012	19,897	20,155	61,924	10	26	32	33
1925	4,176	18,492	13,528	28,225	64,421	7	29	21	44
1930	3,497	15,174	12,560	28,418	59,649	6	25	21	48
1940	2,158	14,392	9,612	58,888	85,050	3	17	11	69
1950	1,508	12,017	5,644	68,226	87,415	2	14	7	78

[1] Percentages may not sum to 100 percent due to rounding into whole numbers.
[2] Includes cigarillos.
[3] Less than 0.5 percent.

Source: Italy, Instituto centrale di statistica, *Sommario di statistiche storiche Italiano.*

and culturally advanced parts of the peninsula. It has been suggested that nasal snuff was primarily taken by old-fashioned country-folk after the 1820s. But, at least in Italy, snuff in fact was preferred in the most urban regions of the nation.

Italian consumers did not remain loyal to snuff throughout the nineteenth century and into the twentieth because they lacked alternatives. The tobacco monopolies always had sold cut pipe tobacco, and they introduced cigars in 1845 and cigarettes in 1884. As we have seen, it is unusual for tobacco consumers to switch readily from smokeless products to smoking tobacco or vice versa. Thus, while cigars immediately gained favor with Italian smokers, they at first did not affect snuff consumption, which reached its peak (as Table 5.12 shows) only in the 1890s. It was the cigarette, however, and not the cigar that ultimately came to dominate the Italian market. Almost from their introduction in 1884, sales of cigarettes soared.[10] By 1931, comparatively earlier than in many other countries (see Table 6.4), cigarettes represented 50 percent of total sales, and they held 80 percent of the market by 1950. Nevertheless, nasal snuff continued to be taken by Italians, who still purchased more than 1.5 million pounds of this product in 1950.

One product that is not cited in the records of the Italian state monopoly is chewing tobacco. Yet we know (Table 5.6) that the Habsburg regie in 1913 sold considerably more than a million pounds of this type of product in the regions of the Tyrol and Istria that were occupied by the Kingdom of Italy after World War I. It is difficult to provide a plausible explanation for this large gap in the Italian archives. Those chewers that lived near the new border could, of course, continue to purchase their favorite brands from the Austrian stores. And some may have taken to consuming snuff as an oral rather than a nasal product, in this way substituting a cut smokeless tobacco for the pressed product. Given that the evidence from Europe and the Americas shows that consumers are generally stable in their habits, it is unlikely that so large a group simply switched from smokeless to smoking tobacco. Yet the Italian records do not mention what would have amounted to more than 2 percent of national sales.

5.5 SWEDEN

The sparsely inhabited nation of Sweden has been characterized by close cooperation between government and industry; as early as the eighteenth century, the government exercised a kind of general overview of the economy found in other states only since World War I. For this reason, although the Swedish government did not erect a tobacco monopoly until 1916, it boasts the oldest continuing records of national production. These records, which begin for tobacco in 1780, are of exceptional value because the patterns of evolution present in Sweden apparently are similar to those found in other Scandinavian countries, where records begin at a much later date. Moreover, these records indicate that, while the same underlying evolutionary processes were occurring in Scandinavia as in other countries, their result was different in the north. The Swedish records thus are valuable not only in suggesting insights into consumption patterns throughout Scandinavia but also in providing the exception that ''probes the rule'' for understanding tobacco usage throughout the Western World.

As also occurred in Austria and France, consumption in Sweden significantly increased during the 1850s. And, as in other countries, the first half of the nineteenth century is marked by a shift from multipurpose plug to products intended for specific purposes. In many countries, however, the nineteenth century witnessed the growing dominance of pipe smoking and the slow eclipse of smokeless tobacco. In Sweden, precisely the opposite happened, as the Swedes adopted snuff as their primary way of using tobacco. At the same time, pipe tobacco, which represented some 40 percent of sales in 1810 (comparable to the ratio in Austria and France), fell to only 10 percent or less by the 1870s.

Throughout Europe, the decisive decade for the adoption of the tobacco habit would seem to be that of the 1850s. In Sweden also, following a period of more than forty years when it had held steady at about one pound a year, per capita consumption suddenly increased by more than 50 percent between 1850 and 1860. In a way again similar to that in other European countries, consumption then leveled off and remained stable during the 1880s and 1890s. As Table 5.13 indicates, the demand for tobacco began to rise again at the end of the century, before again becoming comparatively stable in the 1920s at about three pounds a year. At this level of consumption, the Swedes may be considered

Table 5.13
Tobacco Products Manufactured in Sweden, 1780–1897, and Tobacco Sales by the Swedish Tobacco Monopoly, 1916–1950[1]

	Per Head [3]	Total	Percent of All Products[2]				
			Snuff	Spun[4]	Cut[5]	Cigars[6]	Cigar-ettes
1780	.61	1,286	10%	73%	17%	--%	--%
1800	.77	1,800	12	49	39	--	--
1810	.93	2,238	10	48	41	--	--
1820	.93	2,393	38	24	38	--	--
1830	.96	2,773	44	26	30	--[7]	--
1840	1.10	3,441	57	18	24	1	--
1850	1.17	4,048	60	19	18	4	--
1860	1.61/1.54	6,204	61	15	27	7	--
1870	1.96/1.98	8,178	66	19	10	6	--
1880	1.50/2.70	11,410	62	18	10	10	--
1890	2.49/2.43	11,492	66	22	4	7	--
1897	2.83/2.86	14,140	69	14	7	10	--
1916	3.01/3.31	17,205	73	5	8	7	7
1920	3.49/3.53	20,582	70	4	8	9	9
1925	2.85	17,269	68	3	13	8	8
1930	2.79	17,156	62	2	12	9	14
1940	2.88	18,360	47	1	16	6	29
1950	3.14	22,009	32	--[7]	15	4	49

[1] Does not include small amounts of tobacco products imported for personal use.
[2] Percentages may not sum to 100 percent due to rounding into whole numbers.
[3] Average consumption (not domestic manufacture) during the five-year periods 1856–60, 1866–70, 1876–80, 1886–90, 1896–1900, 1911–15, 1916–20.
[4] "Rull-och presstobak" (1780–1897); "tuggtobak" (1916–1950).
[5] "Kardustobak" (1780–1897); "piptobak" (1916–1950).
[6] Includes cigarillos.
[7] Less than 0.5 percent.

Sources: Svenska tobacs aktiebolaget, *Svenska Tobaks Monopolet 1915–1940*, pp. 77, 108 (1780–1897), and *Om tobak i Sverige Jubileumsskrift 1915–1965*, p. 358 (1916–1950). Statistiska Centralbyrån: *Historisk Statistik*, I:2,3 (population 1780–1840), and *Statistiska Översiktstabeller*, I:122 (average consumption 1856/60–1916/20).

moderate users of tobacco—consuming on average about as much as Austrians and slightly more than the French, but significantly less than the Germans, Americans, or the Dutch.

During the first half of the nineteenth century, consumers in Sweden—as did those in other regions—came to prefer products made for one purpose to the multipurpose rôles and carottes characteristic of the ancien regime. These spun products formed three-fourths of all sales in 1780, and still met half the demand in 1810. During the 1810s, however, the production and sales of spun products fell by 50 percent precisely as sales of snuff quadrupled (Table 5.14).[11] Given that both the population and total tobacco production were relatively stable (the

Table 5.14
Tobacco Products Manufactured in Sweden, 1780–1897 (in thousands of U.S. pounds)

	Snuff	Spun [1]	Cut [2]	Cigars[3]	Total
1780	129	934	223	---	1,286
1800	211	883	706	---	1,800
1810	229	1,116	983	---	2,238
1820	917	578	898	---	2,393
1830	1,207	724	843	1	2,775
1840	1,976	626	821	18	3,441
1850	2,410	783	709	146	4,048
1860	3,756	919	1,072	457	6,204
1870	5,362	1,530	791	495	8,178
1880	7,094	2,027	1,158	1,132	11,411
1890	7,615	2,545	480	852	11,492
1897	9,752	1,972	972	1,443	14,139

[1] "Rull-och presstobak."
[2] "Kardustobak."
[3] Includes cigarillos.
[4] Less than 0.5 percent.

Source: Svenska tobaks aktiebolaget, *Svenska Tobaks Monopolet 1915–1940*, pp. 77, 108.

latter at about 2.25 million pounds), a large number of Swedish purchasers clearly must have substituted one product (snuff) for another (pressed rôles). This comparatively rapid shift in consumer preferences is striking. Tobacco habits normally change at an almost glacial pace, and it is unusual for a consumer of mature years suddenly to drop one product for another.

In fact, however, it is highly unlikely that the switch from plug to snuff initially represented a change from smoking to nasal inhalation. Most of those adopting snuff after 1810 probably did not inhale the product but instead placed moist snuff behind the upper lip, where they allowed it to rest while savoring its flavors. (This way of using tobacco is also found in the United States from the middle of the nineteenth century, but Americans tend to place oral snuff behind the lower lip rather than, as in Sweden, the upper.) The use of moist snuff as an oral product by the Swedes has been comprehensively documented from the end of the nineteenth century.[12] These official production and sales records would suggest that they adopted oral snuff toward the beginning of the nineteenth century—and perhaps from the 1810s—rather than at the end of the nineteenth century.

At first, oral snuff was probably a substitute for chewing tobacco. As Table 5.14 shows, pipe smokers were initially not affected, and sales of cut tobacco were generally stable (at about 8 to 9 million pounds) over the next thirty years. By the 1840s, however, oral snuff had established itself as the dominant tobacco product in Sweden, and it was now preferred over smoking products as

Table 5.15
Sales by the Swedish Tobacco Monopoly, 1916–1950 (in thousands of U.S. pounds) [1]

	Snuff	Spun [2]	Cut [3]	Cigars [4]	Cigar-ettes	Total
1916	12,619	838	1,291	1,254	1,202	17,204
1920	14,383	840	1,709	1,856	1,795	20,583
1925	11,407	494	2,269	1,429	1,371	16,970
1930	10,706	329	2,079	1,612	2,432	17,158
1940	8,647	176	2,998	1,072	5,249	18,142
1950	6,931	86	3,320	990	10,677	22,004

[1] Does not include small amounts of tobacco products imported for personal use.
[2] "Tuggtobak."
[3] "Piptobak."
[4] Includes cigarillos.

Source: Svenska tobaks aktiebolaget *Om tobak i Sverige Jubileumsskrift 1915–1965*, p. 358.

well as over plug by newer generations. While a minority did continue to smoke, sales of cut tobacco stagnated at about 8 million pounds (and 10 percent of the market) from the end of the 1860s until the mid-1920s. In every European country, a small group also remained loyal to pressed plug tobacco. With about 5 to 10 percent of the market between 1885 and 1925, sales of plug are remarkably similar to those in other regions, where pressed products were now purchased largely as chewing tobacco.

In many areas, rising per capita consumption in the 1850s was coincidental with a shift in consumer preferences from pressed products to cut smoking tobacco. And this coincidence has been interpreted by some historians as circumstantial evidence that daily consumption is higher among smokers than among users of smokeless products. In contrast, the Swedish records make it clear that the adoption of oral snuff (beginning in the 1810s) occurred long before an increase in per capita consumption (beginning in the 1850s). Indeed, these data appear to corroborate the hypothesis that smokeless products are used more moderately than smoking tobacco. As summarized in Table 5.14, the rise in per capita consumption in the 1850s is directly tied to a short-term increase in the sale of smoking products; during that decade, for example, the sale of cigars increased more than 200 percent—or more than 12 percent each year.

Oral snuff remained the most popular way of using tobacco among the Swedes for almost exactly a century, from about 1825 to about 1925. As Table 5.15 shows, sales of cigarettes began to climb from the 1920s, and sales of cut pipe tobacco also increased, although more slowly. Since overall consumption again remained relatively stable, the increasing sales of cigarettes again represents a substitution of this product for oral snuff. In the twentieth century, as in the nineteenth, the evolution of tobacco consumption among the Swedes thus is contrary to the patterns found in most other countries. In most of Europe, the

confused

nineteenth century witnessed a shift from smoking tobacco to smokeless products; in Sweden, exactly the reverse happened. Although tobacco preferences are normally slow to change, the remarkably accurate records of their government demonstrate that the Swedes have changed their habits at least twice during the past two centuries, by substituting oral snuff for chewing tobacco in the 1810s and again by substituting cigarettes for oral snuff in the 1920s and 1930s.

NOTES

1. The first systematic censuses in the Habsburg empire were taken in 1857 and 1869. Prior to 1857, the tobacco monopoly published per capita consumption numbers that were based on a long series of guesses. It first estimated how many customers it had, and it then assumed that every snuffer used nine pounds a year compared to every smoker's twelve pounds a year.

2. Because most of the hard carottes sold by the imperial monopoly were grated for snuff by their purchasers, snuff consumption in 1784 amounted to somewhat more than one-third of total sales.

3. As Tables 5.7 and 5.8 indicate, total tobacco consumption during these sixteen years grew from 39 million to 72 million pounds—an increase of 84 percent or about 3.8 percent each year. Since the population of France showed little growth during the nineteenth century, virtually all this rise in tobacco sales can be ascribed either to an increase in the number of tobacco consumers or to greater consumption by those individuals that already used tobacco. During the same sixteen years between 1845 and 1861, per capita sales also show a dramatic rise from slightly over a pound a year to almost two pounds—an increase of 74 percent overall or about 3.5 percent yearly.

4. The rise in overall consumption during the 1850s is striking when it is compared either to the previous two centuries or to sales during subsequent years. Although the enjoyment of tobacco products has continued to increase during the past century, the rate of growth has been much slower. During the some eighty years between 1878 and 1949, as indicated in Table 5.1, tobacco consumption in France rose only 63 percent— and only 47 percent on a per capita basis when the increase in population is taken into account. Consumption of tobacco products thus increased less during these eighty years than was the case during only sixteen years between 1845 and 1861. Put another way, if the use of tobacco had continued to increase after 1861 at the same rate as was witnessed during the previous sixteen years, the French people in 1950 would have consumed more than 2 million pounds of tobacco each year, or about 52 pounds a year per person.

5. Ever since governments began to release national consumption data during the nineteenth century, analysts have noticed an apparent correlation between the higher prices under monopoly regimes and low per capita consumption. See *Staatkundig en Staasthuishoudkundig Jaarboekje voor 1884;* Hutson, *Consumption in Europe,* 12; Gage, *American Tobacco Types,* 101; Gottsegen, *Tobacco,* 5; Gray and Wyckoff, "International Tobacco Trade," 12.

6. Rive, "Consumption of Tobacco since 1600," 63; Price, *France and the Chesapeake,* 788.

7. Gottsegen, *Tobacco,* 6.

8. Price, *France and the Chesapeake*, 465–66.

9. Zeldin, *France,* I:58–59.

10. During the first twenty years of this century, as Table 5.12 indicates, cigarette sales increased 1,000 percent—a growth rate of almost 13 percent each year.

11. Because the government has protected domestic manufacture, imported products have constituted only a small fraction of sales, as is indicated by the per capita consumption data reported in Table 5.11.

12. World Health Organization, *Tobacco Habits Other than Smoking,* 46–47.

Chapter 6

Tobacco Consumption, 1880–1950

6.1 SUMMARY

Chapter 5 has presented and analyzed the substantial evidence from the nineteenth century concerning smokeless tobacco consumption in four separate and disparate regions—the Habsburg empire, France, Italy, and Sweden. While consumer preferences evolved in somewhat different ways in each region, the patterns established by the middle of the century endured in each case for more than fifty years, until the mid-1920s. As Table 6.1 indicates, smokers came to predominate in Austria, France, and Italy. But nasal snuff taking, although it slowly declined in popularity during the nineteenth century, retained the loyalty of significant minorities in each of these four states. In Sweden, in contrast, the oral use of snuff significantly increased during precisely the same years; by 1880, oral moist snuff was the majority preference, with cigars and pipe tobacco tied for second place.

By the beginning of the twentieth century, other countries in the industrialized world also began to keep records of tobacco consumption, and nearly every state did so by 1925. Overall, four main patterns may be distinguished in the tobacco habits of their subjects.

1. As Chapter 5 has shown, cut tobacco had become the most popular form in France, Italy, and the Habsburg empire, but the state monopolies continued to sell significant amounts of nasal snuff.

2. The inhabitants of the Scandinavian states have been especially likely to use tobacco orally. Like the Swedes, the Icelanders primarily have used fine-cut or powdered snuff (Table 6.3). In contrast, the Norwegians and the Danes initially joined with the North Americans in choosing plug chewing tobacco (Table 6.2). After 1925, however, sales of plug fell in Norway while those of snuff remained more stable; by 1950, Norway was second only to Sweden in the use of oral snuff (See Table 6.4).

Table 6.1
Use of Tobacco Products circa 1880[1]

| | Total | Per head[3] | Percent of Total[2] | | | | |
			Snuff	Chewing	Cut	Cigars[4]	Cigarettes
Austria[5,6]	71,245	3.15	7%	3%	69%	18%	1%
France[7]	79,977	2.11	18	3	66	10	2
Germany[6]	154,972	3.60	8	1	63	27	--
Hungary[6]	9,515	--	1	--	88	11	--
Italy[7]	35,228	1.32	21	--	40	39	--
Sweden[6]	11,410	2.65	62	18	10	10	--
U.S.[6]	194,204	3.87	2	55	28	24	1

[1] Data for 1880 except for Austria (1882), France (1885), and Germany (average 1871–1879).
[2] Percentages may not sum to 100 percent due to rounding into whole numbers.
[3] Per capita manufacture/sales in pounds per inhabitant.
[4] Includes cigarillos.
[5] Habsburg empire, excluding Hungary.
[6] Manufacture.
[7] Sales.

    3. At the end of the nineteenth century, North Americans favored chewing tobacco over all types of smoking products; in 1880, plug thus represented more than half of all tobacco sales in the United States, with cigars and cut tobacco more or less tied for second place (Table 6.1). But per capita consumption of chewing tobacco had already reached its peak, and it has fallen in comparison to smoking products in every subsequent year. During the next seventy years, U.S. consumers gradually switched to cigarettes from chewing tobacco as well as from cigars and pipes, with the most rapid increase in cigarette consumption coming during the 1910s (Tables 6.2 and 6.3). Sales of snuff have been more stable over time than those of pressed tobacco; as a consequence, although its sales were only a small fraction of plug sales in 1880, snuff had by 1950 almost overtaken pressed chewing tobacco to become the best-selling smokeless product in the United States (Table 6.4).

    4. With the exception of those in Scandinavia, the majority of European tobacco consumers were smokers by the end of the nineteenth century. Initially, cut pipe tobacco was the best-selling product almost everywhere, with cigarettes generally replacing the pipe by 1950 (Table 6.4). But both chewing tobacco and snuff have also been used in every European country. As Chapter 5 shows, snuff was preferred in Italy and France. Although per capita consumption was much lower than in North America, chewing tobacco was particularly prevalent in the United Kingdom, in Germany, and in the British dominion of Australia (Table 6.2). Almost everywhere, chewing tobacco consumption has declined more precipitously than that of snuff, and snuff thus has replaced plug as the best-selling smokeless product in several of these countries.

in thousands u.s. pounds.

Table 6.2
Use of Tobacco Products circa 1900[1]

	Total	Per Head	Percent of Total[2]				
			Snuff	Chewing	Cut	Cigars[3]	Cigarettes
Austria[4,6]	78,820	3.02	4%	4%	67%	17%	9%
Australia[7]	12,118	2.75	--[8]	---{81}---[9]		17	9
Denmark[5]	9,998	4.17	2	23	40	30	6
France[6]	84,814	2.38	13	3	72	8	5
Germany[7]	196,177	3.02	6	6	30	45	15
Hungary[5]	7,670	.40	1	--	85	8	7
Italy[6]	35,722	1.10	16	--	40	39	5
Norway[5]	7,044	2.86	9	67	18	4	2
Sweden[5]	14,140	2.83	69	14	7	10	--
U.K.[5]	97,725	2.54	1	---{64}---[10]		5	30
U.S.[5]	422,777	5.29	3	44	24	27	2

[1] Data reported for 1900, except for Australia (1908), Denmark (1897), Germany (1913), Norway (1909), Sweden (1897), and the United Kingdom (1907).
[2] Percentages may not sum to 100 percent due to rounding into whole numbers.
[3] Includes cigarillos.
[4] Habsburg empire, excluding Hungary.
[5] Manufacture.
[6] Sales.
[7] Consumption.
[8] Less than 0.5 percent.
[9] Reported together as "manufactured tobacco."
[10] Reported together as "other manufactured tobacco."

Although demand for tobacco products in that region was distorted by governmental regulation, the lowest consumption of smokeless tobacco is seen among Central Europeans, who primarily have been smokers, at first of pipes and later of cigarettes (Table 6.3). Among the European nations, only Greece and Spain do not currently report the consumption of smokeless tobacco, and its prevalence in these countries thus cannot be statistically quantified. Literary evidence clearly indicates that chewing tobacco was found in both regions, and snuff was widely used in Spain during the eighteenth and nineteenth centuries.[1] In part, the use of smokeless tobacco possibly may have dropped in more recent years because the governmental monopolies that control tobacco sales in Greece and Spain did not provide it.

For many of these states, evidence is available only for a comparatively recent stage in the evolution of tobacco habits. Nevertheless, an analysis of this evidence again suggests that tobacco preferences change only very slowly. For many people, the enjoyment of tobacco is a personal matter, and their choices are not directly influenced by fashion. Only a small group, whose size must

Table 6.3
Use of Tobacco Products circa 1925[1]

	Total	Per Head[3]	Snuff	Percent of Total[2] Chewing	Cut	Cigars[4]	Cigar-ettes
Austria[7]	23,699	3.55	1%	3%	49%	10%	37%
Belgium[7]	41,343	5.38	2	--	67	9	22
Canada[7]	30,500	3.28	3	28	40	7	22
Czechoslovakia[7]	44,012	3.24	1	--	43	9	48
Denmark[7]	14,800	4.32	5	19	31	24	21
Finland[7]	6,100	2.01	3	--	18	3	74
France[6]	118,287	3.17	7	2	68	3	20
Germany[7]	213,429	3.17	2	3	34	29	31
Greece[7]	13,300	1.82	--	--	--	--	100
Hungary[7]	23,976	2.20	--[9]	--	75	3	22
Iceland[7]	230	3.40	34	--[8]	17	4	35
Italy[6]	64,201	1.54	7	--	29	21	44
Japan[6]	112,287	1.90	--	--	46[10]	--[9]	54
Netherlands[7]	41,200	6.68	--	1	57	33	10
Norway[6]	7,469	2.58	16	34	29	2	20
Poland[7]	38,309	.88	2	--[8]	65	1	31
Rumania[7]	34,934	2.05	--	--	72	1	24
Spain[7]	59,000	2.36	--	--	72	8	20
Sweden[6]	17,269	2.94	68	3	13	8	8
Turkey[7]	12,700	1.02	--[8]	--	66	--[8]	34
United Kingdom[7]	132,501	2.97	--[8]	7	31	2	61
United States[5]	723,800	7.03	5	18	34	18	11
Yugoslavia[7]	19,654	1.52	--[8]	2	75	2	33

[1] 1925 except for Hungary (1925–1926), Iceland (1932), and Spain (1927).
[2] Percentages may not sum to 100 percent due to rounding into whole numbers.
[3] In some cases, the estimate for 1924 by Hutson (*Production and Consumption of Tobacco in Europe*) has been used as the best available.
[4] Includes cigarillos.
[5] Manufacture.
[6] Sales.
[7] Consumption.
[8] The sources report the use of a small but unspecified amount of chewing tobacco.
[9] Less than 0.5 percent.
[10] Almost all of this pipe tobacco is fine-cut.

vary in response to cultural traditions, seems to be immediately responsive either to fads among the ruling elites or to changes in product composition. For this reason, if a popular product, such as chewing tobacco, comes to be seen as old-fashioned, its consumption will decline only very gradually—often no more than 1 or 2 percent each year. Ultimately, only a small group is left to purchase that product, but the change will have taken decades.

Table 6.4
Use of Tobacco Products in 1950[1]

	Total	Per Head	Percent of Total					Cigarettes[2] 50% of Total
			Snuff	Chew-ing	Cut	Cigars[3]	Cigar-ettes	
Austria[6]	17,300	2.50	1%	2%	19%	4%	76%	1939
Australia[6]	37,953	4.87	--[9]	9	44	1	47	1955
Belgium[6]	42,400	4.93	--[9]	--	51	6	44	1961
Canada[6]	72,800	5.31	1	3	36	3	57	1945
Denmark[4]	25,374	5.93	--[9]	4	22	26	44	1961
Finland[6]	10,000	2.48	--[9]	--[8]	18	--[9]	80	by 1920
France[5]	117,193	2.83	2	1	44	1	53	1943
West Germany[6]	141,126	2.79	1	1	32	30	37	1955
Greece[5]	21,700	2.86	--	--	--	--	100	by 1918
Iceland[6]	480	2.99	17	--[8]	10	4	69	1941
India[5]	461,100	1.29	1	28	26	11	34[10]	--
Italy[5]	87,396	1.85	2	--	14	7	78	1931
Japan[5]	165,687	2.00	--	--	13[11]	--[9]	87	by 1923
Morocco[5]	7,400	.83	12	--	10	--	78	by 1934
Netherlands[4]	62,552	5.91	--	3	28	26	43	1972
Norway[6]	10,700	3.26	11	7	50	1	32	--
Portugal[5]	9,608	1.19	--[9]	--	40	--[9]	60	1943
Russia[4]	344,174	2.01	--	--	34	--	66	--
South Africa[5]	38,300	3.06	1	1	48	--[9]	50	1943
Spain[5]	63,400	2.27	--	--	67	2	31	1955
Sweden[5]	22,009	3.24	32	--[9]	15	4	49	1951
Switzerland[5]	21,700	4.60	--	--	23	23	55	1948
Turkey[6]	40,400	1.93	--[9]	--	14	--[9]	86	1928
United Kingdom[6]	221,500	4.53	--[9]	--[8]	14	--	84	by 1923
United States[4]	1,204,073	7.47	3	7	9	9	72	1941

[1] 1950 except for France (1949), the Netherlands (1956), Portugal (1947), and Russia (1940).
[2] Percentages may not sum to 100 percent due to rounding into whole numbers.
[3] Includes cigarillos.
[4] Manufacture.
[5] Sales.
[6] Consumption.
[7] Recorded sales only; does not include tobacco grown and consumed locally.
[8] The sources report the use of a small but unspecified amount of chewing tobacco.
[9] Less than 0.5 percent.
[10] Includes paper-wrapped cigarettes (12 percent) and tobacco-wrapped bidis (22 percent); see Section 7.3.
[11] Virtually all this pipe tobacco is fine-cut.

At least in the case of tobacco, moreover, the amount of advertising and promotion does not directly affect consumer preferences. Thus, the same changes take place at about the same rate both in countries with competitive market systems and in countries with state monopolies. Almost always, when a new product—cigars in Austria in the 1850s or cigarettes in the United States in the 1910s—is introduced, its sales grow very rapidly. After a few years, the product will have been tried and adopted by the comparatively small number of consumers that either are adventurous in trying new things or that are responsive to changes in fashion. Henceforth, sales either grow at a much slower rate or decline as quickly if this product proves not to appeal to the fundamental habits of the nation.

Tobacco habits thus change slowly, but they do vary over time. When evidence is lacking, it would be foolish to read current patterns back into the past. Just before World War I, for example, chewing tobacco formed about 14 percent of all sales in England, and snuff represented a comparable portion of the Italian market (Tables 6.2 and 6.14). Through the accidents of history, we have nineteenth-century sources from Italy but not from the United Kingdom. The Italian data show that snuff provided more than half of all sales in the northern regions fifty years earlier—precisely what we would expect assuming that the normal growth rate is plus or minus 2 percent a year. If we had comparable evidence from the nineteenth century for England, these sources conceivably might show that chewing tobacco had been as widely used in some regions of that nation as snuff was in Venetia.

6.2 SCANDINAVIA: SUMMARY

Table 6.5 ranks the eleven Western nations with the highest consumption of smokeless tobacco in proportion to sales of all manufactured tobacco products.

Table 6.5
Smokeless Tobacco Products as a Percentage of Total Tobacco Production or Sales

	1880 [1]	1900	1913	1925 [2]	1950 [3]
Sweden	80%	83%	78%	71%	32%
Norway	--	--	53	50	18
Iceland	--	--	--	35	17
Canada	--	--	--	31	4
United States	57	47	34	23	10
Denmark	--	38	25	24	4
Australia	--	--	--	11	9
France	21	16	14	9	3
United Kingdom	--	--	15	8	--
Italy	21	16	9	7	2
Germany	9	--	12	5	2

[1] 1880 except for France (1885) and Germany (1878–1879).
[2] 1925 except for Iceland (1932) and Australia (1936–1937).
[3] 1950 except for Australia (1949–1950) and France (1949).

As it indicates, smokeless products historically have been most prevalent in the Scandinavian countries of Sweden, Norway, and Iceland; although the Danes, like their German neighbors to the south, primarily have tended to smoke, chewing tobacco has been used by a comparatively larger minority than in most European countries. These four states are culturally homogeneous, geographically contiguous, and from time to time have been united under one crown. Nevertheless, one cannot assume an ethnic propensity to snuff or to chew tobacco. The Finns, who share the same climate and traditions and have been separated from Sweden only since 1815, use comparatively few smokeless products (Tables 6.2 through 6.4).

Moreover, although the Scandinavians are comparatively more likely than others to use tobacco orally, they have differed significantly over the years in choosing between oral snuff and pressed plug. Like the Swedes, the Icelanders primarily have used fine-cut or powdered snuff. The Danes, in contrast, have gone along with Americans and Canadians in choosing pressed plug. At the beginning of this century, the Norwegians also tended to prefer chewing tobacco. After 1925, however, sales of plug fell in Norway while those of oral snuff remained stable; by 1950 snuff was more popular in Norway than in any other country except Sweden.

Although our records from the other three Scandinavian countries begin later than those from Sweden, consumption patterns again tend to be relatively stable over time, and it is likely that these patterns already were established during the nineteenth century. In recent years, as in other countries, cigarettes have tended to replace all other tobacco products—with a concomitant increase in per capita consumption. Perhaps because of their penchant for oral smokeless products, however, the Scandinavians have adopted the cigarette habit more slowly than the residents of other regions; the Norwegians were the very last of the industrialized nations to take up cigarettes, which captured 50 percent of the market decades later than in most other countries.

6.2.1 Norway

As Table 6.6 indicates, the Norwegians have been among the most loyal consumers of smokeless products, which represented more than half of all sales in 1913 and which continued to take about 20 percent of the market in 1950. They also are distinguished, even among the Scandinavians, by the slowness with which they have adopted the cigarette. The residents of Norway thus ranked third, after the Swedes and inhabitants of the United States, in consumption of smokeless products. And, as shown in Table 6.4, the Norwegians were the very last of the industrialized nations to take up cigarettes—which had captured less than 50 percent of the market as late as the 1970s.

Overall, with a per capita consumption of about three pounds a year, the Norwegians are moderate users of tobacco products. Economic conditions have had a large effect on demand, which shows a substantial decline during the

Table 6.6
Tobacco Products Manufactured in Norway, 1909 and 1916, and Consumed in Norway, 1913 and 1920–1950

	Thousands of U.S Pounds						Percent of Total Sales				
	Snuff²	Chewing²	Cut³	Cigars⁴	Cigarettes	Total	Snuff	Chewing²	Cut³	Cigars⁴	Cigarettes
1885	14,519	2,701	52,811	7,993	1,952	79,977	18%	3%	66%	10%	2%
1892	12,076	2,717	55,612	7,209	2,367	79,981	15	3	70	9	3
1900	10,843	2,504	61,148	6,350	3,971	84,814	13	3	72	8	5
1910	10,557	2,537	66,050	5,220	7,166	91,529	12	3	72	6	8
1913	10,395	2,530	69,561	5,717	8,926	97,128	11	3	72	6	9
1920	7,366	2,407	74,752	5,410	12,004	101,928	7	2	74	5	12
1925	8,502	2,318	80,609	3,440	23,368	118,297	7	2	68	3	20
1930	6,205	2,254	73,370	2,955	39,382	124,166	5	2	60	2	32
1938	3,473	1,720	65,291	735	40,742	111,962	3	2	58	1	36
1949	1,729	1,419	50,976	949	62,109	117,139	2	1	44	1	53

[1] "Skråtobakk."
[2] "Røyktobakk."
[3] Includes cigarillos.
[4] Percentgaes may not sum to 100 percent due to rounding into whole numbers.

Sources: Norway, Statistisk Sentralalbyrå, *Norges Offisielle Statistikk, Norges Industri, Fabriktelling* (1909); *Produksjonsstatistikk* (1916). Hutson, *Consumption and Production of Tobacco in Europe* (1913, 1920–1930); Lee, *Tobacco Consumption in Various Countries* (1940–1950).

1930s and a slow but steady increase since World War II. Although small amounts of foreign brands (including smokeless products) continued to be imported, Norwegian industry has provided a full range of manufactured tobacco since World War I, and the government has encouraged self-sufficiency by maintaining the tariff on imported tobacco at a much higher level than that on imported leaf. Since overall consumption is stable and governmental regulation does not discriminate among domestic products, the demand for smoking and smokeless tobacco is primarily affected by changes in consumer preferences.

Toward the end of the 1920s, some Norwegians began to prefer the lighter flue-cured tobaccos to the darker types, and sales of smoking tobacco and cigarettes tended to increase at the expense of pressed chewing tobacco.[2] As in Sweden, some of the snuff purchased in Norway is consumed orally instead of being inhaled. To some extent, therefore, the continuing fall in demand for plug also represents a shift to oral snuff. Although demand for snuff also declined during the economic depression of the 1930s, Norwegians subsequently returned to the use of oral snuff but not to plug. Indeed, as Table 6.6 shows, at more than 1 million pounds, snuff sales were slightly higher in 1950 than in 1913. And, with 11 percent of the overall market in 1950, oral snuff remained more popular in Norway than in any other country except Sweden.

6.2.2 Iceland

The small nation of Iceland was under Norwegian suzerainty from the 1260s, passed with Norway under the Swedish crown from 1380 to 1918, and gained full sovereignty only in 1944. Given the close cultural and economic as well as political ties uniting them to the Scandinavian states, it is not surprising that Icelanders also share similar tobacco habits. When separate records for Iceland become available in 1932, its inhabitants were second only to the Swedes and Norwegians in their consumption of smokeless tobacco, primarily in the form of oral snuff. In 1932, as summarized in Table 6.7, snuff thus represented about a third (35 percent) of all sales in Iceland—less than in Sweden (60 percent in 1930) but about equal to the proportion of total consumption represented by smokeless products in Norway (40 percent in 1930).

In 1932, cigarette consumption in Iceland already was higher than in Norway or Sweden, and cigarette sales continued to increase in subsequent years. At 80,000 pounds a year, sales of snuff were almost exactly the same in 1950 as in 1932. But because of population growth and the rise in per capita cigarette consumption during those years, by 1950 snuff represented only 17 percent of all sales compared to 35 percent a year earlier.

As in other countries, the rise in cigarette smoking in Iceland was accompanied by a significant increase in per capita consumption. And since the sales of all other products were stable, almost all the overall increase in the demand for tobacco can be attributed to cigarettes. As Table 6.7 shows, total tobacco consumption doubled during these eighteen years while cigarette consumption

Table 6.7
Consumption of Tobacco Products in Iceland, 1932–1950

	Thousands of U.S Pounds					Percent of Total			
	Snuff	Cut	Cigars[2]	Cigar-ettes	Total[3]	Per Head	Snuff	Cut	Cigars[2]	Cigar-ettes
1932	80	40	10	80	230	2.09	35%	17%	4%	35%
1940	40	70	10	120	250	2.07	16	28	4	48
1945	70	30	10	250	370	2.85	19	8	3	68
1950	80	50	20	330	480	2.99	17	10	4	69

[1] Percentages may not sum to 100 percent due to rounding into whole numbers.
[2] Includes cigarillos.
[3] Included in the total amount is a small amount—not specified in the sources—of pressed chewing tobacco.

Source: Lee, *Tobacco Consumption in Various Countries.*

increased threefold. Even when population gains are taken into account, higher cigarette sales led in turn to a rise in per capita consumption of more than 40 percent in only eighteen years—a rate of growth rarely found in an industrialized country.

6.2.3 Denmark

By the end of the nineteenth century, tobacco habits were relatively fixed. Although certain exceptions can be identified, consistent regional patterns had been established that are slow to change. Scandinavian consumers thus were fairly moderate users of tobacco and preferred smokeless products while residents of the German empire tended both to smoke and to consume greater amounts overall. Denmark, which historically has joined the Scandinavian states to Germany, would seem to show a mix of both regional patterns. The Danish records also provide additional evidence for the consistency over time of consumer habits. As Table 6.2 indicates, for example, the Danes already purchased more than four pounds of tobacco on average in 1913, with per capita consumption gradually rising to almost six pounds a year by 1950—at least a third more each year than their neighbors to the north.

When the Danish records begin in 1897, cut smoking tobacco represented about half of all manufactured products. At one-third of production, smokeless products were the choice of a minority that was much larger than in most countries although comparatively smaller than in Sweden or Norway (see Table 6.5). Throughout the twentieth century, cigars and later cigarettes gradually replaced the pipe, with an accompanying increase in per capita consumption. As is normally the case, however, this change in preferences took several decades to accomplish, and smokeless products were particularly slow to lose market share. At about 3 million pounds, sales of snuff and chewing tobacco were slightly higher in 1930 than in 1913, and almost 2 million pounds of smokeless products were sold as late as 1950 (Table 6.8). The substantial rise in cigarette consumption, particularly in the 1940s, may thus represent the addition to the market of new smokers rather than a shift by existing consumers away from smokeless products.

Although sales of smokeless tobacco remained stable or declined overall during the first half of this century, the demand for snuff in particular has increased in Denmark. As discussed in Chapter 4, a sharp decline in sales of pressed plug occurred in Austria, France, and Sweden during the nineteenth century that was substantially complete by 1850. Since the Danish records begin only in 1897, we do not know whether a similar shift away from plug also had taken place in that country. Whether this evolution represents a continuation of earlier trends, sales of pressed tobacco have fallen substantially since 1913. At the same time, as summarized in Table 6.9 production and sales of snuff have risen more than five times during the same years. By 1950, powdered and cut tobaccos thus met more than three-fourths of the total demand for smokeless products.

6.3 NORTH AMERICA: SUMMARY

During the nineteenth century, European visitors commented—usually unfavorably—on the fondness of those in the United States for chewing tobacco.[3] In fact, as Table 6.5 indicates, smokeless tobacco represented a larger portion of total sales in Scandinavia; plug in particular took a smaller share of the total market in the United States (18 percent in 1925) than in Norway (34 percent; see Table 6.4). Moreover, these critics might have added that certain kinds of smoking tobacco, such as cigars, also were more widely used in the United States than in many European nations. In a sense, however, these European writers were on the mark. Chewing tobacco must have been more noticeable in the United States than elsewhere because those Americans that used it used more of it, and per capita consumption was higher than in Norway or Denmark. Even though they now largely have abandoned chewing tobacco for cigarettes, Americans have been and remain the most enthusiastic users of tobacco in the Western world. While consumption has increased as cigarettes have replaced smokeless products, it already was higher than in other countries when accurate records became common at the end of the nineteenth century (Table 6.1).

The overriding story of the fifty years between 1900 and 1950 is the gradual replacement by cigarettes of most other tobacco products. Cigarette consumption in the United States rose dramatically during the 1910s and increased steadily in every subsequent decade. At first, sales of chewing tobacco, cigars, and pipe tobacco increased along with those of cigarettes. Because of rapid population growth, the plug industry especially prospered, and the all-time record for production (206 million pounds) was not reached until 1917. But per capita consumption of chewing tobacco had already reached its peak in 1880. After 1925,

Table 6.8
Tobacco Products Manufactured in Denmark, 1897, 1907, 1920, 1925, and 1950, and Consumed in Denmark, 1913 and 1930–1940[1]

Thousands of U.S Pounds[1]

	Snuff[2]	Chewing[3]	Cut[4]	Cigars[5]	Cigar-ettes	Total
1897	660	3,086	4,519	1,706	28	9,999
1907	110	2,734	4,795	3,113	3	10,755
1913	327	2,618	4,613	3,419	691	11,688
1920	551	3,270	5,963	4,613	2,329	16,726
1925	717	2,626	4,442	3,399	3,028	14,212
1930	829	2,121	5,106	4,448	3,629	16,133
1940	1,109	1,266	5,717	5,231	4,570	17,893
1950	1,098	926	5,648	6,601	11,101	25,374

Percent of Total[6]

	Per Head	Snuff[2]	Chew-ing[3]	Cut[4]	Cigars[5]	Cigar-ettes
1897	4.17	7%	31%	45%	17%	--[7]
1907	4.15	1	25	45	29	--[7]
1913	4.24	2	23	40	30	6
1920	5.12	3	20	36	28	14
1925	4.32	5	19	31	24	21
1930	4.54	5	13	32	28	23
1940	4.66	6	7	32	29	26
1950	5.93	--[7]	4	22	26	44

Source: Produktionsstatistik for the years cited as reported in the respective volumes of the *Statistiske Meddelelser* (Denmark, Statistiske Department).

the population did not increase sufficiently to offset the effects of decreasing consumption per capita, and the trend in overall sales of chewing tobacco (and also of cigars and cut tobacco) has been almost continuously downward (Table 6.10). As in other countries, changes in tobacco habits tend to be gradual, and the decline in sales of chewing tobacco in any one year often was quite small. Nevertheless, the cumulative change from 1880 to 1950 is dramatic, with chewing tobacco falling during those years from more than 50 percent of total sales to less than 10 percent (Table 6.10).[4]

Consumption of snuff has been more stable over time than that of pressed tobacco. As a consequence, although snuff sales were only a small fraction of plug sales in 1880, snuff had by 1950 almost overtaken pressed chewing tobacco to become the best selling smokeless product in the United States (Table 6.12). At the same time, this change really represents the substitution of one oral product for another. As in Sweden (and in contrast to France or Italy), most snuff in the United States has been used orally rather than being inhaled through the nose. Given the absence of quantitative evidence before 1880, we cannot establish precisely when snuff first came to be used as an oral product in the United States. However, literary evidence suggests that Southerners have taken it in this way at least since the middle of the nineteenth century and perhaps during the eighteenth. As indicated above, the Swedes and other Scandinavians also began to use snuff orally during the same years. Given the small number of Swedes migrating to Georgia or West Virginia, it would be difficult to trace a direct connection between Scandinavia and the Confederacy; and the practice most likely arose spontaneously in the two regions that historically have witnessed the highest consumption of oral snuff.[5]

When sources from that country become available in 1920, Canadians were to be found among those with a particular fondness for chewing tobacco. Al-

---

Notes to Table 6.8

[1]These tables summarize for the years cited either production or tax-paid consumption as reported by the Danish government's statistical bureau; the single exception is 1913, for which the statistical bureau cites production and consumption of cigars, cigarillos, and cigarettes in 1,000 pieces. As indicated by Lee (*Tobacco Consumption*, p. 23), the following conversion factors have been used to calculate the weight of these products for those years: 1,000 cigars equals 11 pounds; 1,000 cigarillos equals 5.5 pounds; 1,000 cigarettes equals 2.75 pounds. For 1913, the government reports total consumption (production plus imports less exports) of each product already converted into kilograms.

[2]Products the statistical bureau lists as intended for consumption as nasal snuff, including both "snustobak" and "spunden snustobak."

[3]Products listed as intended for oral use, including both pressed "skråtobak" and cut "kardus-skrå."

[4]"Røgtobak."

[5]Includes cigarillos.

[6]Percentages may not sum to 100 percent due to rounding into whole numbers.

[7]Less than 0.5 percent.

[8]From 1921, includes the part of Schleswig acquired from Germany in that year.

Table 6.9
Smokeless Tobacco Products Manufactured in Denmark, 1913–1950

| | Thousands of U.S. Pounds | | | | | Percent of Total Products[5] | | | | Percent of | |
| | Snuff | | "Chewing Tobacco" | | | Snuff | | Chewing Tobacco | | Chewing Tobacco | |
	Powder[1]	Twist[2]	Plug[3]	Cut[4]	Total	Powder[1]	Twist[2]	Plug[3]	Cut[4]	Plug[3]	Cut[4]
1913	221	34	1,786	1,034	3,075	7%	1%	58%	34%	63%	37%
1920	428	124	1,951	1,391	3,894	11	3	50	36	58	42
1925	717	--	1,349	1,277	3,343	22	--	40	38	49	51
1930	829	--	975	1,147	2,951	28	--	33	39	46	54
1940	1,109	--	650	620	2,379	47	--	27	26	51	49
1950	1,098	--	540	386	2,024	54	--	27	19	58	42

[1] "Snustobak."

[2] "Spunden snustobak."

[3] "Skråtobak."

[4] "Kardusskrå."

[5] Percentages may not sum to 100 percent due to rounding into whole numbers.

Source: Produktionsstatistik for the years cited as reported in the respective volumes of the *Statistiske Meddelelser* (Denmark, Statistiske Department).

though it formed a smaller portion of tobacco sales than in the United States, chewing tobacco was considerably more popular in Canada than in England or France. As it has in other countries, chewing tobacco consumption fell steadily between 1920 and 1950; snuff, in contrast, has continued to enjoy relatively small but consistent sales during these three decades. As plug fell from favor, pipe tobacco became the most popular form of smoking tobacco among Canadians. Cigars have been comparatively little used, and cigarette consumption has risen only since the 1940s.

6.3.1 The United States

Compared to other Western nations, the United States forms a uniquely large market for consumer products, including tobacco. As reported in Table 6.10, U.S. manufacturers produced almost 200 million pounds of tobacco products in 1880, and total production rose to more than 1 trillion pounds by 1950. Only the German empire provided a market of comparable size in 1880, and the breakup of that empire in 1945 left no European market equal to that of the United States. (See Tables 6.1 through 6.4; if the European states carry through their current schemes of economic unification, their manufacturers will ultimately have a domestic market comparable to the United States.) It is thus somewhat imprecise to compare consumption in the United States to that in a smaller state such as Sweden, whose industries produced only one-twentieth the quantity of tobacco products made in the former nation.

Although they can provide useful insights, we must also be careful in making comparisons to European states that are ethnically and culturally more homogeneous. Because of its enormous expanse, the United States is, like the Habsburg regime prior to 1918, comprised of a congeries of races that speak many languages, practice scores of religions, and remain loyal to widely variant cultural norms. Undoubtedly, for example, there are regions in the United States whose citizens enjoy snuff in quantities equal to those consumed by the Swedes, just as there must be other regions where the per capita consumption of cigars is higher than in Germany or the Netherlands. Unfortunately, however, the U.S. government does not publish regional statistics on tobacco consumption, and these exceptional cases are thus caught up in the aggregated totals.

At the same time, because of the relatively more competitive nature of the U.S. tobacco industry, these aggregated national records may measure consumer preferences as accurately as those of the European monopolies, even when the latter offer greater detail. If America undoubtedly contains several regional markets, the demands of those markets have been met by several national producers that respond to large-scale changes in consumer tastes. When accurate records begin in 1880, the tobacco industry was entering a period both of rapid mechanization and also of increasing concentration, with both trends continuing into the twentieth century. From 1890 to 1910, the tobacco trust controlled the output of more than three-fourths of all manufactured products

Table 6.10
Tobacco Products Manufactured in the United States, 1880–1950[1]

Thousands of U.S Pounds[1]

	Snuff	Plug[2]	Cut[3]	Cigars[4]	Cigar-ettes[5]	Total
1880	3,977	107,169	35,283	46,680	1,175	194,284
1890	9,435	173,616	69,829	78,651	5,524	337,055
1900	13,805	185,354	101,548	114,884	7,186	422,777
1910	31,445	201,791	214,056	147,465	19,445	614,202
1920	34,349	150,329	219,271	162,378	104,645	670,972
1925	37,841	128,292	247,740	128,531	181,393	723,797
1930	40,766	98,987	232,013	116,752	273,000	761,518
1940	37,900	101,400[6]	205,100	99,900	417,600	861,900
1950	39,992	87,466[7]	107,732	104,619	864,264	1,204,073

Percent of Total Products[8]

	Snuff	Plug[2]	Cut[3]	Cigars[4]	Cigar-ettes[5]
1880	2%	55%	18%	24%	1%
1890	3	52	21	23	2
1900	3	44	24	27	2
1910	5	33	35	24	3
1920	5	22	33	24	16
1925	5	18	34	18	25
1930	5	13	31	15	36
1940	4	12[9]	24	12	49
1950	3	7[9]	9	9	72

Sources: United States, Department of Agriculture: *First Annual Report on Tobacco Statistics,* p. 90 (1880–1930), and *Annual Report on Tobacco Statistics, 1952* (1950). Gage, *American Tobacco Types, Uses and Markets,* p. 112 (1940).

except cigars;[6] since the trust's breakup, half a dozen companies have continued to manufacture most of the products consumed in the United States.[7]

Several independent companies inherently are more responsive to consumer demands than the European monopolies that control the only legal source of tobacco. U.S. companies have competed in marketing, in advertising, and in introducing new products; during the first decades of this century, they sometimes also competed on price, cutting the cost of their products to capture market share. This more competitive industry has had several consequences. The U.S. consumer has spent a smaller proportion of his or her daily wage for the better-quality products. Unlike the state monopolies, U.S. companies have spent heavily on advertising and promotion, and they also have been quicker to introduce new products. It is logical to assume that those products with high sales probably are what many consumers want, even if they may be more popular in some regions than in others.

As described in Chapter 3, all the tobacco products consumed today in the United States already existed in a recognizable form by the middle of the nineteenth century. But the years between 1880 and 1910 witnessed the rapid mechanization of the industry, with the consequent introduction of more uniform and sometimes improved products as well as an overall reduction in prices. During the 1890s, the plug industry saw the introduction both of machines that could produce more than two hundred pieces an hour and also of a more intense and consistent sweetener in the form of saccharin.[8] A fully automatic machine to make cigarettes similarly was patented in 1881 and was widely adopted; only in the case of cigars was mechanization delayed, with the shift to machine manufacture not occurring until the 1930s.[9]

Prior to 1950, per capita tobacco consumption in the United States went through three main cycles. As summarized in Table 6.10, total production rap-

---

Notes to Table 6.10

[1] Following Lee (*Tobacco Consumption*, p. 84), these conversion factors consistently have been used to calculate the weight of cigars and cigarettes, which the Bureau of Internal Revenue reports in 1,000 pieces: 1,000 cigars equal 18.6 pounds; 1,000 cigarettes equal 2.205 pounds.

[2] Includes "plug" and smaller amounts of "twist" and "fine-cut" tobacco that are reported as intended for use as chewing tobacco; see Table 5.12.

[3] Prior to 1931, the Revenue Bureau's reports included "scrap tobacco" under "smoking tobacco"; beginning with 1931, scrap tobacco has been reported under chewing tobacco together with plug, twist, and fine-cut. By including all scrap with smoking tobacco in earlier years, the bureau consistently overstated the manufacture of smoking tobacco and understated that of chewing tobacco by a factor that now cannot be measured.

[4] From 1897, includes small cigars or cigarillos.

[5] Prior to 1897, includes small cigars or cigarillos.

[6] Includes 42,900 scrap tobacco.

[7] Includes 39,098 scrap tobacco.

[8] Percentages may not sum to 100 percent due to rounding into whole numbers.

[9] Includes scrap tobacco.

Table 6.11

Per Capita Consumption of Tobacco Products in the United States, 1880–1950

	Number		U.S. Pounds[1]					
	Cigars	Cigar-ettes	Snuff	Plug[2,3]	Cut[4]	Cigars	Cigar-ettes	Total
1900	70	35	0.20	2.64	1.06	1.31	0.08	5.29
1910	77	94	0.34	2.71	1.76	1.43	0.21	6.45
1920	80	419	0.34	2.05	1.36	1.49	0.93	6.17
1925	60	696	0.33	1.79	1.45	1.12	1.54	6.23
1930	50	972	0.33	1.35	1.32	.93	2.14	6.07
1940	42	1,370	0.29	0.78	1.53	.79	3.02	6.41
1950	37	2,479	0.26	.57	.69	.69	5.26	7.47

[1] The weight of cigars and cigarettes has been calculated using the conversion factors: cited in Note 1 to Table 6.10.

[2] Includes "plug" and smaller amounts of "twist" and "fine-cut" tobacco that were reported as intended for use as chewing tobacco; see Table 6.12.

[3] Includes Gage's estimate for the years 1900 to 1930 of the amount of scrap chewing tobacco, which the government reported under "smoking tobacco" prior to 1931; see Note 3 to Table 6.10.

[4] Estimated consumption has been reduced by the amount of scrap tobacco estimated to have been used for chewing products rather than smoking products; see previous note.

Sources: Gage, *American Tobacco Types, Uses and Markets,* p. 115 (1880–1940); United States, Department of Agriculture, *Annual Report on Tobacco Statistics, 1952* (1950).

idly increased from 1880 to 1910. In large part, this increase responded to the rapid population growth and succeeding waves of emigration during these years as well as a significant rise in per capita consumption (see Table 6.11) between 1900 and 1910. Between the two world wars, production stabilized as emigration ceased; and per capita consumption actually declined during the 1930s, reflecting the economic depression during that decade. A new period of growth in both production and consumption then began during World War II. Reflecting these trends in the overall demand for tobacco, production of every type of product also rose phenomenally between 1880 and 1890. Since World War I, the overriding trend, during both good times and bad, has been a shift to cigarettes at the expense of every other type of manufactured product—except for oral snuff.

When accurate records began in 1880 (Table 6.10), pressed or plug chewing tobacco, with more than half (55 percent) of all sales, was unquestionably the most popular product, followed by cigars (24 percent) and cut pipe mixtures (18 percent).[10] Even though cigarettes had been available for perhaps twenty years, their national sales in 1880 were still insignificant, amounting to only 1 percent of all manufactured tobacco.[11] Between 1880 and 1910, as Table 6.10 shows, production of plug declined in relation to the total market; whereas chewing tobacco represented more than half of all production in 1880, its share had fallen to about a third by 1910. Plug production crested during these years because sales of other forms of tobacco grew at a more rapid rate. A particularly sharp increase was recorded in the production of snuff, which grew a remarkable 700 percent from 1880 to 1910. With other products becoming more popular after 1880, the per capita consumption of plug never again reached the 2.8 pounds estimated for that year; nevertheless, because chewing tobacco began with a larger market, the all-time record for production was not set until 1917, when 206 million pounds were produced.[12]

A turning point in preferences occurred during or just prior to World War I. In 1910, for example, manufacturers produced more than 200 million pounds of chewing tobacco (Table 6.10) to meet the demand of a population that used, on average, about two and three-quarters of a pound each year (Table 6.11). Per capita consumption of both smoking tobacco and cigars were also near their high points just before World War I. In contrast, although total production of cigarettes had risen, U.S. consumers still smoked fewer than two cigarettes each week.

The rise of the cigarette during this century thus began during the decade of the 1910s.[13] Since 1920, while the rate of growth has been slower, cigarette consumption has continued to rise. By 1950, cigarettes comprised about three-fourths of all tobacco products made in the United States, and U.S. citizens smoked, on average, more than fifty each week. Many reasons have been advanced for the sudden adoption of the cigarette habit during this decade. Some have suggested that consumers switched from other forms of tobacco to cigarettes because the latter were better suited to the quick pace of life in the industrialized cities. Others attribute the boom in cigarettes to the acceptance of smoking by women. And aggressive advertising in the new mass media—newspapers, magazines, and later radio—also has been credited with forcing up demand.[14] While all these factors may have played a part, a more obvious explanation lies in the introduction of cigarettes with blends that imitated chewing tobacco by primarily including the lighter Burley rather than Oriental tobaccos. Plug chewing tobacco, the most popular product prior to 1910, was now made almost exclusively of the Bright and Burley tobaccos, and the new blended cigarette brands may be said to have responded to established tastes.[15]

In analyzing changes in the composition of tobacco sales during almost two centuries in regions as diverse as France, Central Europe, and Sweden, we have found that tobacco preferences normally change very slowly over the near term. (In the longer run, preferences are highly volatile as small changes accumulate over time.) With the exceptions that have been noted, most consumers tend to be strongly fixed not only in their choice of a product but even in their preference for a particular quality of product. And this stability in consumer habits is also present in the United States. Although cigarette sales jumped between 1910 and 1920 and increased steadily between 1920 and 1950, consumption of other products declined at a relatively slow rate. Indeed, because of population growth, total production continued to increase for up to twenty years after the change in preferences that is signaled by the per capita consumption data.

As we have seen, total production of chewing tobacco peaked in 1917, two decades after per capita consumption began to drop. After 1925, the population did not increase sufficiently to offset the effects of decreasing consumption per capita, and overall sales have tended to drop.[16] Total production (approximately equivalent to consumption) of chewing tobacco thus fell to under 50 million pounds in 1950—less than a forth of the record amount in 1917.[17] Although the decline in production of smoking tobacco and cigars was less precipitous, production of each in 1950 was less than half the record totals reached in 1920 and 1925. In a country with as large a consumer market as the United States, these shifts in preference from other forms to cigarettes are especially noticeable, but they must be kept in perspective. As these statistics again demonstrate, tobacco consumption does not fluctuate wildly. On an annualized basis, the decline each year amounts to a loss of about 3 percent for plug. In planning for the coming year, a manufacturer could thus count on selling about as much as the year before (or even more, if the firm succeeded in increasing its share of the overall market).

Moreover, because so much tobacco is sold each year in the United States, even the small portion of that market now taken by chewing tobacco is significant. As Table 6.4 shows, for example, U.S. sales of chewing tobacco may have fallen dramatically from their peak three decades earlier, but they were still larger than the total sales of all tobacco products in every European country except West Germany, France, and the United Kingdom. Similarly, although snuff represented a large portion of Swedish tobacco consumption and only 3 percent of the U.S. market, that 3 percent amounts to about twice the total sales of all tobacco in Sweden.

Powdered snuff, one of the very oldest, has also been one of the most resilient products. As shown in Table 6.11, per capita consumption increased significantly between 1880 and 1910, and it remained relatively stable at about a third of a pound each year until 1931. Since the 1930s, per capita consumption of snuff has fallen very slowly to about a quarter of a pound. Taking into account a larger population, total production of 40 million pounds in 1950 was only 1 million pounds less than the all-time record set in 1929. As Table 6.12 suggests, by 1950 snuff virtually had overtaken pressed plug as the best-selling form of smokeless tobacco. As in Sweden, Norway, and Denmark, much if not all of the snuff purchased in the United States since the 1830s has been moist, oral snuff. Rather than inhaling it into the nose, the user places the product in the mouth behind the lower lip.[18]

6.3.2 Canada

Although Canadians sometimes worry that their economy and culture will be swallowed up by those of their larger neighbor to the south, in tobacco consumption at least their preferences consistently have differed from those of U.S. consumers—and also from those of the British and the French. When independent records began in 1920, as Table 6.5 indicates, a greater portion of

Table 6.12
Smokeless Tobacco Products Manufactured in the United States, 1880–1950

	Percent of Total Products				
			"Chewing Tobacco"		
	Snuff	Plug	Twist[1]	Fine-cut	Scrap[2]
1880	2%	88%	--%	10%	--%
1890	5	85	--	10	--
1900	7	87	--	6	--
1910	14	75	6	6	--
1920	18	72	6	5	--
1930	29	62	6	4	--
1940	27	35	4	3	31
1950	31	32	4	2	31

[1] Prior to 1903, included in plug tobacco.
[2] Prior to 1931, included in smoking tobacco.

Sources: United States, Department of Agriculture: *First Annual Report on Tobacco Statistics,* p. 90 (1880–1930), and *Annual Report on Tobacco Statistics, 1952* (1950), Gage, *American Tobacco Types, Uses, and Markets,* p. 112 (1940).

tobacco was consumed by Canadians in the form of chewing products than in any other country outside Scandinavia and the United States. Plug thus comprised about a fifth of all sales (22 percent)—significantly less than in the United States (34 percent), but much higher than in Britain (7 percent) or France (2 percent). During the three decades between 1920 and 1950, plug consumption fell sharply from 22 to only 2 percent of all sales (Table 6.13); because of population growth, the quantity sold declined somewhat less dramatically, from more than 6 to only about 2 million pounds (Table 6.13). While chewing tobacco thus has been in rapid decline, snuff has continued to enjoy relatively small but consistent sales of about a million pounds a year throughout these three decades.

As chewing fell from favor, Canadians were slower to adopt cigarettes than either Americans or Britons, and they were more likely to take up the pipe. Until World War II, cut tobacco was the most popular product in Canada, and cigars were comparatively little used. Indeed, smoking tobacco gained in popularity during the 1930s, perhaps because of the economic depression, and the cigarette habit has increased in Canada only since the 1940s. As has also been the case in many other countries, the switch from smokeless products to smoking tobacco has been accompanied by a significant increase in per capita usage.[19]

6.4 OTHER EUROPEAN STATES AND AUSTRALIA: SUMMARY

For the reasons described in Chapter 1, many governments have provided statistical evidence about tobacco consumption in most nations only during this

Table 6.13

Consumption of Tobacco Products in Canada, 1920–1950

| | Thousands of U.S Pounds | | | | | | | Percent of Total Consumption[2] | | | | |
	Snuff	Plug	Cut	Cigars[1]	Cigar-ettes	Total	Per Head	Snuff	Plug	Cut	Cigars[1]	Cigar-ettes
1920	700	6,600	14,100	3,400	5,900	30,700	3.53	2%	22%	46%	11%	19%
1925	800	8,500	12,200	2,200	6,800	30,500	3.28	3	28	40	7	22
1930	1,000	8,500	12,200	2,200	12,100	36,000	3.61	3	24	34	6	34
1940	800	3,100	25,500	2,100	18,200	49,700	4.36	2	6	51	4	37
1950	900	2,300	25,900	2,500	41,200	72,800	5.31	1	2	36	3	57

[1] Includes cigarillos.

[2] Percentages may not sum to 100 percent due to rounding into whole numbers.

Source: Lee, Tobacco Consumption in Various Countries.

century. As Chapter 5 indicates, nasal snuff was widely used in most European states into the nineteenth century. By the time these official governmental records begin, however, most Europeans were smokers. By 1900, cut smoking tobacco was the best-selling product almost everywhere, and cigars were only a distant second to the pipe.[20] Cigarettes ultimately replaced the pipe as the most popular way of using tobacco; they were adopted most rapidly in the United Kingdom and in Central Europe, while the residents of Germany and the Netherlands were among the last in Europe to make the switch from pipes and cigars.

With the notable exceptions of Scandinavia and the United States, sales of smokeless tobacco thus have been smaller than those of smoking products since the end of the nineteenth century. Nevertheless, both chewing tobacco and snuff have been enjoyed in every European country. In Western Europe prior to World War I, chewing tobacco was particularly prevalent in the United Kingdom (where it formed 14 percent of all sales in 1913), in Germany (6 percent of all sales), and in the British dominion of Australia. As is also true in North America, consumption of plug tobacco fell in these nations between the two world wars. Although initially smaller, demand for snuff has been more stable, and snuff actually outsold plug in West Germany by 1950. In Eastern and Central Europe, highly restrictive governmental policies make it more difficult to evaluate consumer preferences. Nevertheless, while they primarily have been smokers, Central Europeans also have used chewing tobacco and snuff, albeit in comparatively limited amounts compared to the inhabitants of North America and the more industrialized nations in Western Europe.

6.4.1 The United Kingdom

Because they taxed imported tobacco leaf at the same rate regardless of the purpose for which it was used, British governments did not keep records of internal domestic tobacco consumption. Beginning in 1907, the government at irregular intervals has conducted censuses of domestic manufacturing production; given the high import duties on manufactured tobacco, it is likely that domestic production approximates consumption. In 1907, as in some subsequent years, however, the value of the census is reduced because it reports production of cut smoking tobacco together with that of pressed plug under the catchall rubric "other manufactured tobacco." Although snuff had taken more than half the market in 1800, the majority of British tobacco consumers were smokers when detailed governmental records began in 1913. Initially, cut tobacco was preferred, but cigarettes were adopted relatively early; cigars always comprised a much smaller portion of tobacco consumption than in Europe or the United States.[21]

Indeed, with 14 percent of sales, pressed chewing tobacco was third in sales in 1913, and it was more widely used in the United Kingdom in 1913 than were cigars. As has also been the case in the United States and Canada, con-

Table 6.14
Consumption of Tobacco Products in the United Kingdom, 1909–1950[1]

	Thousands of U.S Pounds						Per Head	Percent of Total Products[2]				
	Snuff	Chewing	Cut[3]	Cigars[2]	Cigar-ettes	Total		Snuff	Chew-ing	Cut[4]	Cigars[3]	Cigar-ettes
1907	1,198	---{62,126}[3]---		4,833	29,568	97,725	2.54	1%	-(64%)-[4]		5%	30%
1913	956	13,374	46,015	4,796	32,325	97,466	2.38	1	14	47	5	33
1920	500	14,029	56,117	3,007	69,145	142,798	3.39	-[5]	10	39	2	48
1925	551	9,373	42,127	2,050	83,400	137,501	3.04	-[5]	7	31	2	61
1930	808	7,336	37,398	1,745	109,529	156,816	3.37	1	5	24	1	70
1935	852	7,775	42,586	1,703	117,538	170,454	3.65	1	5	25	1	69
1940	1,000	---{40,200}[3]---		800	161,100	203,100	4.32	1	-(20)-[4]		-[5]	79
1950	700	---{38,300}[3]---		800	181,700	221,500	4.53	-[5]	-(17)-[4]		-[5]	84

[1] For 1907 through 1920 includes all of Ireland.
[2] Percentages may not sum to 100 percent due to rounding into whole numbers.
[3] Includes cigarillos.
[4] Reported together as "other manufactured tobacco."
[5] Less than 0.5 percent.

Sources: United Kingdom, Board of Trade, *Final Report of the Census of Production* (1907); Hutson, *Consumption and Pro-duction of Tobacco in Europe* (1913–1935); Todd, *Statistics of Smoking in the U.K.* (1940–1950).

sumption of plug chewing tobacco has fallen during this century—particularly in proportion to sales of other products. As Table 6.14 shows, although Britons consumed almost 8 million pounds of plug in 1935, sales had been cut in half since 1920. Because of the increase in per capita consumption that is often associated with the use of cigarettes, Table 6.14 shows that the percentage of all sales taken by chewing tobacco fell even more rapidly, with plug representing only 5 percent of all sales by 1935.

As has also been the case in other countries, snuff consumption has been more stable during this century than consumption of chewing tobacco. Although snuff production did decline during both world wars, it rebounded after 1920, with consumption literally doubling to a million pounds a year in 1940. In contrast to Scandinavia and the United States, where most snuff is taken orally, many (though not all) purchasers in the United Kingdom continue to use powdered tobacco as a nasal product, particularly in the country towns of the north.

6.4.2 Australia

The sources for tobacco consumption in the British dominions are even scarcer than those for the home country. In Africa and Asia, the native peoples made use of homegrown tobacco, which the imperial governments did not measure because it was not included in the commercial market. The government sometimes did keep records of imports by white colonists, but these are fragmentary, incomplete, and often unpublished. While some of the new states created from the former British colonies do keep track of tobacco consumption, others do not. Among the first Dominions to measure national production was Australia, which followed England in conducting occasional censuses of domestic manufacture beginning in 1908. Given high import duties, these census data effectively are equivalent to consumption.

Nicotiana tabacum is not indigenous to Australia and grows there only with some difficulty. From colonial times, succeeding governments have sought to foster domestic production; since the 1930s, they have encouraged the replacement of dark tobaccos by milder flue-cured Bright. To support domestic growers, high customs duties have been imposed on manufactured products; firms importing unmanufactured tobacco receive rebates if they include a certain minimum amount of local leaf in their own products. These policies have succeeded in fostering domestic tobacco manufacturing—by companies that included branches of U.S. as well as British firms. At the same time, they also have kept prices high for a product consistently characterized with adjectives such as strong, harsh, and bitter. Although quality has improved over the years, Australian leaf and the products made from it probably have little export potential.[22]

Australians customarily have smoked either pipes or home-rolled cigarettes. For the less affluent consumers, there were few alternatives: The local leaf is not appropriate for cigars or snuff, and imported brands have been expensive. Because transportation was slow in this large and thinly populated country, the local leaf was at first pressed into an unsweetened plug (similar to those made in Europe before the 1870s), which the consumer might use as he or she thought best. As in Europe, this multipurpose plug began to be replaced by ready-cut after improved packaging—the introduction of sealed cans about 1902—allowed the latter to be kept moist and fresh over time.[23] Cut tobacco probably outsold plug before 1920; by the 1936–1937 Census of Production, as shown in Table 6.15, fine- and flake-cut products made up two-thirds of total production. Since the introduction of flue-cured tobaccos during the 1930s, cigarettes gradually have replaced pipes among smokers. However, Australians were comparatively slower than smokers in England or the United States to take up cigarettes, and cut tobacco still represented almost half (44 percent) of total consumption in 1949–1950.

Although Australians primarily have used fine-cut smoking tobacco since World War I, pressed plug still is produced and at least in part is used as chewing tobacco. Anecdotal evidence suggests that chewing is common primarily in the outback and among those in occupations that preclude smoking (for example, among sailors, miners, and prison guards).[24] From the 1930s, as Table 6.15 indicates, plug tobacco has held a relatively stable 10 percent of the market—about the same proportion of overall sales as is found in the United States and Canada during these same years.

Because imported nasal snuff is expensive, its sales have always been smaller than those either of plug chewing tobacco or of fine-cut smoking tobacco. Nevertheless, snuff has been present in small quantities from the founding of the first penal settlements. Customs records (which unfortunately are incomplete) from the various colonies that became Australia in 1912 thus list imports of snuff since the 1860s,[25] as does the 1908 Production Census. Although consumption of snuff fell between the census of 1908 and that of 1936, its sales have been relatively stable since the 1930s, Nasal snuff thus enjoys a loyal following, but the small amounts sold represent a diminishing portion of the total market.

6.4.3 The Germanies

Prior to World War I, the German empire formed the third largest market in the Western World for tobacco products, after only the United States and Russia. In 1880, for example, twice as much tobacco was sold in Germany as in the Habsburg empire or France. Although the German state ceded territory and people to other countries after World War I, in 1925 its remaining population still consumed almost twice as much as the French and some 80 million pounds more than the English (see Tables 6.1 through 6.3). Because of the comparatively large volumes of sales, national consumption data may thus, as in the United States, conceal significant regional variations.

Table 6.15

Consumption of Tobacco Products in Australia, 1908, 1936–1937, and 1949–1950[1]

	Thousands of U.S Pounds							Percent of Total Consumption[9]				
	Snuff[2]	Plug	Cut	Cigars[3]	Cigarettes	Total	Per Head	Snuff[2]	Plug	Cut	Cigars[3]	Cigarettes
1908	8	---{9,840}[4]---		645	1,625	12,118	2.75	-[10]	-(81%)--[4]	(81%)--	5%	13%
1936/37[5]	2	2,521[6]	13,838[6]	269	5,771	22,401	3.37	-[10]	11	62	1	26
1949/50	2	3,215[7]	16,763[7,8]	203	17,772	37,953	4.87	-[10]	9	44[11]	1	47

[1] For each product, this table reports domestic production, adding imports and subtracting exports. The amounts imported and exported are included to measure national consumption; except in the case of snuff, removing them would not materially affect totals.

[2] In each year, all snuff was imported.

[3] Includes cigarillos.

[4] Reported together as "manufactured tobacco" in 1908.

[5] July 1 through June 30.

[6] Assuming that imports (555) and exports (1,180) are comprised of plug and cut tobacco in the same ratio as domestic production of plug (2,408) and cut (13,325).

[7] Assuming that imports (774) and exports (413) are comprised of plug and cut tobacco in the same ratio as domestic production of plug (3,143) and cut (16,113).

[8] In 1949–1950, reported domestic production of cut tobacco includes flake-cut (8,129) and fine-cut (7,984) products.

[9] Percentages may not sum to 100 percent due to rounding into whole numbers.

[10] Less than 0.5 percent.

[11] In 1949–1950, reported domestic production of cut tobacco includes flake-cut (21 percent) and fine-cut (21 percent) products.

Source: Australia, Bureau of Census and Statistics, Canberra, *Official Statistics, Commonwealth of Australia, Manufacturing Industries.*

Table 6.16
Tobacco Products Manufactured in Germany, 1871–1879, and Consumed in Germany, 1913–1950[1]

Thousands of U.S Pounds[1]

	Snuff	Chewing[2]	Cut[3]	Cigars[4]	Cigar-ettes	Total	Per Head
1871/72[5]	10,884	1,019	86,073	37,809	---	135,785	3.31
1878/79	18,100	1,627	143,289	64,842	---	227,858	5.06
1871/79[6]	12,423	1,144	97,923	41,277	---	152,767	3.60
1913	10,803	12,346	58,146	88,184	26,698	196,177	3.02
1920[7]	5,631	7,180	55,408	59,015	43,431	170,665	2.82
1925	5,126	7,154	72,487	62,510	65,829	213,106	3.37
1930	4,645	6,217	78,808	80,792	70,283	240,745	3.65
1937/38[8]	3,678	4,542	68,822	98,732	93,337	269,111	3.95
1950[9]	1,143	1,116	45,122	42,415	52,330	142,126	2.79

Percent of Total Products[9]

	Snuff	Chew-ing[2]	Cut[3]	Cigars[4]	Cigar-ettes
1871/72[5]	8%	1%	63%	28%	--%
1878/79	8	1	63	29	--
1871/79[6]	8	1	63	27	--
1913	6	6	30	45	14
1920[7]	3	4	33	35	25
1925	2	3	34	29	31
1930	2	3	33	34	30
1937/38[9]	1	2	26	37	35
1950[9]	1	1	32	30	37

Sources: Germany, Statistisches Reichsamt, *Statistisches Jahrbuch für das Deutsche Reich,* (1871–1879, 1937–1938); Hutson, *Consumption and Production of Tobacco in Europe* (1913–1930); Germany, Statistisches Bundesamt Wiesbaden, *Statistisches Jahrbuch für die Bundesrepublik Deutschland* (1950).

Taken as a group, the Germans are distinguished by the catholicity of their tastes in tobacco. During the twentieth century, all forms of tobacco have found appreciative buyers, and no one product has dominated—as did plug chewing tobacco in the United States, oral snuff in Sweden, and cut tobacco in France, Italy, and the United Kingdom. During the 1920s and 1930s, as Table 6.16 shows, cut tobacco, cigars, and cigarettes thus each represented about one-third of the total market, and this pattern was retained in West Germany in 1950.[26]

Although on average the Germans tend to be smokers, smokeless tobacco products also have enjoyed substantial sales. With 6 percent of the total market in 1913, sales of snuff and chewing tobacco thus were among the highest in any European country outside of Scandinavia (see Table 6.2). Because of the enormous size of the German market, moreover, a larger quantity of both snuff and chewing tobacco actually was purchased than in any of the Scandinavian states. As in other countries, sales of both smokeless products tended to fall between the two world wars. As has been true in other countries also, the rate of decrease was relatively slow (about 2½ percent a year). Thus, more than a million pounds of each product were sold in West Germany as late as 1950. (East Germany did not release sales data.)

Sales of snuff had been larger than those of plug during the 1870s (the only prewar decade from which we have information concerning sales of specific products). With about 8 percent of the overall market, in the 1870s nasal snuff was about as popular as in Austria (although somewhat less in demand than in France or Italy). Given the relatively slow decline in snuff consumption in Germany after 1880, it is reasonable to assume that the demand for nasal powder was higher during the first half of the nineteenth century. Were we, for example, simply to extend the trend line after 1880 backward, snuff would have represented about one-quarter of total sales in the German empire in 1820—about the same proportion as in the neighboring Habsburg empire.

Notes to Table 6.16

[1] In calculating the weight of chewing tobacco, cigars, and cigarettes (reported in 1,000 pieces during the years 1913 through 1950), the following conversion factors were used uniformly for those years: Eighty pieces of chewing tobacco equals 2.205 pounds; 1,000 cigars equals 11 pounds; 1,000 cigarettes equals 2.205 pounds. However, some of the pieces were larger prior to the mid-1920s; thus, these data may understate consumption of those products in 1913 and 1920.

[2] "Kautabak."

[3] "Rauchtabak."

[4] Includes cigarillos.

[5] July 1 through June 30.

[6] Average.

[7] From 1920, excludes territories ceded after World War I.

[8] April 1 through March 31; excludes Austria.

[9] West Germany (Bundesrepublik) only.

[10] Percentages may not sum to 100 percent due to rounding into whole numbers.

6.4.4 The Netherlands

Along with their neighbors in the German states, the inhabitants of the Netherlands long have been reputed to be unusually heavy users of smoking tobacco, and the existing evidence justifies this reputation.[27] By 1950, tobacco consumption throughout the world had risen along with the adoption of the cigarette habit. But the Dutch remained by far the most assiduous consumers of cut smoking tobacco and cigars.[28] In other countries, cigarettes had begun to take the place of cigars by 1925. The Dutch were comparatively slow to make this switch; in 1950, cigars still represented more than a quarter of all products manufactured in the Netherlands.

Although we know from literary sources that the Dutch made use of nasal snuff as well as smoking tobacco during the eighteenth and nineteenth centuries, this smokeless product was no longer manufactured in the Netherlands in 1956.[29] As Table 6.17 indicates, however, at least 300,000 pounds of chewing tobacco continued to be consumed throughout the 1920s and 1930s. And about 2 million pounds of dry and moist chewing tobacco were manufactured in the Netherlands in 1956 for internal consumption and for export. (Some types of moist chewing tobacco are equivalent to products that in other countries are described as oral snuff.)

6.4.5 Central Europe

Five governments ruled over Central Europe between the two world wars—Czechoslovakia, Hungary, Rumania, Poland, and Yugoslavia. (The Republic of Austria, which considered itself part of the West, is discussed in Section 5.2.) In 1925, as shown in Table 6.3, cut smoking tobacco was the dominant product in these five nations, and consumption of cigars was very low compared to Austria or Germany. Between 1925 and the demise of these states at the end of the 1930s, their tobacco monopolies reported a substantial rise in cigarette sales and an accompanying decline in the purchase of pipe tobacco.

Although smokeless products were present in all of these nations except Rumania, reported sales were relatively small. Taken together, snuff and chewing tobacco in 1925 represented about 1 percent of total consumption in Czechoslovakia and Hungary and about 3 percent in Poland and Yugoslavia (Table 6.3). To some extent, the subjects of these states may have reduced their consumption of smokeless tobacco after World War I out of necessity rather than choice. As described in Chapter 4, the regimes established after the war all erected rigid tobacco monopolies, fostered domestic tobacco production, and forbade the import of manufactured products. Although smuggling thrived in the larger cities and near the borders, those individuals living in the interior sections of these nations either bought from the limited range of products offered by the state stores or did without.

Some of those consumers that before the war had purchased smokeless prod-

Table 6.17
Consumption of Tobacco Products in the Netherlands, 1925–1935, and Tobacco Products Manufactured in the Netherlands, 1956

	Thousands of U.S Pounds				Percent of Total[6]				
	Chew-ing[1]	Cut[2]	Cigars[3]	Cigar-ettes	Total[4]	Per Head	Chew-ing	Cut	Cigars[3]	Cigar-ettes
1925	300	27,961	11,474	4,316	44,051	6.68	1%	64%	26%	10%
1930	300	25,523	15,066	7,914	48,803	6.11	1	53	31	16
1935	--{25,523}--		15,749	8,838	50,110	5.68	-{51}--		31	18
1956[5]	2,053	17,703	16,175	26,621	62,552	5.91	3	28	26	43

[1] Includes both dry and moist products ("pruimtabak, droog en nat.")
[2] "Shagtabak" and "rooktabak."
[3] Includes cigarillos.
[4] The sources do not report on the consumption or manufacture of snuff.
[5] Following Lee (*Tobacco Consumption,* p. 57), the following conversion factors are used to calculate the weight of cigars, cigarillos, and cigarettes manufactured in 1956, which the Central Bureau of Statistics reports in 1,000 pieces: 1,000 cigars equals 15 pounds; 1,000 cigarillos equals 5 pounds; 1,000 cigarettes equals 2.205 pounds.
[6] Percentages may not sum to 100 percent due to rounding into whole numbers.

Sources: Hutson, *Consumption and Production of Tobacco in Europe* (1925–1935); The Netherlands, Central bureau voor de statistiek, *Tabakverwerkende industrie 1960* (1956).

ucts may now have shifted to cigarettes because of the low quality of the snuff and chewing tobacco manufactured by the state factories. In 1913 (Table 5.6) the Habsburg tobacco monopoly had sold more than three hundred thousand pounds of chewing tobacco in provinces that later became part of Yugoslavia. Only nine years later, its Yugoslav successor reported selling 25 percent less of this product throughout the entire nation (Table 6.18). Under normal circumstances, tobacco users do not change their habits this rapidly, and the lower quality of the new brands offered to them after 1918 may well have influenced tobacco chewers to reduce their consumption.

While the policies of the state tobacco monopolies in Central Europe placed artificial limits on their choices, it is probable that a majority of tobacco consumers in these states did smoke pipes from the second half of the nineteenth century. As Table 6.19 indicates, cut smoking tobacco consistently formed more than 80 percent of sales by the Habsburg state monopoly for Hungary. Although snuff always was taken, consumption seems to have been lower than in the German-speaking provinces. Production by the monopoly for Austria in 1882 (Table 5.4) can, for example, be compared to production by that for Hungary in 1880. In those years, snuff made up 7 percent of Austrian output and 1 percent of Hungarian. And chewing tobacco, 6 percent of Austrian production, was produced only in limited quantities by the Hungarian factories.

These comparisons must be made with some caution since the per capita

Table 6.18
Tobacco Consumption in Yugoslavia, 1922–1935

	Thousands of U.S Pounds						Per	Percent of Total Consumption [2]				
	Snuff	Chewing	Cut	Cigars[1]	Cigar-ettes	Total	Head	Snuff	Chew-ing	Cut	Cigars[1]	Cigar-ettes
1922	1	249	14,863	346	4,484	19,943	1.66	--[3]	1%	75%	2%	23%
1925	14	287	12,546	489	6,318	19,654	1.52	--[3]	2	75	2	23
1930	6	71	10,505	463	11,175	22,220	1.60	--[3]	--[3]	47	2	50
1935	13	47	5,508	629	9,984	16,181	1.14	--[3]	--[3]	34	4	62

[1]Includes cigarillos.
[2]Percentages may not sum to 100 percent due to rounding into whole numbers.
[3]Less than 0.5 percent.

Source: Hutson, *Consumption and Production of Tobacco in Europe.*

Table 6.19
Tobacco Sales in Hungary, 1850–1861 and 1920–1935, and Tobacco Products Manufactured by the Hungarian Tobacco Monopoly, 1876–1913

	Thousands of U.S Pounds						Percent of Total Sales[1]			
	Snuff	Cut	Cigars[2]	Cigar-ettes	Total	Per Head	Snuff	Cut	Cigars	Cigar-ettes
1850	12	145	43	---	200	--	6%	73%	22%	--%
1861	481	18,643	2,640	---	21,764	--	2	86	12	--
1876	154	7,567	973	---	8,694	--	2	87	11	--
1880	128	8,345	1,043	---	9,516	--	1	91	11	--[3]
1890	122	5,290	619	2	6,033	--	2	88	10	--[3]
1900	71	6,496	586	520	7,673	.40	1	85	8	7
1910	57	7,596	776	1,073	9,502	.46	1	80	8	11
1913	39	6,734	750	706	8,229	.40	1	81	9	9
1920/21[4]	2	7,650	1,257	1,979	10,888	1.36	--[3]	70	12	18
1925/26	3	18,067	1,540	4,366	23,976	2.20	--[3]	75	3	22
1930/31	2	17,439	901	4,410	22,572	2.60	--[3]	77	4	20
1934/35	2	14,671	509	4,316	19,498	2.17	--[3]	75	3	22

[1] Percentages may not sum to 100 percent due to rounding into whole numbers.
[2] Includes cigarillos.
[3] Less than 0.5 percent.
[4] July 1 through June 30.

Sources: Austria, Statistische Central-Commission, *Tafeln zur Statistik der Österreichischen Monarchie* (1850); Austria, Central-Direction der Tabakfabriken und Einlösungsämter, *Tabellen zur Statistik des Österreichischen Tabak-Monopols* (1861); Hungary, Budapest Székesfőváros Statisztikai Hivatal, *Statisztikai Évkönyve* (1876–1913); Hutson, *Consumption and Production of Tobacco in Europe* (1920–1950).

sales of tobacco reported by the Hungarian monopoly were so much lower than those in Austria. Indeed, if the state factories had formed the only source of supply in Hungary, its peoples would have consumed less tobacco each year, on average, than those in any other nation. A substantial second (or black) market clearly existed. As discussed in Chapter 4, the state controlled tobacco growing in Austria but not in Hungary. And the Hungarian government did not (or could not) prevent tobacco growers from selling their leaf in village markets for use as homemade snuff and chewing tobacco.

NOTES

1. See Chapter 3, Notes 45–46.
2. Between 1925 and 1935, as shown in Table 6.6, sales of chewing tobacco declined by 79 percent; during the same years, demand for cut tobacco rose 30 percent, and cigarette sales increased more than 60 percent (although from a low base).

3. Robert, *Story of Tobacco*, 103–4; Heimann, *Tobacco and Americans*, 190; Tennant, *American Cigarette Industry*, 129.

4. Perhaps the most striking aspect of this change is the early replacement of a smokeless product (pressed plug) by a smoking product (cigarettes). Cigarettes were adopted earlier in those nations, such as Austria, where most tobacco users already were smokers. As Table 6.4 shows, however, the United States was an early leader in the switch to cigarettes among nations with a high consumption of smokeless products.

5. See, Section 3.4.

6. Tennant, *American Cigarette Industry*, 27. For the tobacco trust, see in general, Robert, *Story of Tobacco*, 145–53; Jacobstein, *Tobacco Industry*, 103–39. For its arrangements with the British American Tobacco Company (now BAT), see Corina, *Trust in Tobacco*.

7. The 1911 Dissolution Decree divided the trust's businesses among four large companies—American Tobacco, Liggett and Myers, Lorillard, and R. J. Reynolds—as well as dozens of smaller firms, particularly in the smokeless tobacco industries: Tennant, *American Cigarette Industry*, 61. The first three of those companies (called the Big Three) dominated the cigarette industry until after World War II. The 1911 decree did not assign cigarette plants to Reynolds; although the latter company continued to emphasize the sale of chewing tobacco until 1945, it also entered the cigarette industry with Camels in 1913. See ibid., 4–5; Tilley, *R. J. Reynolds*, 363. The history of the multinational corporations from 1911 is sketched by Tucker, *Tobacco: An International Perspective*, 69–105; their holdings and branded products as of 1975 are succinctly listed by Corina, *Trust in Tobacco*, 300–306.

8. The Bright tobacco industry in Virginia and North Carolina remained labor-intensive until the 1890s, when the Adams and Lester-Adams presses were introduced—about 1893 by R. J. Reynolds, and somewhat later by other manufacturers. Because their products made from Bright leaf were naturally less absorbent than Burley plug, North Carolina manufacturers were quicker to adopt saccharin almost as soon as it became commercially available; again Reynolds seems to have led in using this sweetener, which was widely accepted by 1897. See Tilley, *Bright Tobacco*, 580–89, and *R. J. Reynolds*, 83–88.

9. The Bonsack machine, patented in 1881, could turn out more than two hundred cigarettes a minute compared to four a minute produced by well-trained hand workers: Tennant, *American Cigarette Industry*, 21; Heimann, *Tobacco and Americans*, 212; Robert, *Story of Tobacco*, 142. Cigar manufacturers introduced machine production of cigars during the late 1920s (thirty years after the mechanization of the cigarette and plug industries); only 9 percent of cigars were machine-made in 1923, compared to 80 percent ten years later: Gottsegen, *Tobacco: A Study*, 18.

10. Cut tobacco sometimes also was used to make home-rolled cigarettes. A machine for rolling cigarettes at home was offered for sale as early as 1883; since smoking tobacco was less expensive, some cigarette smokers switched either to a pipe or to home rolled cigarettes during the economic downturns of 1907, 1920–1921, and the 1930s: Heimann, *Tobacco and Americans*, 176, 233–34.

11. Cigarettes (tobacco contained in a paper tube) apparently were being produced in New York by the 1860s. Tax was paid on production of 20 million pieces in 1865 (ibid., 206), but this total is inflated because until 1897 the government lumped together cigarettes and small cigars in reporting production. In any case, production had fallen to less than 2 million by 1869: Tilley, *Bright Tobacco*, 507.

12. Gage, *American Tobacco Types,* 113; this estimate does not include scrap chewing tobacco.

13. No matter how it is measured—whether in absolute terms (Table 6.10), in proportion to other production (Table 6.10), or on a per capita basis (Table 6.11)—cigarette production rose more than fourfold during the 1910s.

14. Robert, *Story of Tobacco,* 140; Heimann, *Tobacco and Americans,* 214–17; Gottsegen, *Tobacco: A Study,* 41–42. In the absence of accurate measurements comparing consumption between urban and rural regions or between the genders, none of these explanations is totally persuasive; since cigarette consumption also rose in countries with state monopolies that do not advertise, the direct and immediate influence of advertising would seem to be exaggerated.

15. According to Tilley (*R. J. Reynolds,* 158, 211), Reynolds introduced Camels with a blend (despite their Orientalizing packaging) of Bright, Burley, and only a small amount of Turkish leaf. Reynolds adopted this blend because of his recent success with Prince Albert Smoking tobacco; the latter itself was an adaptation of blends used in chewing tobacco. Robert *(Story of Tobacco)* goes even further and suggests that Camels owed their success to the inclusion of Burley that had been sweetened or flavored much as plug is. According to Robert, the new blend was

largely bright flue-cured, a seasoning of Turkish, and, most distinctive of all, cased or sweetened Burley. The Burley was treated somewhat as though it was being prepared for plug tobacco. Burley had been earlier used in cigarettes, but, so far as can be determined, never in exactly this way. Later, probably about 1916, Maryland leaf was added to the blend for its burning qualities. (p. 230)

See also Heimann, *Tobacco and Americans,* 222–25.

16. A similar pattern is seen in the sales of cigars and cut smoking tobacco. Cigar consumption fell rather rapidly from 1907, when Americans consumed on average eighty-six cigars annually, to a low point of only thirty-seven cigars each year in 1933 during the depths of the Depression; with improving economic conditions, consumption increased, but the overall trend remained downward through 1950. Because of population growth, however, the record for annual production was not reached until 1920, when 162 million pounds of cigars were produced. Per capita consumption of cut tobacco similarly peaked in 1910 (at about one and three-quarters pounds annually), but production continued to increase until 1925.

17. Table 6.10; scrap chewing tobacco has been removed from the 1950 total to permit comparison with the 1917 data.

18. For moist oral snuff, see Section 3.4; for oral snuff in Sweden, see Section 5.5.

19. Between 1940 and 1950, for example, cigarette consumption more than doubled (an annual rate of increase of 8.5 percent). Since sales of all other tobacco products were stable or declining, the 50-percent rise in total consumption during the same decade is entirely due to this more general use of cigarettes (Table 6.13).

20. Cut tobacco formed more than half of all tobacco sales in France and the Habsburg empire from the 1850s (Sections 5.2 and 5.3), and this product also seems to have dominated the market in the United Kingdom, in the British dominions, in the Netherlands, and in Central Europe. However, cigar sales were approximately equal to those of smoking tobacco in Germany and Italy; and cigars were also unusually popular in the Netherlands as well as in Denmark. Perhaps the citizens of these latter countries owe their fondness for cigars to maritime commerce with countries where suitable tobaccos

flourish; certainly, cigars have been used least in landlocked states such as Hungary.

21. As Table 6.4 shows, cigarettes comprised the majority of sales in England by 1923, at least twenty years earlier than in France, Germany, or the United States. For snuff consumption during the nineteenth century, see Chapter 3, Notes 76–78.

22. Akehurst, *Tobacco*, 13, 123–24. For U.S. manufacturers in Australia during the nineteenth century, see Robert, *Story of Tobacco*, 113.

23. Walker, *Under Fire*, 24–25.

24. Ibid., 26.

25. Ibid., 27–31.

26. Germans have been by far among the most enthusiastic consumers of cigars in Western Europe. While cigarettes sales increased at the expense of cigars almost everywhere else between the two wars, Germany was the only country in the West in which sales rose for all three smoking products—cut pipe tobacco, cigars, and cigarettes (Table 6.16). Since per capita consumption also shot up during the same years, it is likely both that more Germans took up smoking and also that many existing smokers now used all three products on more occasions.

27. The sources for earlier years unfortunately give only a total, and they do not list the weight of specific manufactured products. In 1880, however, judging by the amount of raw material used by Dutch manufacturers, the residents of the Netherlands consumed more tobacco per capita than any other nation including the United States. According to the *Staatkundig en Staathusihoudkundig Jaarboekje voor 1884* (p. 113), domestic per capita consumption in the Netherlands during 1880 was equivalent to 7.14 pounds of raw dried tobacco per person. Using the same method of measurement, it was estimated that the Belgians were in second place (5.69 pounds), followed by the Austrians (3.15), Germans (2.87), French (1.98), British (1.43), and Italians (1.32). In the same year (1884; see U.S. Dept. of Agriculture, *First Annual Report*, p. 88), U.S. manufacturers used 4.30 pounds of leaf tobacco per resident. These 1884 comparisons between countries are not totally accurate—for example, manufacturers in some countries may have used more of the stems than was the practice in other countries. Nevertheless, they are consistent with the levels of consumption for manufactured products reported for the Habsburg empire, France, and Italy (see Chapter 5). By 1925, as Table 6.3 above demonstrates, consumption in the United States surpassed that in the Netherlands; but the Dutch remained heavier users of tobacco than the residents of other European countries. While low taxation and limited governmental regulation in the Netherlands undoubtedly facilitated the use of tobacco, cultural and social habits must also have played a role in its acceptance.

28. As Table 6.17 shows, pipe tobacco represented the majority of sales in the Netherlands between the two world wars, but the Dutch also smoked large numbers of cigars and cigarillos, a fondness they shared with the Germans, the Danes, Italians, Swiss, and Americans.

29. See Chapter 3, Note 61.

Chapter 7

Tobacco Consumption in Asia and Africa

7.1 SUMMARY

Tobacco was grown by the European colonists in South and North America from the 1550s, and it was brought to Europe before 1600. For fiscal reasons, its cultivation was prohibited during the seventeenth century in France, the Italian peninsula, Spain, and the German-speaking provinces of the Habsburg Empire. In addition, as discussed in Chapter 4, the rulers of these states also created monopolies—either directly controlled by the crown or farmed to private concessions—over manufacturing, distribution, and sales. Domestic production also was prohibited in England, but the government of that kingdom left manufacturing and retail sales in private hands. A totally free market thus existed primarily in Holland and in Central Europe, including Prussia and Hungary.

These governmental monopolies took away a valuable source of income from their nations' peasantry, and they also may have restricted the total market for tobacco products by raising their prices. However, they did not noticeably influence the consumer in her or his choices between specific types of products. Whether the market was controlled by one monopoly or supplied by a larger number of private firms, overall consumption patterns were the same. From the very beginning, Europeans everywhere chewed tobacco, took it as nasal snuff, and smoked it in clay pipes. Except in Spain and some of its colonies, however, smokers did not use cigars until the 1840s, and they took up cigarettes only after 1880.

Throughout Europe, tobacco habits have been relatively stable over time. Because an individual's tobacco preferences tend to be fixed, consumption patterns change slowly. Because tobacco is a luxury that is not needed for life, the accumulation of these small changes can over the longer term—fifty to a hundred years—lead to radically different customs. In the short term, however, consumption patterns are not affected by wars and political changes, by social and intellectual fads, or by advertising and promotional efforts. Even economic changes seem to affect tobacco consumption only at the margin. In France, for example, because of economic growth during the first half of the nineteenth century, more persons used tobacco, but many of these new consumers simply adopted the snuff habit from their neighbors.

The previous chapters thus show that the tobacco preferences of an individual—or those of a natural community like a rural village or an urban craft—are an independent variable: Over the near term, consumption patterns are affected neither by economic, commercial, and political practices, nor by social, religious, or cultural habits. Hence, it is reasonable to assume that the same general patterns of evolution that are present in Europe will be found in other cultures. In Asia and in Africa, it also is likely that tobacco preferences change slowly but are capable of radical alterations over the centuries. For example, if a cautious and scrupulous explorer in 1850 states that the members of an African tribe primarily use oral snuff, we can assume that they also preferred snuff fifty years earlier. But we would be wrong to speculate that they had used snuff for two or three centuries. And it would be an unwarranted leap of faith to impose the preferences of this one tribe on all Africans everywhere and at all times.

During the greater part of the four centuries discussed by this study, Asia was ruled by five empires. Moving from west to east, Europeans arrived first in the territories ruled by the Muslim emperors of Ottoman Turkey—whose empire, encircling the Mediterranean, also included what today are Hungary, Yugoslavia, Romania, Bulgaria, Albania, and Greece as well as Arabia, Iraq, Syria, Palestine, Egypt, Libya, Tunisia, Algeria, and Morocco. Continuing east, they came in turn to the territories of Persia, Mogul India, China, and Japan. In contrast to the few great empires ruling Asia, smaller kingdoms or tribal confederations governed the continent of Africa south of the Ottoman territories along the Mediterranean.

The two centuries between 1450 and 1650 witnessed continuous if intermittent European expansion by sea into Asia and Africa. Explorers charted new routes to the East, and merchants and priests built warehouses and churches along the coasts. In most cases, however, Europeans did not occupy the inland regions, which were ruled until at least 1850 by the native peoples. During the fifteenth and sixteenth centuries, the Portuguese established trading ports, at which they purchased slaves for shipment to the Americas, along the western coast of Africa and in Angola, Madagascar, and Mozambique. These ports also served as way stations to their ports at Goa in India, Malacca in what today is Malaysia, and Macao on the coast of China. After 1600, the Portuguese were in turn followed by representatives of other European states. The Dutch, the French, and the British all established coastal stations along the West Coast of Africa; and the Dutch additionally controlled the Cape of Good Hope from 1652 to 1815. In Asia, the Spanish began to occupy the Philippines; the Dutch moved into Ceylon, Indonesia, and Taiwan; and the French and British began to dispute control over the decaying Mogul empire in India.

To all of the regions with which they traded, Europeans brought the tobacco plant, which thus reached Asia before it arrived in some regions of Europe. The Portuguese and the Dutch brought tobacco to the East Coast of Africa before 1600, and Dutch traders also carried it to the Ottoman Empire shortly after 1600. It reached China and Japan early in the seventeenth century, from whence it was spread to more remote regions of Asia. During the next few decades, the plant was carried inland from the ports by native merchants. By about 1750, both tobacco and its products were available virtually everywhere in the world.

The first European empires in Asia and Africa were primarily mercantile and did not seek to occupy the hinterland. Only during the brief period from 1870 to 1950 did Europeans colonize and immigrate in substantial numbers to Africa or Asia, and only during the latter period did rulers in the Ottoman or the Japanese realms establish state monopolies on the European pattern. Instead, throughout most of these centuries, they left the tobacco trade to private individuals or companies, whose records largely have disappeared.

Until the twentieth century, it thus is difficult and perhaps impossible to provide a statistical measurement of consumption in Asia and Africa. Literary records in Arabic and in the Asian languages probably provide useful anecdotal evidence, but references to tobacco in these sources have not been systematically collected. In many cases, the historian must thus rely on accounts by European travelers, only some of whom were accurate observers. For example, the accounts of many Europeans describe the Turks, Africans, and Japanese as consuming enormous amounts of tobacco each day.[1] But these descriptions are subjective and reflect the (usually unstated) prejudices of the observer. For example, some early Europeans indiscriminately refered to all the sultan's myriad peoples and races simply as ''Turks.'' And their conceptions of what constitutes ''heavy'' consumption are diverse and incompatible; some observers who do not themselves use tobacco might describe as a ''heavy'' smoker a person smoking as few as two pipefuls during an evening. Even the explorers who provide careful and objective accounts describe only a specific place at a particular era. Nevertheless, because tobacco preferences tend to persist over long periods of time, it is likely that the practices found in a specific region also were prevalent in that area during at least the preceding and the subsequent fifty years. In some cases, moreover, when nineteenth-century accounts can be compared to current data, the consumption patterns described are still present today, suggesting that the earlier descriptions are accurate overall if not in every detail.

7.2 PERSIA, THE OTTOMAN EMPIRE, AND AFRICA

The Ottoman rulers usually did not attempt to influence the beliefs or cultural habits of those they ruled and taxed; given the available technology, such attempts would have failed in any case. At least during their empire's early centuries, however, the Ottomans encouraged commercial and mercantile activities, and the empire was tied together by a network of trade that fostered a growing uniformity of consumer products from Cairo to Belgrade. And either despite or because of its centuries of struggle with the neighboring Persian Empire, both ideas and products frequently traveled between the two realms. From Jidda on the West Coast of the Arabian peninsula, from Cairo, and from the coastal cities of North Africa, Muslim traders (often called "Arabs" although they belong to many nations) spread these luxury goods throughout Africa. An interconnected series of trade routes linked Madagascar on the East Coast to Ghana on the West. Established sea routes linked ports along the East Coast as far south as Madagascar, and camel caravans similarly carried luxury goods, including tobacco, along fixed routes across the Sahara. Each year, caravans set out from Cairo south to Nubia and the Sudan; while others dispatched from Tripoli, Tunis, Algeria, and Morocco moved south and west across the Sahara through fabled Timbuktu to Ghana on the West Coast.

Tobacco reached Istanbul, the capital of the empire, before 1600. Some contemporary sources say it was introduced by Dutch traders, while others suggest that it was brought to the capital from the East Indies or from Egypt, where it had been known by 1550. It must have been common by the early years of the next century, for the Ottoman emperors Ahmed I (1603–1621) and Murad IV (1621–1640) are said to have forbidden tobacco and coffee, possibly because these are not expressly mentioned in the Koran. Like the prohibitions ordained by their fellow rulers in Europe, these Ottoman laws could not be enforced, and they were repealed by Murad's successor, Mohammed IV.[2] Some sources state that Turkish soldiers transmitted tobacco to Persia when Murad IV went to war against his neighbor to the east, but it probably was introduced more peaceably before 1600 by Portuguese traders operating out of their entrepôts at Ormuz and Goa.[3] In either case, tobacco must have been widely available by the reign of the Persian shah Abbas I (1587–1625), to whom contemporary European sources attribute a ferocity against tobacco users similar to that recounted of Murad I.[4]

After lifting these early prohibitions, the Ottoman and Persian governments did not directly regulate tobacco production until the nineteenth century, and the plant was widely grown throughout both empires on small plots as well as on larger plantations. Over the centuries and under very different climate and soil conditions, the leaf imported from the Americas evolved into the Oriental and Semi-Oriental types, which tend to be smaller and to possess characteristic aromatic qualities.[5] Air-cured Oriental leaf was and still is the main crop in Turkey, Persia, and the Middle East, with the more fertile regions of Iran and the Lebanon producing strong and intensely aromatic types, among which is found the distinctive Latakia.[6] And Oriental and Semi-Oriental types also have long been grown in the Ottoman Empire's European provinces and in the Caucasian provinces of the Russian Empire.[7]

Along the Mediterranean coast in Algeria and Tunisia, the leaf apparently did not change in the same way, and the main crop has been a strong, non-aromatic dark leaf, often high in nicotine and sometimes said to possess peculiar flavors. After the French conquered and occupied Algeria during the nineteenth century, the government encouraged the colonists to develop commercial plantations, and these produced large quantities of dark leaf for use by the French state monopoly.[8] In Egypt, a type of tobacco somewhat lighter than North African leaf was frequently cultivated in earlier centuries. However, a government monopoly of the European type was erected in 1810, tobacco cultivation was prohibited in 1890, and Egypt no longer produced tobacco.[9]

As indicated in Section 7.1, the available sources do not provide us with quantitative measurements of consumption. Many Europeans describe the Turks as consuming truly remarkable amounts of tobacco each day. However, these anecdotes are not confirmed by the more recent records of the Turkish state monopoly. In 1925, the residents of the Republic of Turkey consumed on average only about a pound of tobacco a year on average—less than those of any other nation except Poland and much less than British, French, or U.S. consumers. In 1950, although their per capita consumption had increased, the Turks still used less tobacco on average than the inhabitants of any European nation except Portugal. And the consumption of the Moroccans and Indians was also lower than in Europe. While contemporary comparisons are not an infallible guide to past practices, it is unlikely that eighteenth-century residents of Istanbul or Cairo really consumed more tobacco on average than those in Paris or London.[10]

Many growers cultivated tobacco for their own consumption, and the domestic markets were supplied by thousands of local firms. Hence, it is risky to generalize about tobacco habits in empires as large and diverse as those controlled by the Persians and the Ottomans. Based on travelers' reports, the pipe seems to have been preferred in Persia and in the major cities of Turkey, the Balkans, and Egypt. In contrast, the Bedouin population of the Middle East and North Africa seem to have used chewing tobacco and taken nasal and oral snuff. But some snuff was also taken in the cities, and some Arabs smoked pipes as well as taking snuff, and there clearly must have been many local variations in the composition of these products. However, the presence of cigars is never mentioned, and any type of cigarette seems to have been rare before 1850.

Although this type of smoking device may have arisen independently in India, unnamed Persians apparently deserve the credit for inventing the *nargileh* or water pipe, which in various forms quickly spread west to the Ottoman Empire and then south along the caravan routes from Egypt and North Africa to all of Africa. This device—referred to by European travelers as the hookah or hubbly-bubbly—creates a partial vacuum that allows the smoke to be drawn up through water and along a tube, thus cooling the smoke before it is inhaled. Although the precise date is unknown, it must have been invented shortly after 1600.[11] By the eighteenth century, the water pipe was common throughout the bazaars of the Ottoman provinces both in Europe and in North Africa. And it soon was carried along the caravan routes to the African interior—where European explorers mention its presence both in West Africa as well as along the entire east coast from Ethiopia to South Africa.[12]

In addition to smoking it in pipes, the inhabitants of the Near East and Africa also chewed tobacco and took it as nasal and oral snuff. While the sources do not permit a quantitative analysis of preferences, snuff was certainly used in Turkey and in Egypt, and the peoples of the Balkans took both snuff and chewing tobacco during the nineteenth century.[13] But it is the caravan peoples and bedouins of Arabia, North Africa, the Sahara, and West Africa that particularly favor smokeless tobacco. Men of the Arabian tribes are said to have both smoked tobacco and also to take it as finely powdered oral snuff, which they used in a way that resembles the descriptions of dipping in the U.S. South. Pungent snuffs were also produced in Syria and in Palestine, where they sometimes provided an income to Christian monks.

Both snuff and pressed chewing tobacco seem to have been especially common among the pastoral and caravan peoples in the interior regions of North Africa. In Tripoli (in present-day Libya), in Tunisia, and in Algeria, the strong local tobaccos were widely chewed and snuffed as were also those imported into Tripoli and Tunisia by the Ottoman monopoly. In Morocco, powdered tobacco seems to have been preferred; away from the coastal regions, few Moroccan men were seen without their snuff boxes, which often were highly decorated. Among the Berber tribes of the west and central Sahara, the Tuaregs are reported to have used only snuff and chewing tobacco and not to have smoked at all.[14]

Religious leaders sometimes sought to forbid tobacco (as recently as 1887 in Morocco). But these prohibitions were as futile as those by Christian leaders in Europe and the Americas, and tobacco cultivation later was encouraged when Algeria and Morocco were occupied by the French. Although they are comparatively recent, the records of the state monopoly for Morocco provide evidence that supports the accounts of nineteenth-century travelers. Cigarettes—which the French colonial regime introduced—formed by 1935 about 60 percent of total sales in Morocco; their sales have grown in subsequent years at the expense of cut smoking tobacco. At the same time, snuff consumption has remained stable, with about 12 to 15 percent of legal sales (Table 7.1). As a comparison of these data with those reported in Table 6.5 suggests, snuff consumption in proportion to sales of other products thus has been considerably higher in Morocco in recent years than in most regions of Europe.

If the Moroccans remain partial to powdered snuff, use of pressed chewing

Table 7.1
Sales of Tobacco Products in Morocco, 1935–1950

	Thousands of U.S Pounds					Percent of Total[1]				Per Capita			
	Snuff	Cut	Cigars	Cigar-ettes	Total	Snuff	Cut	Cigars	Cigar-ettes	Snuff	Cut	Cigar-ettes	Total
1935	500	1,000	20	2,200	3,720	14%	27%	--[2]	60%	.07	.16	.33	.56
1940	600	1,100	13	3,400	5,113	12	22	--[2]	67	08	.14	.45	.67
1945	800	800	13	3,800	5,413	15	15	--[2]	70	.10	.10	.47	.67
1950	900	700	13	5,800	7,413	12	10	--[2]	78	.10	.08	.65	.83

[1] Percentages may not sum to 100% due to rounding into whole numbers.
[2] Less than 0.5%.

Sources: Régie des Tabacs, as reported by Lee, *Tobacco Consumption in Various Countries*, p. 54.

Table 7.2
Per Capita Manufacture of Chewing Tobacco, 1976 (in U.S. pounds)

```
             Thousands of U.S Pounds
             Algeria   .60
             Tunisia   .29
             Libya     .09
             Pakistan .08
             Mexico    .05
```

Source: World Health Organization, International Agency for Research on Cancer, *Tobacco Habits,* IARC Monographs, p. 56.

tobacco is especially high in the other North African states—Algeria, Tunisia, and Libya. As Table 7.2 shows, these countries now lead in the per capita use of this product; however, their consumption is comparatively light compared to that found in the United States between 1880 and 1940.[15] While the evidence is very recent, it again lends credibility to nineteenth century accounts. The process of modernization and the adoption of European customs encourages cigarette consumption and discourages the use of traditional forms. Hence, it is reasonable to assume that—although they never may have equalled the U.S. record—the North Africans used chewing tobacco more frequently a century ago.

The Negro tribes immediately to the south of the Sahara live at the end of the caravan routes from North Africa, and their habits are strongly influenced by North African ("Arab") culture. Tobacco practices in West Africa are close to those of the Moroccans, while the habits of the Sudanese resemble those of their Egyptian neighbors. Smoking and snuffing are favored; chewing also is found, but it is less common than in Algeria. Mungo Park, who explored what are today Senegal and Mali from 1795 to 1797, described both smoking and snuffing as common among all social classes; tobacco was considered highly valuable and had a fixed worth relative to weapons and iron. Park's impressions are confirmed by later travelers who found the water pipe and strong snuff throughout the region stretching from Timbuktu and Liberia in the West to the Sudan in the East.[16] Most Africans consider nasal snuff and sneezing to be highly refreshing, and they often have mixed piquant substances with powdered tobacco to increase its bite. In the sub-Saharan north, the tribes traditionally have made use of *natron,* a kind of soda made by distilling pond water. In the more southern regions of Africa, many peoples similarly used chili peppers.

From 1850, Europeans also began to explore equatorial and southern Africa, where they again found extensive use of both water and clay pipes. Snuff and chewing tobacco also were prevalent; indeed, chewing tobacco apparently is more common in southern Africa than in the Muslim states of the Sahara or the Sudan. While their reports do not permit precise measurement, specific tribes seem to have made greater use of one form of these than of others. What was never found by European travelers was the cigar or the cigarette. As in North Africa and the Sahara, these were introduced only during this century by European colonists; early accounts describe the Africans as reacting with amusement or confusion when offered cigars.[17]

In coastal Nigeria, the Cameroons, Angola, and the Congo, the pipe seems to have held pride of place. But some inland tribes also used and even preferred oral snuff. Snuff also is found in Uganda and Central Africa, and it apparently was popular among the Zulus at the beginning of the nineteenth century. Like their compatriots in Europe, the Dutch (now Afrikaans) in the Cape of Good Hope have been reputed to be heavy pipe smokers. Some also used snuff, however; and it is impossible to know whether the whites learned this habit from the natives or vice versa.[18] In 1950, smokeless products represented only 2 percent of reported sales in South Africa, but snuff seems to have been more widely used in earlier years.[19]

Smokeless tobacco perhaps was used most extensively along the eastern coast of Africa, where the natives seem to have equalled the Algerians in their consumption of pressed chewing tobacco and moist oral snuff. An ethnological expedition in 1893 found the Gallas enjoying smoking, chewing, and snuffing. But their neighbors, the Somalis and Danakils, used only chewing tobacco, and literally did not know how to smoke. In Madagascar and Zanzibar, some tribes smoked tobacco in stone or water pipes, but all tribes carried snuff boxes. Like the Swedes and Americans, these Africans use snuff as an oral product. "Snuff is taken in the mouth, never in the nose, a pinch of the powder being thrown on the tongue or placed between the lower lip and the gum."[20]

7.3 INDIA

Portuguese merchants brought the tobacco plant to the west and possibly also to the east coast of Africa, but it was carried inland by native merchants along the caravan routes linking Africa to the Muslim states in the north. In India also, the "noble weed" was introduced by the Portuguese and quickly adopted by the native peoples throughout the subcontinent. Traveling around the Cape of Good Hope, Portuguese explorers first reached India in 1497, and in 1510 established Goa as the capital of a protectorate along the southwestern coast. Tobacco reached Portugal itself from Brazil about 1550, and it is possible that merchants carried it to India during the next half century. However, the few commercial records remaining from that era are silent about the plant, and its presence in India first is attested in 1605 by an officer at the court of the Mogul emperor in Delhi; according to his account, the emperor debated with his physician the propriety of essaying this new drug.[21]

Not later than 1620, tobacco was being cultivated throughout the emperor's realm. In the south, it is recorded as growing in Ceylon in 1610 and was sowed near Goa in 1617. By the latter year, tobacco also was raised in the Ganges valley in the Northeast as well in the Gujarat region northwest of Bombay; and it had been carried further north to what are today Pakistan and Afghanistan by 1650. Many regions thus proved hospitable to this new crop, which was exported to Moka and Arecan on the Red Sea by 1619 and harvested in great abundance by 1650. At the end of the eighteenth century, the plant had become so common and familiar to the native peoples that they considered it indigenous to the subcontinent.[22] Various varieties of sun-cured dark leaf formed the majority of the crop, but significant amounts of the stronger *Nicotiana rustica* also have been grown in the northern regions and in the Punjab in what is now Pakistan. As in Africa, the government recently has encouraged the growing of sun-cured light tobacco; at the end of the 1950s, however, only 70 million pounds of light were harvested compared to more than 400 million of the dark varieties.[23]

The Mogul emperors ruled over a congeries of native princes and peoples, both Muslim and Hindu. As the Mogul Empire weakened during the eighteenth century, the French and the British disputed control over the native princes; ultimately, the British East India Company won out, establishing an effective protectorate from 1763 until 1857, when control was assumed by the viceroy for the British crown. Under the raj and until the division of the continent into the two independent states of India and Pakistan in 1948, only the more populous cities were directly administered by the British; many regions remained under native princes, with British residents in effective control. The East India Company established a monopoly over cultivation in the regions it directly controlled (which harvested 375 million pounds about 1895); both production and marketing were free in most of the native states.[24]

Thus, until recently the central administration did not keep track of consumption by the many peoples of widely disparate cultures that inhabited the vast subcontinent, and little is known about practices in the rural villages. Overall, literary evidence suggests that tobacco habits differed between a northern and a southern zone. The northern zone, more or less Muslim in religion and crossed by established trade routes, stretched from northern India west to Persia and the Ottoman Empire and then south to include Africa. In this northern or Muslim zone, the water pipe and snuff prevailed; cigars and cigarettes were rare until the twentieth century, and their use sometimes was considered a sign of low social rank.[25] The Indians either independently invented the nargileh or hookah, or they very quickly imported it from Persia; while it perhaps became most popular among the Muslims in the central and northern provinces, it is mentioned during all periods by travelers to all regions.[26]

As in North Africa, Muslims both smoked and snuffed, but conscientious Hindus avoided smoking. According to a traveler during the 1660s, Portuguese men and women in Goa took snuff with great enthusiasm, and they may have passed this habit to the Indians with whom they traded. During the eighteenth century and the first half of the nineteenth, the snuffs prepared with tobaccos from certain regions were highly esteemed in Europe; these also were taken at the court of the Mogul emperor and the greater princes, for whom were created elaborate snuff-boxes equal to any designed for the courtiers of Louis XIV in

France. By the end of the eighteenth century, according to contemporary travelers' accounts, Hindus of lower rank also used powdered snuff. The latter was the only form of tobacco permitted to members of the Brahmin or priestly caste, who were not allowed to smoke cheroots or pipes; once tobacco had touched a Brahmin's lips, it was said to be defiled by his saliva and could not be returned to his mouth.[27]

In the northern or Muslim zone, the water pipe and snuff were favored, and cigars, cigarettes, and chewing tobacco were less common. In contrast, chewing tobacco is very frequent in a southeastern trade zone that includes southern India, Burma, Ceylon, Malaysia, Sumatra, and Indochina. Since antiquity, the peoples of this southern zone have chewed betel, which is made from slices or pieces of the fruit of the betel palm. Together with lime paste and other aromatic flavorings, these betel pieces are smeared onto the leaf of the betel pepper, which is then rolled up. It was a short step to add tobacco leaves to the other ingredients or simply to chew tobacco with lime.[28]

In addition to enjoying the water pipe, snuff, and chewing tobacco, the peoples of this southern zone are also the only Asians to make significant use of cigars and cigarettes. It is possible that the Spanish brought these forms to the Philippines, where they entered into Asian commerce. However, they also may have been independently developed by the peoples of this zone, who are described as smoking something like a true cigar at the end of the seventeenth century.[29] More popular in India itself was the cheroot, a truncated cigar made from strong dark tobaccos in Manila and at Trinchinopoly in southern India; it has been described as very strong and as possessing an unpleasant aroma. The natives of south India also favor the strong bidi or biri. A cross between a cigarillo and a true cigarette, bidis are made of powered dark tobacco wrapped in a special leaf grown in the states of Andhra Pradesh and Orissa in south India.

Also ancient in parts of this southern zone are true cigarettes—called buncos or bonkos by the Malays—made from strips of tobacco or crushed leaf and wrapped in the dried leaves of the banana, various palms, or maize. Although cigarettes wrapped in vegetable matter also are found under this name in south India as early as the seventeenth century, the Indians generally seem to have made greater use of cheroots or bidis.[30] During the twentieth century, the wealthier classes often have adopted as a sign of high social status cigarettes of the "U.S." type, wrapped in paper and containing milder flue-cured and Burley leaf. As Table 7.3 shows, however, partially because they escaped some excise taxes, the traditional type of cigarette still predominated in the overall market as late as 1950; perhaps half of the paper-wrapped cigarettes resembled the U.S. type, with the rest being made of dark air-cured or *rustica*.[31]

7.4 JAPAN

During the fifteenth century, the Portuguese crown encouraged the establishment of trade with Asia, and explorers operating under its flag were the first to

Table 7.3
Tobacco Consumption in India, 1950

Thousands of U.S Pounds

Snuff	Chewing	Hookah	Cigars[1]	Bidis	Cigar-ettes	Total
5,600	128,900	118,500	50,400	101,600	54,800	454,200

Percent of Total[2]

Snuff	Chewing	Hookah	Cigars[1]	Bidis	Cigar-ettes
1%	28%	26%	11%	22%	12%

[1] Includes cheroots.

[2] Percentages may not sum to 100 percent due to rounding into whole numbers.

Sources: Indian Council of Agricultural Research; Lee, *Tobacco Consumption in Various Countries*, p. 40.

reach the coasts of Africa, Arabia, Persia, India, China, and Japan. Merchants in these areas carried tobacco inland, and their inhabitants sometimes developed novel ways of consuming tobacco. Nevertheless, they owe to the Portuguese the credit for introducing the seeds of the "noble weed." Shortly after the Portuguese crown in 1537 made Macao the center for its trade in China, three merchant junks accidentally discovered Japan in 1542 or 1543. Based on the island of Kyushu, south of the main island of Honshu, the Portuguese established limited commercial contacts, and the Jesuit Francis Xavier began proselytizing for Christian converts in 1549. From the end of the sixteenth century, the shoguns began to restrict Christian missions, and all contacts with Europeans were prohibited (except for one Dutch post at Nagasaki) from 1637 to 1854.

Precisely when the Portuguese first introduced tobacco is not known. Japanese sources state that it was sowed near Nagasaki in 1605, but the plant may already have been introduced in the 1580s or 1590s. Certainly the crop was already flourishing in the 1610s, when the shogun made several ineffective attempts to prohibit its growing. From the southern islands, the Japanese rather quickly carried tobacco cultivation north, and it was cultivated throughout the empire by the 1700s.[32] The southern regions of both China and Japan lie in a belt that is climatically highly suitable for the cultivation of tobacco. During their centuries of isolation from the West, Japanese growers thus developed a number of native types—almost all air- and sun-cured—that are characterized by fine tissue, delicate veins, and the mild flavor that Japanese smokers have always preferred.[33]

Within the context of Japan's relatively rigid system of feudal land ownership, all aspects of the tobacco trade were in private hands until 1904 when the Meiji government erected the Japanese Tobacco and Salt Corporation (JTS) as one of several state monopolies. For many years, the JTS, like several European tobacco monopolies, reported directly to the finance ministry. During the U.S. occupation, it was reorganized in 1949 as a separate nationalized industry. The monopoly has total control over all aspects of cultivation, manufacturing, distribution, and retail sales; until recently, it effectively shut out foreign imports.[34] Under the guidance of the JTS, production is intensive, and crop yields are high, with more than ten thousand peasants cultivating farms that average less than a quarter of an acre in area. In addition to the native light tobaccos, the monopoly has since the 1930s fostered the growing of flue-cured Bright and Burley; by the end of the 1950s, flue-cured tobacco represented more than half the harvest.[35]

Statements about Japanese consumption patterns must be advanced cautiously. During more than two centuries, Japanese governments did not allow foreigners to enter the empire. We thus have no travelers' reports, and observers native to a culture often do not report on or even notice commonplace activities. Overall, the majority of Japanese tobacco consumers seem to have smoked tobacco that was cut very fine. The traditional style of pipe, also frequently found in China, has three parts—a long bamboo tube with a small metal bowl at one end and a metal mouthpiece at the other.[36] Apparently, the Japanese did not use either cigars or cigarettes, and their preference for the pipe may explain why farmers developed several types of mild tobaccos.

By the 1700s, nasal snuff also was taken. The Japanese may have prepared their own snuffs, and they purchased them from Chinese merchants, sometimes preserved in small bottles of clear green glass imported from Portugal. Again, a specific etiquette grew up, and Japanese artists also developed special forms for snuff boxes, generally made of lacquered papier mâché.[37] However, pressed chewing tobacco does not seem to have been present, except perhaps among the Ainu peoples on the northern islands.[38]

During the Meiji era, the Japanese sought to adapt aspects of Western technology to their own needs, and the state monopoly offered its customers Western-style cigars (made from native dark tobaccos) and cigarettes. As Table 7.4 indicates, Japanese tobacco consumers have adopted cigarettes more rapidly than in most European countries.[39] The traditional pipes using fine-cut smoking tobacco are now rarely found, and the JTS no longer sells snuff, although courtiers still took it at the beginning of this century. Some seventeenth-century sources and more recent observers describe the Japanese as heavy smokers; however, their per capita usage during this century has been lower than that in the United States and in several European nations.

7.5 CHINA

Up to the second half of the nineteenth century, the suzerainty of the Ming (1368–1644) and Manchu (1644–1922) emperors was recognized by several hundred million souls within an empire that extended as far as Tibet to the west,

Table 7.4
Tobacco Sales in Japan, 1925–1950

	Thousands of U.S Pounds				Percent of Total[1]		
			Cigar-				Cigar-
	Cut	Cigars	ettes	Total	Cut	Cigars	ettes
1925	52,100	60	60,127	112,287	46%	--[2]	54%
1930	51,900	15	66,581	118,496	44	--	46
1940	43,200	30	113,276	156,506	28	--	72
1950	21,700	30	143,957	165,687	13	--	87

[1]Percentages may not sum to 100 percent due to rounding into whole numbers.
[2]Less than 0.5 percent.

Sources: Japanese Tobacco and Salt Corporation; Lee, *Tobacco Consumption in Various Countries*, p. 46.

Indochina to the south, Korea and Taiwan to the east, and parts of Mongolia and Manchuria to the north. Within this vast realm, the emperor's subjects raised excellent tobacco of several types and consumed it in all the usual ways. From China, merchants carried tobacco south as well as north to eastern Siberia, where the native peoples adopted Chinese practices.[40]

The tobacco plant was carried from South America to China by 1600 along one or more of several possible routes.[41] However it reached China, tobacco was extensively cultivated in the southern provinces by the 1630s, when the new crop attracted the attention of the crown. Like the rulers of virtually every other state into which it was introduced, the Chinese emperors in 1638 and 1641 prohibited its cultivation (under penalty of decapitation); as in every other country where this was attempted, prohibition could not be enforced. Much of China lies in a zone that is favorable to the cultivation of tobacco, and the highly skilled Chinese peasants developed effective techniques for producing both sun- and air-cured varieties. Not later than the end of the seventeenth century, *Nicotiana tabacum* was grown throughout the empire, and *Nicotiana rustica* was also raised to a limited extent in northern Shensi and in the mountainous districts of Hopeh and Szechwan, where *tabacum* could not be grown.[42] Since the 1920s, as in several other regions, flue-cured Burley has also been introduced; as Table 7.5 shows, it today accounts for perhaps a third or more of the crop.

Table 7.5
Tobacco Production in China, 1955–1959 (average) (in thousands of U.S. pounds)

Flue-cured	603,681
Light sun-cured	513,202
Dark air-cured	469,429
Dark sun-cured	101,318

Source: Akehurst, *Tobacco*, pp. 117, 489–98.

As in Japan, cigars and cigarettes were comparatively rare, and the pipe provided the main way in which the Chinese enjoyed tobacco prior to the twentieth century. Both the dry pipe and the water pipe were present throughout the empire, with both forms carried to a high state of design and finish among the wealthy.[43] Although it is likely that more Chinese were smokers than were snuffers, a significant number have taken nasal snuff from at least the 1640s to the present. The introduction of snuff often is attributed to Portuguese merchants trading in Macao and Canton from the sixteenth century, or to the Jesuits, who established a mission at the court in Peking about 1601. However, it is also possible that the Chinese themselves discovered this way of enjoying tobacco. As in Europe, Chinese physicians and apothecaries studied the medicinal uses of tobacco, and it would have been natural to reduce it to a powder as was done with other herbs or even with tea.

We cannot establish precisely when the Chinese first began to use manufactured snuff for pleasure. A missionary writing in 1726 stated that the Chinese nobility had used snuff for about a century, which would push its introduction back to the 1620s. And collectors of snuff bottles attribute some early examples to the early seventeenth or even the late sixteenth century. By 1685 snuff was imported throughout Canton, and it was regularly presented to the emperor by the Peking Jesuits on ceremonial occasions between 1684 and 1752.[44] These first references to snuff cite its use by the courtier and mandarin classes. But both imported and domestic snuffs also were taken by members of the middling and lower classes.

The first packages containing snuffs imported from Europe were marked with the French fleur-de-lis; since the exotic sells, this insignia provided the traditional emblem of snuff shops into the twentieth century, much as statues of Indians, Scotsmen, and Blackamoors marked the entrance to tobacconists in the United States. According to the *Hiang tsu pi ki,* published in 1705, snuff was manufactured both in Peking and Canton, with snuff from Canton even surpassing "that made for the Palace. It is manufactured in five different colors, that of apple color taking the first rank." Lower grades also were sold, both plain and perfumed. Since the eighteenth century, mint, camphor, and jasmine have been the most popular aromatics, and essence of rose also is used. At the beginning of the twentieth century, tobacco from Shantung with a distinctive aroma was preferred. After it had been fermented or sweated, the dried leaves were carefully freed from the stems and ribs, crushed in a mill or mortar, and then winnowed through sieves before being scented.[45]

Although Europeans preferred boxes, wealthy Chinese carried snuff in small bottles, which developed out of the phials used by druggists. Many of these have been preserved, in an endless variety of shapes and designs made out of glass, porcelain, ivory, coral, mother of pearl, amber, crystal, and semiprecious gemstones; among the most highly prized are glass bottles with beneficent statements written on the inside. Traditionally, the bottles are closed by a stopper shaped like a small knob and often made of a different material, and the snuff was removed from the bottle with spoons of silver, ivory, bone, horn, or bamboo. Many of these bottles are of exquisite workmanship, with connoisseurs generally preferring those made under the Chi'ien Lung emperor (1736–1795).[46]

Snuff seems to have lost some of its mystique after 1850, and the quality of snuff bottles is said to have declined. As in France and Italy, however, snuff continued to be taken in China up to the present day. At the end of the nineteenth and the beginning of the twentieth centuries, European visitors to Peking found a number of special shops selling only snuff and displaying the traditional fleur-de-lis insignia. By 1937, snuff was still sold, but the French emblem had disappeared, perhaps in response to the nationalistic sentiment of the period.[47] Most European sources refer to snuff in Peking simply because this region was most frequently visited. While snuff may have been more popular in the capital than in the provinces, the location of factories in southern China suggests that it was also used in that region. In any case, large snuff firms still existed in Shanghai in 1923 when a U.S. anthropologist purchased ten different varieties from the proprietor of the most important shop, which was run by Muslims from Lan-chou.[48]

NOTES

1. See Chapter 3, Note 92.

2. Comes, *Histoire*, 117–20, 165–78; Laufer, *Introduction of Tobacco*, 61–63.

3. Laufer, *Tobacco in Asia*, 15.

4. Most of the popular histories describe the attempts—ferocious and colorful but ineffective—by the Ottoman and Persian sultans to enforce these bans; according to European observers, they routinely cut off ears and noses and, in one case, forced a pipe through a poor smoker's nostrils. While these reports may well be exaggerated, they do prove that at least some of the sultans' subjects used tobacco. See Brooks, *Tobacco in Arents*, 71–75; Mackenzie, *Sublime Tobacco*, 124–25; Comes, *Histoire*, 217–25; Corti, *History of Smoking*, 138–39.

5. See Section 2.3.

6. Akehurst, (*Tobacco*, 488–501) provides an estimate of average production (during the years 1954–1959) throughout the world of the eight main types of tobacco—light (flue-cured, air-cured Burley, other air-cured, and sun-cured); Oriental and Semi-Oriental; and dark (air-cured, sun-cured, and fire-cured). For the earlier centuries, see Billings, *Tobacco*, 369–74.

7. See Chapter 2, Note 26; Price, *Tobacco adventure*, 52; Mavor, *Economic History of Russia*, I:104, II:203–4.

8. As part of their policy to achieve autarky after World War I, the French colonial administration increased Algerian production; according to Huston (*Consumption*, 71), an average of 18 million pounds were exported to France each year from 1926 to 1935. For the nineteenth century, see Billings, *Tobacco*, 170, 360; Comes, *Histoire*, 169–70.

9. Comes, *Histoire*, 167.

10. See Tables 6.3 and 6.4, which list tobacco consumption in 1925 and 1950 in those nations that provide plausible records.

11. Johann Neander's *Tabacologia*, published in Leiden in 1622, contains two en-

gravings of the Persian nargileh, which already was in use in the Comoros Islands near Madagascar in 1622 and in Madagascar itself by 1638; Fairholt, *Tobacco,* 204; Laufer, Hambly, and Linton, *Tobacco in Africa,* 11; Laufer, *Tobacco in Asia,* 27–28.

12. The water pipe always has been something of a luxury. As in Europe, the less affluent smokers in Turkey, Egypt, and Africa used pipes with clay bowls, with the stems sometimes made of horn or maple, or of aromatic woods such as cherry or jasmine. See Fairholt, *Tobacco,* 204–12; Laufer, Hambly, and Linton, *Tobacco in Africa,* 16–17, 21, 37; Billings, *Tobacco,* 157–58, 167–70; Comes, *Histoire,* 165, 173.

13. Comes, *Histoire,* 119, 165; Table 5.6 above.

14. Comes, *Histoire,* 168–172, 232; Billings, *Tobacco,* 364; Fairholt, *Tobacco,* 291; Laufer, Hambly, and Linton, *Tobacco in Africa,* 18–19; Charles Doughty, *Travels in Arabia Deserta,* passim.

15. Table 6.11 above. For chewing tobacco in Algeria, see also Tucker, *Tobacco: An International Perspective,* 68.

16. Park, *Travels in the Interior of Africa,* 164 and passim; Laufer, Hambly, and Linton, *Tobacco in Africa,* 19–21; Comes, *Histoire,* 173–77.

17. We can only speculate why these forms are absent. Many African tobaccos produce leaves unsuitable for cigar wrappers, and cigars could not be kept fresh during the long months of caravan travel. But these technical factors do not explain why the Africans never developed the cigarette wrapped in maize or palm leaves such as is found in South America and Southeast Asia.

18. Billings, *Tobacco,* 169–70; Comes, *Histoire,* 178–85; Laufer, Hambly 22–37; Mackenzie, *Sublime Tobacco,* 314–17.

19. Table 6.4. The statistics cited report only sales in the commercial market, and they do not include local consumption of homegrown leaf.

20. Quoting Ralph Linton, in Laufer, Hambly, and Linton, *Tobacco in Africa,* 41.

21. Laufer, *Asia,* 11–15.

22. Ibid.; Comes, *Histoire,* 195–208.

23. Comes, *Histoire,* 208–9; Tucker, *Tobacco: An International Perspective,* 42; Akehurst, *Tobacco,* 9, 491–98. The harvest at the end of the 1950s had fallen from almost 800 million pounds twenty years earlier.

24. Comes, *Histoire,* 209.

25. Comes, *Histoire,* 204.

26. Edward Terry, who lived in India from 1616 to 1619, thus described its use, as did Peter Mundy, who worked for the East India Company from 1628 to 1634: Laufer, *Tobacco in Asia,* 11–12, Comes, *Histoire,* 197–205.

27. See Chapter 3, Note 21; Comes, *Histoire,* 202, 208; Laufer, *Tobacco in Asia,* 39. For snuff consumption in India, see also World Health Organization, *Tobacco Habits,* 61.

28. Brooks, *Tobacco in Arents,* I:149.

29. Ibid., I:166, Note 19; Laufer, *Tobacco in Asia,* 18.

30. Comes, *Histoire,* 199 (1779), 208; Tucker, *Tobacco: An International Perspective,* 41–42; Laufer, *Tobacco in Asia,* 19–20.

31. Tucker, *Tobacco: An International Perspective,* and 37, 127, 130. Compared to the European nations (see Table 6.4), tobacco consumption in India would seem to be low, but these governmental statistics do not include a significant but unknown amount of homegrown tobacco.

32. Comes, *Histoire,* 247–253; Laufer, *Tobacco in Asia,* 1–2.

33. See Chapter 2, Note 7; Akehurst, *Tobacco,* 38, 210–11; Billings, *Tobacco,* 371; Comes, *Histoire,* 253–54; Akehurst, *Tobacco,* 210–11.

34. Tucker, *Tobacco: An International Perspective,* 106–7; Akehurst, *Tobacco,* 127.

35. Ibid., 32, 120, 210. During the years 1955–1959, Japanese farmers harvested, on average, about 200 million pounds of flue-cured Bright, 9 million pounds of Burley, and more than 100 million pounds of native sun-cured light tobaccos: ibid., 489–97.

36. As is normal in this culture, these pipes often were highly decorated, and ceremonial forms of smoking had been developed by the 1690s: Comes, *Histoire,* 251–52; Billings, *Tobacco,* 173.

37. Comes, *Histoire,* 253; Curtis, *Snuff and Snuff-Boxes,* 88.

38. Comes, *Histoire,* 255; Laufer, *Tobacco in Asia,* 31.

39. See Table 6.4. By 1925 (Table 7.4), cigarettes represented more than half the monopoly's sales; their share rose to 90 percent by 1950 after a rapid increase in sales during the 1940s.

40. Brooks, *Tobacco in Arents,* I:146–47, 154; Laufer, *Tobacco in Asia,* 15–17.

41. The Portuguese, who brought tobacco seeds to Japan, probably also introduced them to China, where they had established trading centers on the southern coast at Macao (1537) and Canton (1567). The Dutch, who receive credit for having introduced tobacco to Istanbul in 1605, may have shipped it to Taiwan, which they occupied from 1624 to 1662. It is possible that the Japanese simultaneously introduced tobacco to the northern provinces of China via Korea and Manchuria, with which they traded. In addition, Chinese merchants themselves, sailing from Fukein province in the southeast, by 1600 were carrying tobacco from Luzon in the Philippines, where it had earlier been introduced by the Spanish. See Comes, *Histoire,* 256–65; Laufer, *Tobacco in Asia,* 2–4.

42. Laufer, *Tobacco in Asia,* 4–5; Comes, *Histoire,* 268–69, 274–77; Billings, *Tobacco,* 373–74; Akehurst, *Tobacco,* 11, 37–48.

43. The dry pipe, also used in Japan, has three separate parts, allowing it to be easily cleaned: A stem (made of bamboo or other woods) connects a small bowl (of copper, alloy, or brass) to a mouthpiece (of stone, ivory, or milk-white glass). By 1700 the water pipe had been brought from India to Kansu province and Chinese Turkestan, whence it was carried throughout the empire—although it always was most common in the Muslim regions in the southwest. Although they borrowed the principle, Chinese artisans created several new types of water pipes, usually in copper or brass and sometimes decorated with ivory or precious stones. See Laufer, *Tobacco in Asia,* 20–23, 28–31; Billings, *Tobacco,* 172; Comes, *Histoire,* 260, 274.

44. Comes, *Histoire,* 271–72; Laufer, *Tobacco in Asia,* 32; Carrington, "Ancient Snuff Boxes," 13; Curtis, *Snuff and Snuff-Boxes,* 93.

45. Laufer, *Tobacco in Asia,* 33–34; Comes, *Histoire,* 268.

46. Laufer, *Tobacco in Asia,* 35–36; Curtis, *Snuff and Snuff-Boxes,* 93–97.

47. Comes, *Histoire,* 268; Carrington, "Ancient Snuff Boxes," 14.

48. Laufer, *Tobacco in Asia,* 32.

Glossary

AGING. After it has been dried or *cured,* tobacco undergoes a process variously called aging, fermentation, or sweating. This additional step serves to develop the desired odor and aroma and to eliminate a raw, harsh, or bitter taste found in freshly cured leaf. The precise nature of the aging process varies depending on the variety of leaf, and the distinction between aging and fermentation is one of degree or intensity. Aging is a relatively slow and gentle process, largely uncontrolled and involving low heat and moisture content. Fermentation describes a more vigorous method, which today is usually controlled, in which the tobacco is subjected to a higher moisture content and larger temperature changes; because the tobacco becomes heated and gives off moisture during active fermentation, the latter process also is called sweating.

The methods used to age tobacco have changed little over the centuries. The process of natural aging undergone by today's flue-cured and Burley cigarette tobaccos is not substantially different from that used for the air-dried dark tobaccos prevalent during the eighteenth century. In both cases, the cured leaf is pressed or "prized" into large hogsheads weighing nine hundred to one thousand pounds. These are then stored in large, well-ventilated warehouses for twelve to thirty months while the leaf undergoes the desired chemical changes. In earlier times, care was taken to prize the leaf during a dry season. Today it may be mechanically "redried" prior to aging through the application of heat and sometimes steam; this ensures a more uniform moisture content at the desired level.

Leaf destined for cigars, pressed chewing tobacco, and snuff generally undergoes a more intense fermentation after it is aged. In making nasal snuff, aged leaf is subjected to active fermentation or sweating for several months before it is ground into powder. Eighteenth-century sources speak of three weeks of fermentation; current manufacturing processes call for two to four months. In manufacturing moist oral snuff, the aged and conditioned leaf may first be chopped or cut into ribbons before it is repacked to undergo fermentation or sweating for two to twelve months. For pressed or *plug* chewing tobacco, fermentation is somewhat briefer (as little as a week during the eighteenth century); in the United States, the leaf usually is fermented in a "sauce" or sweetening agent.

In the case of cigar leaf, active fermentation precedes aging. In Cuba, cigar leaves traditionally were carefully piled into heaps to ferment in their own heat and then were hung to age for six months to three years. In the United States and in Europe, this traditional ''bulk'' sweating method still is used for leaf of high value, with faster mechanized methods being employed for less expensive brands. After an initial sweat, which lasts six to twelve months, the piles are broken and may be remoistened. Ultimately the leaf is repacked in cases or bales and allowed to age for as long as several years.

AIR CURING. After they are harvested, tobacco leaves are dried or cured. With air curing, this is accomplished by exposing the leaves to the surrounding atmosphere, usually by hanging or suspending them in some sort of structure that protects them from rain and direct sunlight. Over the centuries, these structures have evolved from simple huts to large barns, sometimes covering several acres, in which humidity, temperature, and air circulation can be controlled. Originally, almost all tobacco was air-cured, and this method still accounts for about 20 percent of the leaf in the world market.

Both *dark* and *light* tobaccos are air-cured. Historically, air-cured dark types are very common. Air-cured dark can be grown in a variety of soil types, usually of a heavy texture. The leaf is heavy, dark, and thick, and it sometimes is described as having a strong or even harsh flavor.

Until the middle of the nineteenth century, the majority of the tobacco produced in Virginia (under the name Oronoko) was dark air-cured, and the tobacco grown in Europe was also of this type. Thus, air-cured dark varieties were the basis of most of the snuff, chewing tobacco, and pipe tobacco consumed in the United States and Europe prior to the 1830s. With the development of other varieties, dark air-cured leaf came to be used in the United States mainly for chewing tobacco and as one element of blended pipe tobaccos; in France, Spain, and Italy, it also has been used to make the less-expensive ''black'' cigarettes. Most of the tobacco used in cigars is also of this type.

The best-known light air-cured varieties are *Burley* and *Maryland,* which are used to manufacture cigarettes and pipe tobacco. Both were developed in the United States during the nineteenth century and today also are cultivated in other parts of the world. Depending on the climate and soil, Burley is more or less mild.

APALTO. A term used in parts of the Germanies and Central Europe to refer to the *farmed monopolies* controlling the manufacture, distribution, and retail sales of tobacco products.

BIDI. A cross between a cigarillo and a cigarette, the strong-tasting bidi (or biri) is made of powdered dark tobacco wrapped in a special leaf grown in the states of Andhra Pradesh and Orissa; they are consumed throughout southern India.

BRIGHT TOBACCO. Together with the process of *flue curing,* which is essential to its production, Bright tobacco was developed in North Carolina during the first half of the nineteenth century; it also is raised in South Carolina, Georgia, and Virginia. It grows best in an environment characterized by relatively infertile soil with a low nitrogen content, a mild climate, and reliable rainfall, which is found in these states. When subjected to flue curing, the leaf grown in this environment becomes light in color (often a pure yellow) and possesses a smooth, oily texture; it characteristically is light-bodied, low in nicotine, and high in sugar.

Flue-cured Bright leaf at first was grown to provide an attractive wrapper for *pressed* or *plug chewing tobacco,* and it is still used for this purpose and also for pipe tobacco. Toward the end of the nineteenth century, its mild and lightly aromatic taste was also found to be highly suitable in blended *cigarettes.* As the demand for cigarettes increased, so also did cultivation of Bright, which now provides almost half of world tobacco production. Bright (often called *Virginia* outside the United States) today is raised on every continent, sometimes in environments not wholly suitable to production of the true type.

BURLEY. Burley (earlier called White Burley) is a true mutation of a dark air-cured type (Red Burley), and was first noticed in 1864 in Brown County, Ohio. Although farm management and soil types can produce Burley that is darker or lighter, it characteristically is a relatively light and mild tobacco that is grown on deep, fairly rich loamy soils and is *air cured.* Because it can absorb large amounts of sugar and other sweeteners (up to 25 percent of its own weight), Burley was rapidly developed as an alternative to *Bright* and ultimately came to dominate the U.S. chewing tobacco market. It is today grown throughout the world for use in cigarettes and as pipe tobacco.

CAROTTE. From the end of the seventeenth century, large blocks of pressed tobacco which were so called in France because they were shaped something like the root vegetable of the same name (carrot). This name also was used in other European countries as well as in Colonial America, where carottes up to twenty inches in length were manufactured. In contrast to the smaller and softer *rôles,* carottes were generally sold in a dry, hard form; in France, from the 1720s on, the carrot-shaped product was wound with string along its full length, and it thus is also referred to as *tabac ficelé* (tied tobacco). Leaf intended for sale as carottes was first twisted or spun (and might also be sweetened or flavored) before being placed under pressure in iron molds for twenty-four to forty-eight hours.

CHEWING TOBACCO. One of the original ways of consuming tobacco is "chewing," in which the consumer places the leaf or prepared tobacco in the corner of the mouth in order to absorb its flavors. Users sometimes move this lump or "quid," moistened by their saliva, around in the mouth; but few actually chew it in a vigorous manner.

It is possible to chew many forms of prepared tobacco, and the forms used for this purpose have changed over the centuries. Prior to the nineteenth century, European and American manufacturers generally offered only three types of products. In addition to powdered nasal snuff and cut smoking tobacco, they produced a variety of multipurpose twisted or pressed products—the most common being the softer *rôles* and harder *carottes*—that the consumer might grate for snuff, cut up for chewing, or slice for smoking tobacco. Since these twisted or pressed products were purchased by both smokers and snuffers, it is difficult to estimate the popularity of chewing. However, literary evidence shows that chewing was practiced in Europe and the Americas from the introduction of tobacco itself.

From the 1840s and 1850s, these multipurpose pressed products were eclipsed by those intended specifically for chewing. (Coarsely cut chewing products also are available, but these are less common than pressed.) In America, this change was signaled by the introduction of the oblong-shaped *plug,* which increasingly came to be sweetened and flavored. In Europe, special products destined for this market also appeared about the middle of the century; in contrast to the U.S. products, however, these often were not artificially flavored. Judging by sales, chewing tobacco was most popular in the United States and in parts of Scandinavia; although it is present in almost all European countries, it generally has represented less than 10 percent of total sales of tobacco products.

Chewing tobacco, both flavored and unflavored, is found in most parts of the world. In Africa it was especially common among the caravan peoples and bedouins of North Africa, the Sahara, and West Africa. In Asia, chewing was practiced particularly in a southeastern trade zone that includes southern India, Burma, Ceylon, Malaysia, Sumatra, and Indochina. It also was used in China and among the native peoples to the north of China, but it apparently always has been rare in Japan.

CIGAR. Strictly speaking, what the Spanish call a true cigar *(cigarro puro)* is a cylindrical roll that is made solely of tobacco leaves in three different forms—the filler, the binder, and the wrapper. In the manufacturing process, the filler leaves are formed into the shape of the cigar; the binder leaf is then wrapped around the filler to create a bundle called a "bunch." This composite bunch then is covered with the wrapper leaf, which is wound on spirally (either clockwise or counterclockwise), starting at the fire end and ending at the head. Until the late 1920s, all this was done by hand; today in Europe and the United States the making of the filler bunch usually is mechanized, but the wrapper leaf still is applied by hand to the best grades.

Cigars are common only in Europe, the Americas, and East Asia, where they have provided a relatively new way of consuming tobacco. North Americans and Europeans did not smoke cigars until the middle of the nineteenth century, some three hundred years after they adopted chewing tobacco, snuff, and the pipe. When the Spanish reached the Americas, the native peoples (in parts of the West Indies, Mexico, and Brazil) smoked something like the modern cigar (tobacco wrapped in tobacco) as well as both large and small cigarettes (tobacco wrapped or contained in a sheath of vegetable matter). However, the Spanish colonists were slow to accept this habit: Although the cigar reached Spain by the end of the seventeenth century, nasal snuff and pipes remained more popular until 1750 or even 1800. In other European countries and in the United States, the cigar became relatively common only during the 1840s. Cigars (and cigarettes) were not found in Africa prior to European colonization at the end of the nineteenth century. They also are rare in the northern or Muslim regions of Asia, and they are found in significant numbers only in the southern trade zone that includes southern India, Burma, Ceylon, Malaysia, Sumatra, and Indochina.

CIGARETTES. The true cigarette (tobacco tightly rolled and wrapped in paper) was developed in Spain during the 1600s. The native peoples in Brazil, Mexico, and the Caribbean Islands sometimes smoked tobacco loosely contained in sheaths of vegetable matter, including reeds, sugar cane, banana leaves, and corn silk. By the end of the sixteenth century, Spanish colonists in these regions also smoked tobacco wrapped in corn silk (as well as pipes and possibly cigars). Sometime after 1600 it became apparent, probably in Spain, that a fine paper was preferable, and the hand-wrapped *papelate* came into existence. Although the maize cigarette continues to exist, papelates slowly gained popularity and were common in Spain and Spanish America by the end of the eighteenth century.

Cigarettes were introduced in other European countries in the 1840s, but they became popular among smokers only starting in the 1880s, with the introduction of machine-made brands; they reached the United States by 1860, where they became common during the first quarter of this century. Like cigars, cigarettes were unknown in Africa and rare in the Muslim regions of the Middle East, Asia, and India; prior to this century, they were used only in a southeastern trade zone that includes southern India, Burma, Ceylon, Malaysia, Sumatra, and Indochina. In addition to true cigarettes, the natives of South India also smoke the native *bidi.*

CIGARILLO. This name is given in the United States to a small *cigar* (tobacco rolled and wrapped in a tobacco leaf).

CURING. Terms like "curing" and *aging* sometimes are applied to various of the stages through which the leaf passes between harvesting and consumption; for example, retailers may speak somewhat loosely of "aging" or "curing" manufactured products such as cigars. Strictly speaking, however, curing refers to the systematic drying of the leaf after it is harvested and before it is aged and goes to the manufacturer. Through the curing process, the fresh leaves are gradually dried under controlled conditions of temperature, humidity, and air supply. As it comes from the field, as much as 80 to 90 percent of tobacco leaf is water, and curing reduces this to 10 to 25 percent. Obviously, the dried leaves are more easily stored and shipped. More important, during the curing process the chemical composition of the leaf changes in ways that bring out and enhance its characteristic flavors and aroma. Each of the four curing processes in common use thus is fully appropriate only with some varieties and is unsuitable for drying other types.

In a sense, all tobacco is cured by allowing warm air to pass over the leaf. However, the term *air-cured* is reserved for a method in which the tobacco is placed under a roof and dries at the ambient air temperature (during bad weather, some heat may be supplied). During the other commonly used processes—*fire curing, sun curing,* and *flue curing*—the temperature of the air surrounding the leaves is raised above that of the surrounding atmosphere. Air curing thus provides the slowest method of drying the leaf, with flue curing being the most rapid.

CUT SMOKING TOBACCO. Along with nasal snuff and chewing tobacco, cut tobacco intended to be smoked in a *pipe* or *water pipe* (more recently, also in home-rolled cigarettes) is one of the original forms in which tobacco has been consumed since its discovery early in the sixteenth century. Smoking tobacco originally was manufactured from air-, sun-, or fire-cured dark leaf; since its discovery in 1864, the heavier grades of flue-cured Burley also have been used, particularly in the United States. After they are cured and aged, the leaves are *spun* into a ribbon or cord and then cut or sliced into small strips or cubes; depending on the size and shape of the latter, they are variously described by names such as flake-cut, fine-cut, and ribbon-cut.

Together with various forms of the pipe, cut smoking tobacco is present everywhere throughout the world. Most has been made of one type of leaf, with the blends of mixtures that combine two or more different varieties appearing in Europe during the second half of the nineteenth century. Since the same era, U.S. manufacturers have sometimes added sweetening or flavoring agents.

DARK TOBACCOS. All tobacco leaf can be described as either *light* or *dark,* with dark tobaccos generally being perceived as stronger in flavor and light tobacco as more mild.

These qualities are affected both by the soil type and by the curing method. Dark tobaccos are grown on heavier soils, which are often rich in organic matter and contain substantial amounts of nitrogen. In the United States and Europe, they are either *air-* or *fire-cured;* in India and Pakistan, they also are *sun-cured.* Air and sun curing produce a heavy, large, thick leaf that is dark brown in color and possesses a strong flavor and aroma; fire-cured dark may be somewhat more oily with a smoky flavor.

It is likely that all tobacco originally was of the dark air-cured variety (called Oronoco in colonial Virginia), with the light varieties *(Burley, Bright,* and *Oriental)* having developed through cultivation on lighter soils and the use of flue and sun curing. Thus, prior to about 1830, all tobacco consumed (whether as snuff, by chewing, or in pipes) was of this type. With the trend toward cigarettes during this century, dark tobaccos now represent a smaller share of the world market. In the West, air-cured dark leaf today primarily is found in chewing tobacco, nasal snuff, cigars, and in the "black" cigarettes smoked in Spain, Italy, and France; in India and East Asia, it also is grown for domestic consumption in *water pipes* and *bidis.* Fire-cured dark leaf primarily is consumed in strong cigars, chewing tobacco, and nasal and oral snuff.

DIPPING. In the United States, a term used in the Southern states to describe the use of moist *oral snuff.* It presumably refers to the process by which the user first "dips" into the container with the fingers or a small spoon or stick and then carries the snuff into the mouth, placing it between the lip and the gums.

FARMED MONOPOLY. A system in which the government of a region or nation (1) abrogates to itself control over one or more aspects of the cultivation and import of tobacco leaf, and the manufacture, distribution, and retail sale of tobacco products, and (2) sells or farms its monopoly powers to one or more corporations. In theory, the state's monopoly powers are auctioned off to the highest bidder for a set number of years. The company holding the farm almost always sets up its own manufacturing plants. In some cases, it also owns the retail outlets; in others, it wholesales its products under license to private retailers, who are required to sell at a set minimum price.

FERMENTATION. See *aging*

FIRE CURING. Toward the end of the seventeenth century or the beginning of the eighteenth, farmers in Virginia began to build small fires on the floors of their drying barns. The increased heat cured the tobacco more rapidly during periods of bad weather. Moreover, depending on the type of wood used, the smoke imparted an additional flavor and aroma to the leaf. Only dark tobaccos are fire-cured, and the leaf produced through this process is described as dark brown in color, with a heavy, oily texture and a strong, often smoky taste and aroma. Originally used both for smoking and for chewing tobacco, fire-cured dark types are still produced in Virginia, Kentucky, Tennessee, Italy, and parts of Africa for use in *cigars, chewing tobacco,* and *oral snuff.*

FLUE CURING. All curing methods serve to dry tobacco after it is harvested. Since flue curing uses the highest temperature, it provides the most rapid way of drying the leaf. In contrast to air curing, artificial heat is used throughout to raise the temperature well above that of the outside air; unlike fire curing, this heat is carried through pipes or flues, and no gasses or smoke enter the curing barn.

This method is comparatively recent, having been generally adopted only in the 1870s. It is both essential to and the only method used in the production of a particular variety of mild light leaf. In the United States this variety is called *Bright;* in Europe, it is given the name *Virginia,* although mainly it is not produced in that state.

GROS RÔLE. A French term ("large roll") for manufactured tobacco sold in the form of a large semisoft *rôle.*

HABSBURG EMPIRE. From 1558 to 1918, the Austrian branch of the Habsburg family ruled over a congeries of polyglot territories primarily located in Central Europe and the Balkans. At various times, these included regions now found in Austria, Czechoslovakia (Bohemia and Moravia), Hungary, Italy (Lombardy, Venetia, and the Tyrol), Poland (Galicia and Silesia), Rumania, and Yugoslavia (Bosnia, Croatia, Dalmatia, Herzegovina, and Istria).

HOOKAH. See *water pipe*

KAU-UND KÜBELTABAK. A German term referring to *chewing tobacco* both cut and *pressed.*

LATAKIA. Latakia is an *Oriental* tobacco originally grown in Syria near a port city of that name. After it is sun-cured in the usual way, it is hung in smoke to add additional flavors, producing a distinctive and highly pungent aroma and taste. It is added in small quantities to pipe mixtures and to a few cigarette brands; in prior centuries, it also was made into *nasal snuff.*

LIGHT TOBACCOS. All tobacco leaf can be described as either *light* or *dark,* with dark tobaccos generally being perceived as stronger in flavor and light tobacco as more mild. These qualities are affected by the soil, climate, and methods of cultivation used. With the exception of *Burley* (which is produced on relatively heavy silt loam soils), light leaf usually is grown on light, open soils; some varieties need soil that is relatively low in nitrogen. Light tobaccos may be air-cured (Burley), flue-cured *(Bright),* or sun-cured *(Oriental).* They generally are characterized by a thin leaf, light in weight and color, and a mild or "weak" taste; they may be more or less aromatic.

MAKHORKA. See *Nicotiana rustica*

MARYLAND. An *air-cured light* leaf grown in the southern counties of that state since the 1820s. Maryland is light in color, fluffy in texture, and mild in taste; it primarily is used in cigarettes.

MENU FILÉ. The French name for the type of chewing tobacco called *twist* in the United States.

MONOPOLY. See *farmed monopoly* and *state monopoly*

NARGILEH. See *water pipe*

NASAL SNUFF. From its introduction into Europe about 1550 to the present, tobacco has been consumed in the form of a powder that is sniffed up into the nostrils. Nasal snuff today is usually made from *air-cured* or *fire-cured, dark tobaccos,* and this always seems to have been the case. Before it is ground, the aged leaf is allowed to ferment or "sweat" for up to several months; flavorings may be added during fermentation, and snuff may also be perfumed after it is ground.

Snuffing has been more prevalent in some regions than in others; in all cases, it began to decline in importance relative to smoking during the second quarter of the nineteenth century. During the centuries of its greatest popularity, manufacturers offered many more kinds of snuff than is the case today. In eighteenth-century England, where there was no retail *farmed* or *state monopoly,* snuff thus was prepared and mixed to order by retailers in hundreds of varieties—flavored and unflavored, perfumed and unperfumed—which were available in coarse, medium, or fine grinds, according to taste.

Nasal snuff has been taken in almost all parts of the world, and it has been especially prevalent among the caravan peoples of the Middle East and North Africa, among the Muslim and Hindu peoples of the Indian subcontinent, and throughout Black Africa. In China and Japan (as also in eighteenth-century Europe), snuff taking was developed into an aristocratic art form, and a variety of snuffs of high quality were produced.

NICOTIANA RUSTICA. With *Nicotiana tabacum, N. rustica* is one of the two species that, under the common name *tobacco,* have been cultivated throughout the world during the past five centuries. Like *N. tabacum, rustica* is native to the Americas, where it was grown by the peoples living in the eastern half of what is today the United States. It resembles the *air-cured, dark* varieties of *N. tabacum,* but it is somewhat coarser in flavor and aroma and has a higher nicotine content. *Rustica* is grown on the heavier, more fertile soils also favored by *air-cured dark,* and it is cultivated and harvested in similar ways. But it prefers a somewhat colder climate than *tabacum* and can be grown at higher altitudes.

Rustica has seldom entered into the world market, but it has been cultivated for local consumption in at least three regions. (1) In Europe, it was widely grown (under the name *makhorka* or *mahorka*) until World War II in eastern Russia and in central and northern Poland, where it was smoked in pipes by the rural population. (2) It is cultivated in significant amounts in the north and northeastern regions of what today are India and Pakistan (the Punjab, Uttar Pradesh, Bihar, West Bengal, and Assam), where it is manufactured into products both for chewing and for smoking in *water pipes.* (3) In China it has been raised for use as smoking tobacco in dry pipes, in northern Shensi and in the mountainous districts of Hopeh and Szechwan, where *tabacum* could not be grown.

NICOTIANA TABACUM. The biological genus *Nicotiana* contains fifty or sixty species. However, the name *tobacco* refers only to *N. tabacum* and *Nicotiana rustica.* Both species originally were native to the New World, where *N. tabacum* was cultivated by the native peoples of the West Indies, Mexico, Central America, Venezuela, the Guianas, and Brazil. We cannot be precise about the characteristics of this early form of *N. tabacum,* but its leaf apparently was not unlike the modern *air* and *fire-cured dark* types.

Virtually all tobacco cultivated at the present time belongs to this species. The many varieties existing today—differing in the number, shape, size, color, and texture of their leaves—apparently developed in response to varying climates and soil types as *N. tabacum* has been spread throughout the world during the past five centuries. The only true mutation of economic importance is White *Burley*. The great range of types assembled under this single species name has led to several attempts at subclassification, but none of these are universally accepted.

ORAL SNUFF. Oral snuff is a type of moist, coarse- or ribbon-cut tobacco that consumers allow to rest between the lip and the gums—with Americans traditionally placing it behind the lower lip, and Swedes behind the upper lip. Oral snuff apparently represents a development of snuff intended for nasal use, some of which was sold in a coarse-cut and moistened form during the eighteenth century. Since at least the first third of the nineteenth century, products specifically intended for this use have been sold, especially in the United States and in the Scandinavian countries. (In Sweden, for example, moist oral snuff represented more than half of all tobacco sales between 1840 and 1930.)

Like *nasal snuffs,* snuffs intended for oral use generally have been made from *air-cured* or *fire-cured dark* leaf. After being aged and conditioned for handling, the leaf is chopped or cut, often into short ribbons or strips. The chopped leaf is then packed in hogsheads or other containers to undergo active fermentation or sweating for up to two months (see *aging*). Some products or brands are flavored, and all contain a relatively high moisture content when they are packed into retail containers.

ORIENTAL TOBACCOS. The Oriental tobaccos represent fundamental changes in the original American varieties of *Nicotiana tabacum* that have evolved over the centuries in response to the infertile soils, cool wet winters, and hot dry summers associated with the Mediterranean climate in what are today Turkey, Greece, and the southern provinces of the USSR. True Oriental leaf is characterized by its small size, mild taste, and sweet-spicy aroma; it is comparatively low in tar and nicotine. The aromatic oils are produced through the slow growth of small-leaved plants in soils with low fertility and little nitrogen.

Oriental tobaccos are sun-cured to dry them as quickly as possible without excessive heat. Through curing, the small leaves become tan or yellow and take on their distinctive aroma and taste. Oriental leaf today is used primarily in smoking tobacco and especially in blended cigarettes; thus, it was not widely imported into Western Europe or the United States until cigarettes were adopted at the end of the nineteenth century. In earlier centuries, it also was made into naturally aromatic *nasal snuffs,* which were esteemed in the Middle East but rarely exported to the West.

OTTOMAN EMPIRE. The territories ruled by the Ottoman state were most numerous at the end of the seventeenth century. In Europe, these then included the current nations of Bulgaria, Greece, Hungary, Rumania, and Yugoslavia; Hungary was lost in 1699, the other regions during the nineteenth century. In Asia and Africa, the empire included what are today Turkey, Iraq, Syria, Lebanon, Israel, Jordan, Egypt, Libya, and Tunisia; Egypt was lost in 1839, and the other Asian provinces with the demise of the empire following World War I.

PAPELATE. Spanish name for a *cigarette* hand-rolled in paper.

PIPE. The word used to describe the container in which cut tobacco is placed before it is set afire so that the smoke may be inhaled. Along with the dry pipe, *water pipes* also are used throughout much of Asia and Africa. In Europe and the United States, most pipes consist of two pieces (although these are in some cases carved from one block). The tobacco is placed into a bowl (usually round) and allowed to burn, and the user inhales the smoke into the mouth through a narrow, hollow "stem" that fits into the side of the bowl near its base. Until the 1870s, pipes most frequently were made of clay, although fragrant hard woods or (in the United States) corncobs were also used. Since then, the wood of the briar plant has become the most common material.

In Africa and in the provinces of the *Ottoman Empire, water pipes* were popular but expensive; as in Europe, the less affluent consumers often smoked tobacco in pipes with clay bowls, with the stems sometimes made of horn, maple, or aromatic woods such as cherry or jasmine. In China and Japan, dry pipes instead are made of three distinct and separate parts, allowing them to be easily cleaned. A stem, made of bamboo or other woods, connects a small bowl of copper, alloy, or brass to a mouthpiece of stone, ivory, or milk-white glass; in contrast to Europe and the Middle East, clay rarely was used prior to the end of the nineteenth century.

PIPE TOBACCO. See *cut smoking tobacco*

PLUG. Small oblong blocks of semisoft *chewing tobacco* have been manufactured in the United States since the beginning of the nineteenth century. At first the leaf was *spun* or twisted before it was pressed into plugs; later, moistened strips of leaf were used to form the "lump" or inside filler. From the 1840s or 1850s, this filler usually has been immersed in some kind of "sauce" that contains agents—such as licorice, sugar, or saccharine—that add a sweet flavor. It is then dried (and may be sprinkled with additional flavorings), trimmed, wrapped in a leaf of smooth texture and agreeable color, and pressed to form a plug of uniform weight.

PRESSED TOBACCO. This term refers to a process by which moistened tobacco leaves, which usually are first spun or cut up, are placed in a mold and pressed together under high pressure to form a semi-hard block. Depending on their shape, various names have been given to the resulting products; in Europe, they have been referred to as carottes and *rôles;* in the United States, the most common pressed product has been the oblong-shaped *plug.*

PRUIMTABAK (Dutch). See *chewing tobacco*

RAUCHTOBAK. German for *cut smoking tobacco* intended to be used in a pipe; cognate terms are used in several Germanic languages, including Danish *(røgtabak)* and Norwegian *(røyketabakk).*

RÉGIE. A French word that means "public administration" or "public corporation." It is used in France and also in some other European countries to refer to the *state monopoly* over tobacco sales.

RÔLES. This French name also was used in other European countries and in Colonial America to describe spun or twisted tobacco products that left the factory in a relatively soft state. Tobacco leaves first were cleaned and had their stems removed. They then were dampened and twisted or spun into large rolls weighing from ten to as much as one hundred pounds. Some rolls were sold to retailers at this stage; others, often those containing more expensive leaf, were then cut up and pressed for sale as the harder, string-wrapped *carottes*.

SCAFERLATI. The French name for *cut smoking tobacco* manufactured to be used in a *pipe*.

SEMI-ORIENTAL TOBACCOS. The so-called Semi-Oriental varieties resemble low-quality *Oriental* leaf; they are produced when Oriental seed is cultivated in environments or climates that are not wholly suitable, such as are found in Macedonia, the coast of what is today Yugoslavia, or southern Italy. As one moves away from the coasts in these areas, the leaves become larger and less aromatic.

SKRÅTOBAK (Danish) and SKRÅTOBAKK (Norwegian). See *chewing tobacco*

SMOKING TOBACCO. See *cut smoking tobacco*

SNUFF. See *nasal snuff; oral snuff*

SPUN TOBACCO. After they are *cured* and *aged,* moistened tobacco leaves may be spun or woven into a ribbon or *twist* by hand, on a spinning wheel, or mechanically. Until the 1850s, manufacturers often supplied retailers both with large spun rolls weighing from ten to as many as one hundred pounds (see *rôles*) and also with smaller rolls or *twists* that the consumer could grate or cut up at home. To facilitate these subsequent manufacturing processes, the leaves also may be spun before they are pressed into *carottes* or *plug,* or cut up to make smoking or cigarette tobacco.

STATE MONOPOLY. A system in which the government of a region or nation (1) abrogates control over one or more aspects of the cultivation and import of tobacco leaf, and the manufacture, distribution, and retail sale of tobacco products, and (2) directly administers and manages their manufacturing and distribution. In some cases, retail sales also are carried out by state employees; in others (notably in France and under the *Habsburg Empire*), private retailers purchase a license to sell tobacco products and generally are required to sell at prices fixed by the state tobacco administration.

SUN CURING. Sun curing is the simplest and least expensive method of drying freshly harvested tobacco leaves, but it requires long periods of sunshine and the expectation that there will be little or no rain for at least three weeks. During most of the curing process, the leaf is laid on the ground or hung on racks and exposed to the full rays of the sun; it may be covered at night. Although sun curing has been little used in the United States, elsewhere this method today accounts for as much as a third of world production. Typical sun curing dries the leaf more rapidly than air curing, and lightens its color. It is essential in producing the light-colored *Oriental leaf,* which formerly was used in snuff and which today is an ingredient in pipe tobacco and blended cigarettes. It also has been used in India and China to cure other tobaccos, both *light* and *dark,* whose qualities are generally similar to air-cured leaf of the same variety.

SWEATING. See *aging*

TABAC À CHIQUER (French). See *chewing tobacco*

TABAC À MÂCHER (French). See *chewing tobacco*

TABAC FICELÉ (French). See *carotte*

TOBACCO. The name used in many languages (although variously spelled) both for (1) any plant of the two species *Nicotiana tabacum* and *Nicotiana rustica* (biological genus *Nicotiana* of the *Solanaceae* family); and (2) the products manufactured from or containing the leaves of these plants, such as *cigars, cigarettes, snuff, cut smoking tobacco,* and *chewing tobacco.*

The biological genus *Nicotiana* contains fifty or sixty species, but the name *tobacco* refers only to *N. tabacum* and *N. rustica.* From the time of its discovery in the sixteenth century, almost all the tobacco commercially grown in the United States and perhaps 90 percent of world tobacco production has been some form of *Nicotiana tabacum; N. rustica* has been grown for consumption only in a few regions. Over the past five centuries, many varieties have developed, but biologically all are varieties of this one species.

Although potentially a perennial, tobacco is usually cultivated as an annual. Its leaves, which form the only commercially valuable part of the plant, are very large in comparison both to its root structure and to its relatively small (usually light pink) flowers and minute seeds.

Broadly speaking, all tobacco leaf is described as either *light* or *dark.* These terms refer to the color of the leaf after it has been picked and dried, but they also are relevant to its characteristic flavor, taste, and aroma. Generally, dark tobaccos are perceived as stronger and light tobaccos as more mild. These qualities are affected by the soil, climate, and methods of cultivation used. With the exception of *Burley* (which is grown on relatively heavy silt loam soils), light open soils tend to produce a thin leaf that is mild, light in weight and color, and weak in aroma; heavy soils generally produce thick, heavy, strong leaf of darker colors.

These qualities also are brought out by the method used to cure the leaf, with four methods being commonly used—*air, fire, sun,* and *flue curing.* All these factors are interdependent, with a particular method of curing bringing out the characteristic flavor and taste of a variety grown in a specific way in a specific environment. Thus, there are many varieties of tobacco with differences that have been appreciated by both producer and consumer. Several of the historically most important varieties are listed separately, including *dark* leaf and *Burley, Bright,* and *Oriental* (which are all types of *light* leaf).

TUGGTOBAK (Swedish). See *chewing tobacco*

TWIST. After they are cured and aged, tobacco leaves may be spun either into rolls or into a twisted shape with this name. Prior to the 1850s, manufacturers often supplied tobacco in the form of both semisoft rolls and harder twists that consumers then cut up for smoking, chewing, or snuffing. Today, small twists in a dry, hard state are made primarily for use as *chewing tobacco.*

VIRGINIA. A name used in the United Kingdom (and in its former colonies) to refer to mild cigarette tobaccos, including air-cured *Burley* and flue-cured *Bright*. Although they now mainly are grown in other states, the term has been used to refer to these tobaccos since they first became available in Britain in the late 1860s.

WATER PIPE. The *nargileh* or water pipe—referred to by European travelers as a "hookah" or "hubbly-bubbly"—consists of three parts. Tobacco is placed in a bowl above a container which is filled with water. When the water pipe is in service, a partial vacuum is created that allows the user to draw the smoke up through the water and along a pipe or tube, thus cooling the smoke before it is inhaled. Although the precise date is unknown, the water pipe probably was invented shortly after 1600 in Persia; it soon was spread both west to the *Ottoman Empire* and east to India and China. By the eighteenth century the water pipe was common throughout the Ottoman provinces in Europe, the Middle East, Egypt, and North Africa. It also was prevalent in many regions of Africa as well as throughout the Chinese Empire and the Muslim regions of the Indian subcontinent.

References

GOVERNMENTAL AND INDUSTRY SOURCES

Several Countries

Hutson, J. B. *Consumption and Production of Tobacco in Europe*. United States Department of Agriculture, Technical Bulletin No. 587. Washington, D.C., 1937.

Lee, P. N., ed. *Tobacco Consumption in Various Countries*. London, 1975.

Mitchell, B. R. *European Historical Statistics 1750–1970*. New York, 1978.

———. *International Historical Statistics: The Americas and Australasia*. Detroit, 1983.

Staatkundig en Staathuishoudkundig Jaarboekje voor 1884; Uitgegeven door de Vereeniging Voor de Statistiek in Nederland. Amsterdam, 1884.

Austria

Central-Direction der Tabakfabriken und Einlösungsämter. *Tabellen zur Statistik des Österreichischen Tabak-Monopols*. Vienna, 1861–1873.

Statistische Central-Commission. *Österreichisches statistisches Handbuch für die im Reichsrat vertretenen königreiche und länder*. Vienna, 1880–1917.

———. *Statistisches Jahrbuch der Österreichischen Monarchie*. Vienna, 1861–1881.

———. *Tafeln zur Statistik der Österreichischen Monarchie*. Vienna, 1840–1861.

Statistisches Zentralamt. *Geschicte und Ergenbuisse der Zentralen Amtlichen Statistik in Österreich 1829–1979*. Vienna, 1979.

Australia

Bureau of Census and Statistics, Canberra. *Official Statistics, Commonwealth of Australia. Manufacturing Industries*. Canberra, 1938–1951.

Brazil

Centre National de la Recherche Scientifique (Paris). *L'Histoire quantitative du Brésil de 1800 à 1930*. Paris, 1973.

Canada

Dominion Bureau of Statistics, Agricultural Division. *Historical Series of Tobacco Statistics: Production, Process and Trade.* Ottowa, 1950.
Urqhart, M. C., and V. A. Buckley. *Historical Statistics of Canada.* Cambridge, 1965.

Denmark

Statistiske Department. *Statistiske Meddelelser.* 4th Series. Vols. 30, 50, 55, 57, 59–60, 66, 75, 89, 101, 114, 129, 145. Copenhagen, 1907–1952.

France

Chambre des députés. *Session 1837; Enquête sur les tabacs.* Paris, 1837.
Direction générale des manufactures de l'État. *Compte du produit de la fabrication et de la vente exclusives du tabac.* Paris, 1862–1880.
———. *Rapport concernant la fabrication et la vente exclusives du tabac . . .* Paris, 1820–1846.
Hamille, Victor. *Enquête parlementaire sur l'exploitation du monopole des tabacs et des poudres.* Versailles, 1875.
Institut National de la Statistique. *Annuaire statistique de la France.* Paris, 1878– .

Germany

Bericht der Taback-Enquete-Commission über den Tabackbau, den Kandel mit Rohtabak, de Tabackfabrikation und den handel mit Tabackfabrication, so wie uber die Tabackbesteuerung im Deutschen Reich. Berlin, 1878.
Statistisches Bundesamt Wiesbaden. *Bevölkerung und Wirtschaft 1872–1972.* Stuttgart, 1972.
———. *Statistisches Jahrbuch für die Bundesrepublik Deutschland.* Wiesbaden, 1952– .
Statistisches Reichsamt. *Statistisches Jahrbuch für das Deutsche Reich.* Berlin, 1880–1941.

Hungary

Budapest Székesfőváros Statisztikai Hivatal. *Tatisztikai Évkönyve.* Budapest and Berlin, 1896– .

Ireland

Central Statistics Office. *Statistical Abstract of Ireland.* Dublin, 1931– .

Italy

Instituto centrale di statistica. *Sommario di statistiche storiche italiano 1861–1955.* Rome, 1958.

The Netherlands

Central bureau voor de statistiek. *Tabakverwerkende industrie 1960.* Zeist, 1962.
――――. *1899–1979 tachtig jaren statistiek in tijdreeksen.* 's-Gravenhage, 1979.

New Zealand

Department of Census and Statistics. *Statistical Report on the Factory Production of New Zealand.* Wellington, 1923–1952.

Norway

Statistisk Sentralalbyrå. *Norges Offisielle Statistikk. Norges Industri, Fabriktelling.* Oslo, 1909– .
――――. *Norges Offisielle Statistikk. Norges Industri, Produksjonsstatistikk.* Oslo, 1909– .

Sweden

Guinchard, J., ed. *Sweden Historical and Statistical Handbook.* 2 vols. Stockholm, 1914.
Statistiska Centralbyrån. *Historisk Statistik för Sverige.* 3 vols. Stockholm and Lund, 1955–1972.
――――. *Statistiska Översikstabeller.* 2 vols. Stockholm, 1960.
Sundborj, Gustav, ed., *Sweden: Its People and Its Industry, Historical and Statistical.* Stockholm, 1904.

United Kingdom

Board of Trade. *Final Report on the Census of Production of the United Kingdom . . . 1907* (1912, 1924, 1930, 1945, 1948).
Mitchell, B. R., and Phyllis Deane. *Abstract of British Historical Statistics.* Cambridge, 1962.
Mitchell, B. R., and H. G. James. *Second Abstract of British Historical Statistics.* Cambridge, 1971.
Todd, G. F., ed. *Statistics of Smoking in the U.K.* London, 1957.

United States

Department of Agriculture. *Annual Report on Tobacco Statistics, 1952.* Washington, D.C., 1952.
――――. *First Annual Report on Tobacco Statistics (with Basic Data).* Statistical Bulletin No. 58. Washington, D.C., 1937.
Holmes, George. "Three Centuries of Tobacco." In *Yearbook of the United States Department of Agriculture 1919,* pp. 151–75.
Internal Revenue Service. *Report of the Commissioner of Internal Revenue on the Operations of the Internal Revenue System.* Washington, D.C., 1865–1880.
(See also the studies by Gage and Garner cited in the next section.)

HISTORIES AND STUDIES

Akehurst, B. G. *Tobacco.* London, 1968.

Alford, B. W. E. *W. D. & H. O. Wills and the Development of the UK Tobacco Industry 1786–1965.* London, 1973.

American Tobacco Company. *"Sold American"—The First Fifty Years.* New York, 1954.

Apperson, G. L. *The Social History of Smoking.* London, 1914.

Arlott, John. *The Snuff Shop.* London, 1974.

Arnold, B. W. *History of the Tobacco Industry in Virginia from 1860 to 1894.* Baltimore, 1897.

Axton, W. F. *Tobacco and Kentucky.* Lexington, Ky., 1975.

Badger, Anthony. *Prosperity Road: The New Deal, Tobacco and North Carolina.* Chapel Hill, N.C., 1980.

Bain, John. *Tobacco in Song and Story.* New York, 1896.

Barbour, Violet. *Capitalism in Amsterdam in the Seventeenth Century.* Baltimore, 1950.

Beckett, J. V. *Coal and Tobacco: The Lowthers and the Economic Development of West Cumberland 1660–1760.* Cambridge, 1981.

Beer, G. L. *The Commercial Policy of England toward the American Colonies.* Columbia University Studies 3, no. 2. New York, 1893.

———. *The Old Colonial System, 1660–1754.* New York, 1912.

———. *The Origins of the British Colonial System, 1578–1660.* New York, 1908.

Beltchev, Koitcho. *Tobacco in Bulgaria.* Finland, 1950.

Benesch, Fritz. *150 Jahre Österreichischen Tabakregie, 1784–1934.* Innsbruck, Austria, 1934.

Besant, Walter. *London in the Time of the Stuarts.* London, 1903.

Bierck, H. A. "Tobacco Marketing in Venezuela, 1798–1799: An Aspect of Spanish Mercantilistic Revisionism," *Business History Review* 39 (1965): 489–502.

Billings, E. R. *Tobacco: Its History, Varieties, Culture, Manufacture, and Commerce, with an Account of Its Various Modes of Use from Its First Discoveries to Now.* Hartford, Conn., 1875.

Blackwell, William. *The Beginnings of Russian Industrialization, 1800–1860.* Princeton, N.J., 1968.

Blondel, Spire. *Le Tabac: Le livre des Fumeurs et des Priseurs.* Paris, 1891.

Bloom, Herbert. *The Economic Activities of the Jews of Amsterdam in the 17th and 18th Centuries.* Williamsport, Pa., 1937.

Bouant, E. *Le Tabac, culture et industrie.* Paris, 1901.

Bragge, William. *Bibliotheca Nicotiana: A Catalogue of Books About Tobacco, together with a Catalogue of Objects Connected with the Use of Tobacco in all Its Forms.* Birmingham, Ala., 1880.

Brennan, William. *Tobacco Leaves: Being a Book of Facts for Smokers.* Menasha, Wisconsin, 1915.

Broeze, Frank. "The New Economic History, the Navigation Acts, and the Continental Tobacco Market, 1770–1790," *Economic History Review,* Second Series, 26 (1973): 668–678.

Brongers, Georg. *Nicotiana Tabacum: The History of Tobacco and Tobacco Smoking in the Netherlands.* Groningen, 1964.

———. *Van gouwenaar tot bruyerè pijp.* Amerongen, 1978.

Brooks, Jerome. *The Mighty Leaf: Tobacco Through the Centuries.* Boston, 1952.

———. *Tobacco: Its History Illustrated by the Books, Manuscripts, and Engravings in the Library of George Arents Junior.* 5 vols. New York, 1937–1952.

Brunet, J. *Le bon usage du tabac en poudre, Les diférentes manières de la préparer et de le parfumer* . . . Paris, 1700.

Brunet, Raymond. *Manuel Pratique de la culture et fabrication du Tabac.* Paris, 1903.

Chuard, Jean, and O. Dessemontet. *Le 250e anniversaire de la culture du tabac en pays romand 1719–1969.* Lausanne, Switzerland, 1970.

Cochran, Sherman. *Big Business in China: Sino-Foreign Rivalry in the Cigarette Industry, 1890–1930.* Cambridge, Mass., 1980.

Cohausen, Johann Heinrich. *Satyrische Dedancken von der Pica Nasi.* Leipzig, 1720.

Cole, W. A. "Trends in Eighteenth-Century Smuggling," *Economic History Review* (second series) 10 (1958): 395–410.

Comes, Orazio. *Delle Razze dei Tabacchi, Filogenesi, Qualità ed Uso.* Naples, 1905.

———. *Histoire, géographie, statistique du tabac.* Naples, 1900.

Congard, Roger. *Étude économetrique de la demande de tabac.* Paris, 1955.

Corina, Maurice. *Trust in Tobacco: The Anglo-American Struggle for Power.* London, 1975.

Corti, Egon. *A History of Smoking,* trans. Paul England. New York, 1932.

Curtis, Matton. *The Story of Snuff and Snuff Boxes.* New York, 1935.

Davis, Ralph. "English Foreign Trade 1660–1700," *Economic History Review* (second series) 7 (1954–1955): 150–66.

DeCoin, Robert. *History and Cultivation of Cotton and Tobacco.* New York, 1864; repr., Wilmington, Del., 1973.

de Jesus, Edward. *The Tobacco Monopoly in the Philippines: Bureaucratic Enterprise and Social Change, 1766–1880.* Quezon City, Philippines, 1980.

Devine, Thomas. *The Tobacco Lords: A Study of the Tobacco Merchants of Glasgow and Their Trading Activities, circa 1740–1790.* Edinburgh, Scotland, 1975.

Dickson, Sarah. *Panacea or Precious Bane: Tobacco in Sixteenth Century Literature.* New York, 1954.

———. *Tobacco: A Catalogue of the Books, Manuscripts, and Engravings Acquired since 1942 in the Arents Tobacco Collection at the New York Public Library.* New York, 1958.

Doughty, Charles. *Travels in Arabia Deserta.* London, 1921.

Encyclopédie du tabac et des fumeurs. Paris, 1975.

Evans, George. *The Old Snuff House of Fribourg and Treyer.* London, 1921.

Fairholt, Frederick. *Tobacco: Its History and Associations, Including an Account of the Plant and its Manufacture, with its Modes of Use in All Ages and Countries.* London, 1859.

Falass, Marco Antonio. *La factoria de tabaccos de Costa Rica.* San Jose, Costa Rica, 1972.

Fermond, Charles. *Monographie du Tabac, comprenant l'historique, les propriétés thérapeutiques, physiologiques, et toxicologiques du tabac.* Paris, 1857.

Fernandez-Diaz, Edouard. *Le Tabac en Bulgarie.* Paris, 1926.

Frederiksen, O. J. "Virginia Tobacco in Russia under Peter the Great," *The Slavonic and East European Review* 21 (1943): 40–56.

Gage, Charles E. *American Tobacco Types, Uses and Markets.* United States Department of Agriculture, Circular No. 249. Washington, D.C., 1933–1942.

Garner, W. W., et al. "History and Status of Tobacco Culture." In *United States Department of Agriculture Yearbook 1922*, pp. 395–468.

Garner, Wrightman. *The Production of Tobacco*. Philadelphia, 1946.

Gayvallet, Prosper. *Le Monopole du tabac en France*. Tonneins, France, 1905.

George, M. D. *London Life in the Eighteenth Century*. London, 1925.

Gisquet, P., and H. I. Hitier. *Le Production de tabac: principes et méthodes*. Paris, 1961.

Gokhale, B. H. "Tobacco in Seventeenth-Century India," *Agricultural History* 48 (1974): 484–92.

Gondolff, E. *Le tabac sous l'ancienne Monarchie: La Ferme royale 1629–1791*. Vesoul, France, 1914.

Goodrich, Luther. "Snuff in China," *China* 18 (February 15, 1942): 12–14.

Gottsegen, Jack. *Tobacco, a Study of Its Consumption in the United States*. New York, 1940.

Gray, Lewis. *History of Agriculture in the Southern United States to 1860*. 2 vols. Washington, D.C., 1933.

Gray, Stanley, and V. J. Wyckoff. "The International Tobacco Trade in the Seventeenth Century," *Southern Economic Journal* 7 (1940): 18–25.

Hamilton, Albert. *This Smoking World*. New York and London, 1928.

Hamilton, H. *The Industrial Revolution in Scotland*. Repr., London, 1966.

Hanauer, A. *Études économiques sur l'Alsace ancienne et moderne*. 2 vols. Paris, 1876–1877.

Harley, Laurence. *The Clay Tobacco Pipe in Britain*. Stratford, England, 1976.

Heimann, Robert. *Tobacco and Americans*. New York, 1960.

Herndon, G. M. *William Tatham and the Culture of Tobacco*. Coral Gables, Fla., 1969.

Hess, Mary Anthonita. *American Tobacco and Central European Policy: Early Nineteenth Century*. Washington, D.C., 1948.

Hill, Benson. *A Pinch—of Snuff: Composed of Curious Particulars and Original Anecdotes of Snuff Taking . . .* London, 1840.

Hitier, H. I., and L. Sabourin. *Le Tabac*. 2nd ed. Paris, 1970.

Hitz, Harald, and Hugo Huber. *Geschichte der Österreichischen Tabakregie 1784–1835*. Wien, Austria, 1975.

Hovde, Brynjoff. *The Scandinavian Countries, 1720–1865*. 2 vols. Boston, 1943.

Israel, Maurice. *Le Tabac en France et dans le monde*. Paris, 1973.

Jacobstein, Meyer. *The Tobacco Industry in the United States*. New York, 1907.

Jahn, Raymond. *Tobacco Dictionary*. New York, 1954.

Johnson, Paul R. *The Economics of the Tobacco Industry*. New York, 1984.

Joubert, Charles. *Nouveau Manuel complet du fabricant et de l'amateur de Tabac*. Paris, 1844.

Jubilaumsschrift anlasslich der Feier 400; i.e. vierhundert Jahre Tabakanbau in Hatzenbuhl. Hatzenbuhl, 1973.

Julien, Pierre. "La Chique et le Marin," *Revue des Tabacs* 199 (1952): 25–27.

Killebrew, J. B. *Tobacco Leaf: Its Culture and Cure, Marketing and Manufacture*. New York, 1897.

Kish, Bruno. *Scales and Weights: A Historical Outline*. New Haven and London, 1965.

Krükl, Josef. *Das Tabak-Monopol in Oesterreich und Frankreich*. Wien, Vienna, 1878.

Laufer, Berthold. *The Introduction of Tobacco into Europe*. Field Museum of Natural History, Anthropology Leaflet Number 19. Chicago, 1924.

————. *Tobacco and Its Use in Asia.* Field Museum of Natural History, Anthropology Leaflet Number 18. Chicago, 1924.

Laufer, Berthold, with Wilfrid Hambly and Ralph Linton. *Tobacco and Its Use in Africa.* Field Museum of Natural History, Anthropology Leaflet Number 29. Chicago, 1930.

Laurent, L. *Le Tabac; sa culture et sa préparation, production, et consummation dans les divers pays.* Paris, 1900.

Le Corbeiller, Clare. *European and American Snuff Boxes 1730–1830.* New York, 1966.

Lewis, Albert B. *Use of Tobacco in New Guinea and Neighboring Regions.* Field Museum of Natural History, Anthropology Leaflet Number 17. Chicago, 1924.

Libert, Lutz. *Tobacco, Snuff-boxes and Pipes,* trans. Sheila Marnie. London, 1986.

Liebault, Jean. *L'Agriculture et la maison rustique.* Paris, 1567.

Linck, O. *Das Tabaksmonopol in Württemberg 1750–1890.* Stuttgart, 1894.

Linton, R. *Use of Tobacco among North American Indians.* Field Museum of Natural History, Anthropology Leaflet Number 15. Chicago, 1924.

Lorillard and Tobacco—200th Anniversary P. Lorillard Company, 1760–1960. New York, 1960.

McCausland, H. *Snuff and Snuff-Boxes.* London, 1951.

McDonald, A. F. *The History of Tobacco Production in Connecticut.* New Haven, 1936.

MacInnes, C. M. *The Early English Tobacco Trade.* London, 1926.

Mackenzie, Compton. *Sublime Tobacco.* London, 1957.

Mann, Charles. *Tobacco: The Ants and the Elephants.* Salt Lake City, Utah, 1975.

Mason, J. Alden. *Use of Tobacco in Mexico and South America.* Field Museum of Natural History, Anthropology Leaflet Number 16. Chicago, 1924.

Mathieu-Dairnvaell, Georges. *Le Tabac vengé: Physiologie du tabac, de la pipe, du cigare, de la cigarette et de la tabatière.* Paris, 1845.

Mavor, James. *An Economic History of Russia.* 2nd ed., 2 vols. London, 1925.

Nash, R. C. "The English and Scottish Tobacco Trades in the Seventeenth and Eighteenth Centuries: Legal and Illegal Trade," *Economic History Review* (second series) 35 (1982): 345–72.

Neander, Johann. *Tabacologia.* Leiden, the Netherlands, 1622.

Nikula, Oscar. *Strengbergs, 1762–1962.* Jakobstad, 1962.

Ortiz, F. *Cuban Counterpoint: Tobacco and Sugar,* trans. H. de Onís.

Park, Mungo. *Travels in the Interior of Africa.* London, 1984.

Pasetti Thommaso. *Cenni Storico Statistica sul Monopolo del Tabacco in Italia.* Rome, 1900.

Penn, W. A. *The Soverane Herbe: A History of Tobacco.* London, 1901.

Perez-Vidal, José. *España en la historia del Tabaco.* Madrid, 1959.

Price, Jacob. *France and the Chesapeake: A History of the French Tobacco Monopoly, 1674–1791, and of its Relationship to the British and American Tobacco Trades.* 2 vols. Ann Arbor, Mich., 1973.

————. *The Tobacco adventure to Russia, Enterprise, politics, and diplomacy in the quest for a Northern market for English colonial Tobacco, 1676–1722.* Transactions of the American Philosophical Society, New Style, 51, part 1. Philadelphia, 1961.

Provost, André. *L'Industrie du tabac. Généralités—Scaferlatis—Cigarettes.* Paris, 1935.

Puisieux, René. *L'Impôt du Tabac sous l'ancien Régime.* Paris. 1906.

Ramsey, Elizabeth. *The History of Tobacco Production in the Connecticut Valley.* Smith College Studies in History, 15, nos 3–4. Northampton, Mass., 1930.

Rival, Ned. *Tabac, miroir du temps.* Paris, 1981.

Rive, Alfred. "The Consumption of Tobacco since 1600." *The Economic Journal,* Economic History Series, 1 (1926–1929): 57–75.

———. "A Short History of Tobacco Smuggling," *The Economic Journal,* Economic History Series, 1 (1926–1929): 554–569.

Rivero Muñiz, José. *Tabaco, su historia en Cuba.* 2 vols. Havana, Cuba, 1964–1965.

Robert, Joseph. *The Story of Tobacco in America.* New York, 1952.

———. *The Tobacco Kingdom: Plantation, Market, and Factory in Virginia and North Carolina, 1800–1860.* Glouster, Mass. 1969. (repr. of 1938 ed.)

Roessingh, H. K. *Inlandse tabak: expansie en contractie van een handelsgewas in de 17ᵉ en 18ᵉ eeuw in Nederland.* Wageningen, Netherlands, 1976.

Sebillot, Paul. *Le Tabac dans les Traditions, les superstitions, et les coutumes.* Paris, 1893.

Sejersted, Francis. *Blader av tobakkens historie J. L. Tiedemans Tobaksfabrik 1778–1978.* Oslo, 1978.

Shepherd, C. W. *Snuff Yesterday and Today.* London, 1963.

Slicher van Bath, B. H. "Agriculture in the Low Countries (ca. 1600–1800)," *Relazioni del Xᵉ Congresso Internazionale di Scienza Storiche.* Vol. 4, pp. 169–203. Florence, 1955.

Smith, R. E. F., and David Christian. *Bread and Salt: A Social and Economic History of Food and Drink in Russia.* Cambridge, 1984.

Sobel, Robert. *They Satisfy: The Cigarette in American Life.* Garden City, N.Y., 1978.

Svenska tobaks aktiebolaget. *Om tobak i Sverige Jubileumsskrift 1915–1965.* Stockholm, 1965.

———. *Svenska Tobaks Monopolet 1915–1940 Minnesskrift utgiven med anledning av Svenska Tobaksmonopolets tjngofemariga verksamket den 1 Juni 1940.* Stockholm, 1940.

Tanner, A. E. *Tobacco from the Grower to the Smoker.* London, 1912.

Tatham, William. *An Historical and Practical Essay on the Culture and Commerce of Tobacco.* London, 1800. Reprinted 1969 in G. M. Herndon, *William Tatham and the Culture of Tobacco,* Coral Gables, Fla.

Tennant, Richard. *The American Cigarette Industry.* New Haven, Conn., 1950.

Thomas, James A. *A Pioneer Tobacco Merchant in the Orient.* Durham, N. C., 1928.

Tiedemann, Friedrich. *Geschichte des Tabaks und anderer ähnlicher Genussmittel.* Frankfurt, 1854.

Tilley, Nannie May. *The Bright Tobacco Industry.* Chapel Hill, N.C., 1948.

———. *The R. J. Reynolds Tobacco Company.* Chapel Hill, N.C., 1985.

Tollison, Robert. *Smoking and the State: Social Costs, Rent Seeking, and Public Policy.* Lexington, Mass., 1988.

Tso, T. C. *Physiology and Biochemistry of Tobacco Plants.* Stroudsburg, Pa., 1972.

Tucker, David. *Tobacco: An International Perspective.* London, 1983.

Walker, Robin. *Under Fire: A History of Tobacco.* Carlton, Australia, 1983.

White, Charles. *The Operation of Tennessee Tobacco Taxes.* University of Tennessee, School of Business Administration, Study No. 1. Knoxville, 1937.

Wilbert, Johannes. *Tobacco and Shamanism in South America.* New Haven, Conn., 1987.

Winkler, John. *Tobacco Tycoon, the Story of James Buchanan Duke*. New York, 1942.

Wolf, Jakob. *Der Tabak und die Tabakfabrikate*. Leipzig, Austria, 1912.

World Health Organization, International Agency for Research on Cancer. *IARC Monographs on the Evaluation of the Carcinogenic Risk of Chemicals to Humans.* Vol. 37: *Tobacco Habits Other than Smoking*. New York, 1985.

Zeldin, Theodore. *France 1848–1945*. 2 vols. Oxford, 1973–77.

Index

ABOUT THE AUTHOR

JAN ROGOZIŃSKI, a writer specializing in historical and technical subjects, lives in Fort Lauderdale, Florida. Rogoziński received a Ph.D. in social and cultural history from Princeton University. In addition to numerous articles and reports on research findings published in magazines and professional journals, he is the author of *Caste, Power, and Law: Social Conflict in Fourteenth Century Montpellier* (1982).

re buy'k v z z

vrh w 18th. c. Va.
29